Greg Byrd, Lynn Byrd and Chris Pearce

Cambridge Checkpoint

Mathematics

Coursebook

9

CAMBRIDGE
UNIVERSITY PRESS

University Printing House, Cambridge CB2 8BS, United Kingdom

Cambridge University Press is part of the University of Cambridge.

It furthers the University's mission by disseminating knowledge in the pursuit of education, learning and research at the highest international levels of excellence.

www.cambridge.org
Information on this title: www.cambridge.org/9781107668010
© Cambridge University Press 2013

First published 2013
Reprinted 2013

Printed in the United Kingdom by Latimer Trend

A catalogue record for this publication is available from the British Library

ISBN 978-1-107-66801-0 Paperback

Cover image © Cosmo Condina concepts/Alamy

Contents

Contents

Introduction

Welcome to Cambridge Checkpoint Mathematics stage 9

The *Cambridge Checkpoint Mathematics* course covers the Cambridge Secondary 1 mathematics framework and is divided into three stages: 7, 8 and 9. This book covers all you need to know for stage 9.

There are two more books in the series to cover stages 7 and 8. Together they will give you a firm foundation in mathematics.

At the end of the year, your teacher may ask you to take a **Progression test** to find out how well you have done. This book will help you to learn how to apply your mathematical knowledge and to do well in the test.

The curriculum is presented in six content areas:

- Number
- Algebra
- Measures
- Handling data
- Geometry
- Problem solving.

This book has 19 units, each related to one of the first five content areas. Problem solving is included in all units. There are no clear dividing lines between the five areas of mathematics; skills learned in one unit are often used in other units.

Each unit starts with an introduction, with **key words** listed in a blue box. This will prepare you for what you will learn in the unit. At the end of each unit is a **summary** box, to remind you what you've learned.

Each unit is divided into several topics. Each topic has an introduction explaining the topic content, usually with worked examples. Helpful hints are given in blue rounded boxes. At the end of each topic there is an exercise. Each unit ends with a review exercise. The questions in the exercises encourage you to apply your mathematical knowledge and develop your understanding of the subject.

As well as learning mathematical skills you need to learn when and how to use them. One of the most important mathematical skills you must learn is how to solve problems.

 When you see this symbol, it means that the question will help you to develop your problem-solving skills.

During your course, you will learn a lot of facts, information and techniques. You will start to think like a mathematician. You will discuss ideas and methods with other students as well as your teacher. These discussions are an important part of developing your mathematical skills and understanding.

Look out for these students, who will be asking questions, making suggestions and taking part in the activities throughout the units.

Acknowledgements

The authors and publishers acknowledge the following sources of copyright material and are grateful for the permissions granted. While every effort has been made, it has not always been possible to identify the sources of all the material used, or to trace all copyright holders. If any omissions are brought to our notice, we will be happy to include the appropriate acknowledgements on reprinting.

p. 15 Ivan Vdovin/Alamy; p. 23*tl* zsschreiner/Shutterstock; p. 23*tr* Leon Ritter/Shutterstock;

p. 29 Carl De Souza/AFP/Getty Images; p. 33*t* Chuyu/Shutterstock;

p. 33*ml* Angyalosi Beata/Shutterstock; p. 33*mr* Cedric Weber/Shutterstock;

p. 33*bl* Ruzanna/Shutterstock; p. 33*br* Foodpics/Shutterstock; p. 37*t* Steven Allan/iStock;

p. 37*m* Mikael Damkier/Shutterstock; p. 37*b* Christopher Parypa/Shutterstock;

p. 41 *TT*photo/Shutterstock; p. 55*t* Dusit/Shutterstock; p. 55*m* Steven Coburn/Shutterstock;

p. 55*b* Alexander Kirch/Shutterstock; p. 57 Jacek Chabraszewski/iStock; p. 73*m* Rich Legg/iStock;

p. 73*b* Lance Ballers/iStock; p. 97 David Burrows/Shutterstock; p. 103 Dar Yasin/AP Photo;

p. 110*t* Katia Karpei/Shutterstock; p. 110*b* Aleksey VI B/Shutterstock;

p. 124 The Art Archive/Alamy; p. 127 Edhar/Shutterstock; p. 135 Sura Nualpradid/Shutterstock;

p. 137 Dana E.Fry/Shutterstock; p. 137*m* Dana E.Fry/Shutterstock; p. 138t NASTYApro/Shutterstock;

p. 138*m* Adisa/Shutterstock; p. 139*m* EHStock/iStock; p. 139*b* Zubin li/iStock;

p. 140*t* Christopher Futcher/iStock; p. 140*b* Pavel L Photo and Video/Shutterstock;

p. 144 Eoghan McNally/Shutterstock; p. 146 Pecold/Shutterstock; p. 158*tl* Jumpingsack/Shutterstock;

p. 158*tr* Triff/Shutterstock; p. 158*ml* Volina/Shutterstock; p. 158*mr* Gordan/Shutterstock;

p. 185 Vale Stock/Shutterstock

The publisher would like to thank Ángel Cubero of the International School Santo Tomás de Aquino, Madrid, for reviewing the language level.

1 Integers, powers and roots

Mathematics is about finding patterns.

How did you first learn to add and multiply negative integers? Perhaps you started with an addition table or a multiplication table for positive integers and then extended it. The patterns in the tables help you to do this.

+	3	2	1	0	−1	−2	−3
3	6	5	4	3	2	1	0
2	5	4	3	2	1	0	−1
1	4	3	2	1	0	−1	−2
0	3	2	1	0	−1	−2	−3
−1	2	1	0	−1	−2	−3	−4
−2	1	0	−1	−2	−3	−4	−5
−3	0	−1	−2	−3	−4	−5	−6

This shows
$1 + -3 = -2$.
You can also subtract.
$-2 - 1 = -3$ and
$-2 - -3 = 1$.

×	3	2	1	0	−1	−2	−3
3	9	6	3	0	−3	−6	−9
2	6	4	2	0	−2	−4	−6
1	3	2	1	0	−1	−2	−3
0	0	0	0	0	0	0	0
−1	−3	−2	−1	0	1	2	3
−2	−6	−4	−2	0	2	4	6
−3	−9	−6	−3	0	3	6	9

This shows
$2 × -3 = -6$.
You can also divide.
$-6 ÷ 2 = -3$ and
$-6 ÷ -3 = 2$.

Square numbers show a visual pattern.
$1 + 3 = 4 = 2^2$
$1 + 3 + 5 = 9 = 3^2$
$1 + 3 + 5 + 7 = 16 = 4^2$
Can you continue this pattern?

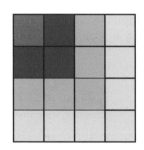

1.1 Directed numbers

Directed numbers have direction; they can be positive or negative. Directed numbers can be integers (whole numbers) or they can be decimal numbers.

Here is a quick reminder of some important things to remember when you add, subtract, multiply and divide integers. These methods can also be used with any directed numbers.

What is $3 + -5$?

> Think of a number line. Start at 0. Moving 3 to the right, then 5 to the left is the same as moving 2 to the left.

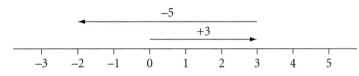

Or you can change it to a subtraction: $3 + -5 = 3 - 5$.

Either way, the answer is -2.

> add negative → subtract positive
>
> subtract negative → add positive

What about $3 - -5$?

Perhaps the easiest way is to add the inverse.

$3 - -5 = 3 + 5 = 8$

What about multiplication?

$3 \times 5 = 15$ $3 \times -5 = -15$ $-3 \times 5 = -15$ $-3 \times -5 = 15$

Multiply the corresponding positive numbers and decide whether the answer is positive or negative.

Division is similar.

> Remember for multiplication and division:
>
> same signs → positive answer
>
> different signs → negative answer

$15 \div 3 = 5$ $-15 \div 3 = -5$ $-15 \div -3 = 5$ $15 \div -3 = -5$

These are the methods for integers.

You can use exactly the same methods for any directed numbers, even if they are not integers.

Worked example 1.1

Complete these calculations.   **a** $3.5 + -4.1$ **b** $3.5 - -2.8$ **c** 6.3×-3 **d** $-7.5 \div -2.5$

a $3.5 - 4.1 = -0.6$ You could draw a number line but it is easier to subtract the inverse (which is 4.1).
b $3.5 + 2.8 = 6.3$ Change the subtraction to an addition. Add the inverse of -2.8 which is 2.8.
c $6.3 \times -3 = -18.9$ First multiply 6.3 by 3. The answer must be negative because 6.3 and -3 have opposite signs.
d $-7.5 \div -2.5 = 3$ $7.5 \div 2.5 = 3$. The answer is positive because -7.5 and -2.5 have the same sign.

◆ **Exercise 1.1**

> Do not use a calculator in this exercise.

1 Work these out.
   a $5 + -3$ **b** $5 + -0.3$ **c** $-5 + -0.3$ **d** $-0.5 + 0.3$ **e** $0.5 + -3$

2 Work these out.
   a $2.8 + -1.3$ **b** $0.6 + -4.1$ **c** $-5.8 + 0.3$ **d** $-0.7 + 6.2$ **e** $-2.25 + -0.12$

3 Work these out.
   a $7 - {-4}$ **b** $-7 - 0.4$ **c** $-0.4 - {-7}$ **d** $-0.4 - 0.7$ **e** $-4 - {-0.7}$

4 Work these out.
   a $2.8 - {-1.3}$ **b** $0.6 - {-4.1}$ **c** $-5.8 - 0.3$ **d** $-0.7 - 6.2$ **e** $-2.25 - {-0.12}$

5 The midday temperature, in Celsius degrees (°C), on four successive days is 1.5, −2.6, −3.4 and 0.5. Calculate the mean temperature.

6 Find the missing numbers.
   a $\square + 4 = 1.5$ **b** $\square + {-6.3} = -5.9$ **c** $4.3 + \square = -2.1$ **d** $12.5 + \square = 3.5$

7 Find the missing numbers.
   a $\square - 3.5 = -11.6$ **b** $\square - {-2.1} = 4.1$ **c** $\square - 8.2 = 7.2$ **d** $\square - {-8.2} = 7.2$

8 Copy and complete this addition table.

+	−3.4	−1.2
5.1		
	−4.7	

9 Use the information in the box to work these out.

$$2.3 \times 9.6 = 22.08$$

   a $-2.3 \times {-9.6}$ **b** $-22.08 \div 2.3$ **c** $22.08 \div {-9.6}$
   d $-4.6 \times {-9.6}$ **e** $-11.04 \div {-2.3}$

10 Work these out.
   a $2.7 \times {-3}$ **b** $2.7 \div {-3}$ **c** $-1.2 \times {-1.2}$ **d** $-3.25 \times {-4}$ **e** $17.5 \div {-2.5}$

11 Copy and complete this multiplication table.

×	3.2	−0.6
−1.5		
		1.5

12 Complete these calculations.
   a $-2 \times {-3}$ **b** $(-2 \times {-3}) \times {-4}$ **c** $(-3 \times 4) \div {-8}$

13 Use the values given in the box to work out the value of each expression.
   a $p - q$ **b** $(p + q) \times r$
   c $(q + r) \times p$ **d** $(r - q) \div (q - p)$

$$p = -4.5 \quad q = 5.5 \quad r = -7.5$$

14 Here is a multiplication table.
Use the table to calculate these.
   a $(-2.4)^2$ **b** $13.44 \div {-4.6}$
   c $-16.1 \div {-3.5}$ **d** $-84 \div 2.4$

×	2.4	3.5	4.6
2.4	5.76	8.4	13.44
3.5	8.4	12.25	16.1
4.6	13.44	16.1	21.16

15 p and q are numbers, $p + q = 1$ and $pq = -20$. What are the values of p and q?

1.2 Square roots and cube roots

You should be able to recognise:

- the squares of whole numbers up to 20×20 and their corresponding square roots
- the cubes of whole numbers up to $5 \times 5 \times 5$ and their corresponding cube roots.

> Only squares or cubes of integers have integer square roots or cube roots.

You can use a calculator to find square roots and cube roots, but you can estimate them without one.

Worked example 1.1

Estimate each root, to the nearest whole number. **a** $\sqrt{295}$ **b** $\sqrt[3]{60}$

a $17^2 = 289$ and $18^2 = 324$

$\sqrt{295}$ is 17 to the nearest whole number.

295 is between 289 and 324 so $\sqrt{295}$ is between 17 and 18.
It will be a bit larger than 17.

b $3^3 = 27$ and $4^3 = 64$
$\sqrt[3]{60}$ is 4, to the nearest whole number.

60 is between 27 and 64 so $\sqrt[3]{60}$ is between 3 and 4.
It will be a bit less than 4. A calculator gives 3.91 to 2 d.p.

◆ **Exercise 1.2**

> Do not use a calculator in this exercise, unless you are told to.

1 Read the statement on the right. Write a similar statement for each root.
  a $\sqrt{20}$ **b** $\sqrt{248}$ **c** $\sqrt{314}$ **d** $\sqrt{83.5}$ **e** $\sqrt{157}$

> $2 < \sqrt{8} < 3$

2 Explain why $\sqrt[3]{305}$ is between 6 and 7.

3 Estimate each root, to the nearest whole number.
  a $\sqrt{171}$ **b** $\sqrt{35}$ **c** $\sqrt{407}$ **d** $\sqrt{26.3}$ **e** $\sqrt{292}$

4 Read the statement on the right. Write a similar statement for each root.
  a $\sqrt[3]{100}$ **b** $\sqrt[3]{222}$ **c** $\sqrt[3]{825}$ **d** $\sqrt[3]{326}$ **e** $\sqrt[3]{58.8}$

> $10 < \sqrt[3]{1200} < 11$

5 What Ahmad says is not correct.
  a Show that $\sqrt{160}$ is between 12 and 13.
  b Write down the number of which 40 is square root.

> $\sqrt{16} = 4$ so $\sqrt{160} = 40$.

6 a Find $\sqrt{1225}$.   **b** Estimate $\sqrt[3]{1225}$ to the nearest whole number.

> $35^2 = 1225$

7 Show that $\sqrt[3]{125}$ is less than half of $\sqrt{125}$.

8 Use a calculator to find these square roots and cube roots.
  a $\sqrt{625}$ **b** $\sqrt{20.25}$ **c** $\sqrt{46.24}$ **d** $\sqrt[3]{1728}$ **e** $\sqrt[3]{6.859}$

9 Use a calculator to find these square roots and cube roots. Round your answers to 2 d.p.
  a $\sqrt{55}$ **b** $\sqrt{108}$ **c** $\sqrt[3]{200}$ **d** $\sqrt[3]{629}$ **e** $\sqrt[3]{10\,000}$

1.3 Indices

This table shows powers of 3. Look at the patterns in the table.

> 3^4 is 3 to the **power** 4.
>
> 4 is called the **index**.
>
> The plural of index is **indices**.

Power	3^{-4}	3^{-3}	3^{-2}	3^{-1}	3^0	3^1	3^2	3^3	3^4	3^5
Value	$\frac{1}{81}$	$\frac{1}{27}$	$\frac{1}{9}$	$\frac{1}{3}$	1	3	9	27	81	243

Negative powers of any positive integer are fractions. Here are some more examples.

$2^4 = 2 \times 2 \times 2 \times 2 = 16$ $2^{-4} = \frac{1}{16}$ $7^3 = 7 \times 7 \times 7 = 353$ $7^{-3} = \frac{1}{343}$

Any positive integer to the power 0 is 1. $2^0 = 1$ $7^0 = 1$ $12^0 = 1$

Worked example 1.3

Write these as fractions.   **a** 2^{-6} **b** 6^{-2}

a $2^{-6} = \frac{1}{2^6} = \frac{1}{64}$ $2^6 = 2 \times 2 \times 2 \times 2 \times 2 \times 2 = 64$

b $6^{-2} = \frac{1}{6^2} = \frac{1}{36}$ $6^2 = 36$

◆ Exercise 1.3

1 Write each number as a fraction.   **a** 5^{-1} **b** 5^{-2} **c** 5^{-3} **d** 5^{-4}

2 Write each number as a fraction or as an integer.
   a 7^2 **b** 7^{-2} **c** 7^{-1} **d** 7^0 **e** 7^3

3 Write each number as a fraction.
   a 4^{-1} **b** 10^{-2} **c** 2^{-3} **d** 12^{-1} **e** 15^{-2} **f** 20^{-2}

4 **a** Simplify each number.   **i** 2^0 **ii** 5^0 **iii** 10^0 **iv** 20^0
   b Write the results in part **a** as a generalised rule.

5 Write each expression as a single number.
   a $2^0 + 2^{-1} + 2^{-2}$ **b** $3^2 + 3 + 3^0 + 3^{-1}$ **c** $5 - 5^0 - 5^{-1}$

6 Write each number as a decimal.
   a 5^{-1} **b** 5^{-2} **c** 10^{-1} **d** 10^{-2} **e** 10^{-3}

7 Write each number as a power of 2.
   a 8   **b** $\frac{1}{2}$ **c** $\frac{1}{4}$ **d** $\frac{1}{16}$ **e** 1

8 $2^{10} = 1024$. In computing this is called 1K. Write each of these as a power of 2.
   a 2K   **b** 0.5K   **c** $\frac{1}{1K}$

1.4 Working with indices

You can write the numbers in the boxes as powers.
Look at the indices. $2 + 3 = 5$ and $5 + 3 = 8$.

$9 \times 27 = 243$	$32 \times 8 = 256$
$3^2 \times 3^3 = 3^5$	$2^5 \times 2^3 = 2^8$

This is an example of a general result.

> To <u>multiply</u> powers of a number, <u>add</u> the indices. $A^m \times A^n = A^{m+n}$

$9 \times 9 = 81 \quad \Rightarrow \quad 3^2 \times 3^2 = 3^4 \qquad 2 + 2 = 4$

$4 \times 8 = 32 \quad \Rightarrow \quad 2^2 \times 2^3 = 2^5 \qquad 2 + 3 = 5$

The multiplications above can be written as divisions.
You can write the numbers as powers.
Again, look at the indices. $5 - 3 = 2$ and $8 - 3 = 5$.
This shows that:

$243 \div 27 = 9$	$256 \div 8 = 32$
$3^5 \div 3^3 = 3^2$	$2^8 \div 2^3 = 2^5$

> To <u>divide</u> powers of a number, <u>subtract</u> the indices. $A^m \div A^n = A^{m-n}$

$27 \div 3 = 9 \quad \Rightarrow \quad 3^3 \div 3^1 = 3^2 \qquad 3 - 1 = 2$

$4 \div 8 = \frac{1}{2} \quad \Rightarrow \quad 2^2 \div 2^3 = 2^{-1} \qquad 2 - 3 = -1$

Worked example 1.4

a Write each expression as a power of 5.   i $5^2 \times 5^3$ ii $5^2 \div 5^3$
b Check your answers by writing the numbers as decimals.

a i $5^2 \times 5^3 = 5^{2+3} = 5^5$ $2 + 3 = 5$
   ii $5^2 \div 5^3 = 5^{2-3} = 5^{-1} = \frac{1}{5}$ $2 - 3 = -1$
b i $25 \times 125 = 3125$ 3125 is 5^5
   ii $25 \div 125 = \frac{1}{5} = 0.2$

◆ Exercise 1.4

1 Simplify each expression. Write your answers in index form.
   a $5^2 \times 5^3$ b $6^4 \times 6^3$ c $10^4 \times 10^2$ d $a^2 \times a^2 \times a^3$ e $4^5 \times 4$

2 Simplify each expression. Leave your answers in index form where appropriate.
   a $2^5 \times 2^3$ b $8^2 \times 8^4$ c $a^3 \times a^2$ d $2^3 \times 2^3$ e $b^3 \times b^4$

3 Simplify each expression.
   a $3^5 \div 3^2$ b $k^4 \div k^3$ c $10^6 \div 10^4$ d $5^2 \div 5^4$ e $7 \div 7^1$

4 Simplify each expression.
   a $2^2 \div 2^2$ b $2^2 \div 2^3$ c $2^2 \div 2^4$ d $2^4 \div 2^2$ e $2^4 \div 2^6$

5 Write each expression as a power or fraction.

   a $8^3 \times 8^4$ **b** $5^2 \times 5$ **c** $4^2 \times 4^4$ **d** $9^2 \div 9^3$ **e** $12^2 \div 12^4$

6 Find the value of N in each part.

   a $10^2 \times 10^N = 10^4$ **b** $10^2 \div 10^N = 10$ **c** $10^2 \times 10^N = 10^7$ **d** $10^2 \div 10^N = 10^{-1}$

7 This table shows values of powers of 7.
   Use the table to find the value of:

7^1	7^2	7^3	7^4	7^5	7^6
7	49	343	2401	16 807	117 649

   a 49×2401 **b** $16\,807 \div 343$ **c** 343^2.

8 a Write the numbers in the box as powers of 4. Check that the division rule for indices is correct.

   $$1024 \div 16 = 64$$

   b Write the numbers as powers of 2 and check that the division rule for indices is correct.

9 a Write 9 and 243 as powers of 3.

   b Use your answers to part **a** to find, as powers of 3:   **i** 9×243 **ii** $9 \div 243$.

10 Simplify each fraction.

   a $\dfrac{2^3 \times 2^4}{2^5}$ **b** $\dfrac{a^3 \times a^2}{a^2}$ **c** $\dfrac{d^3 \times d}{d^1}$ **d** $\dfrac{10^6 \times 10^4}{10^2 \times 10^3}$

11 a Write each of these as a power of 2.

   i $(2^2)^2$ **ii** $(2^2)^3$ **iii** $(2^4)^2$ **iv** $(2^4)^3$ **v** $(2^2)^4$

   b What can you say about $(2^m)^n$ if m and n are positive integers?

12 In computing, $1K = 2^{10} = 1024$. Write each of these in K.

   a 2^{12} **b** 2^{15} **c** 2^{20} **d** 2^7

13 Find the value of n in each equation.

   a $3^n \times 3^2 = 81$ **b** $5^n \times 25 = 625$ **c** $2^n \div 2 = 8$ **d** $n^2 \times n = 216$

Summary

You should now know that:

★ You can add, subtract, multiply or divide directed numbers in the same way as integers.

★ Using inverses can simplify calculations with directed numbers.

★ Only square numbers or cube numbers have square roots or cube roots that are integers.

★ $A^0 = 1$ if A is a positive integer.

★ $A^{-n} = \dfrac{1}{A^n}$ if A and n are positive integers.

★ $A^m \times A^n = A^{m+n}$

★ $A^m \div A^n = A^{m-n}$

You should be able to:

★ Add, subtract, multiply and divide directed numbers.

★ Estimate square roots and cube roots.

★ Use positive, negative and zero indices.

★ Use the index laws for multiplication and division of positive integer powers.

★ Use the rules of arithmetic and inverse operations to simplify calculations.

★ Calculate accurately, choosing operations and mental or written methods appropriate to the number and context.

★ Manipulate numbers and apply routine algorithms.

End-of-unit review

1 Complete these additions.

   a $-3 + 6$ **b** $12 + -14.5$ **c** $-3.5 + -5.7$ **d** $-3.6 + 2.8 + -1.3$

2 Subtract.

   a $12 - -4$ **b** $-6.4 - 8.3$ **c** $3.7 - -8.3$ **d** $-5.1 - -5.2$

3 $2.5 \times 4.5 = 11.25$. Use this to find the value of each expression.

   a -2.5×-4.5 **b** $-11.25 \div -4.5$ **c** -4.5×1.25

4 Solve these equations.

   a $x + 17.8 = 14.2$ **b** $y - 3.4 = -9.7$ **c** $3y + -4.9 = 2.6$

5 Look at the statement in the box. Write a similar statement for each number.

   a $\sqrt{111}$ **b** $\sqrt{333}$ **c** $\sqrt{111}$ **d** $\sqrt[3]{333}$

$4 < \sqrt{19} < 5$

6 a Estimate $\sqrt{200}$ to the nearest whole number.

   b Estimate $\sqrt[3]{200}$ to the nearest whole number.

7 Choose the number that is closest to $\sqrt{250}$.

   14.9   15.1   15.4   15.8   16.2

8 Choose the number that is closest to $\sqrt[3]{550}$.

   7.6   7.8   8.2   8.5   8.8

9 Show that $\sqrt{1000}$ is more than three times $\sqrt[3]{1000}$.

10 Write each of these numbers as a decimal.

   a 2^{-1} **b** 4^{-1} **c** 2^{-2} **d** 5^{-2}

11 Write each number as a fraction.

   a 3^{-2} **b** 2^{-3} **c** 6^{-1} **d** 12^{-2}

12 Write each expression as a single number.

   a $2^2 + 2^0 + 2^{-2}$ **b** $10^{-1} + 10^0 + 10^3$

13 Write each number as a power of 10.

   a 100 **b** 1000 **c** 0.01 **d** 0.001 **e** 1

14 Write each expression as a single power.

   a $9^2 \times 9^3$ **b** 8×8^2 **c** $7^5 \div 7^2$ **d** $a \div a^3$ **e** $n^1 \div n^2$

15 Simplify each expression.

   a $2^4 \div 2^5$ **b** $15^0 \times 15^2$ **c** $20^5 \div 20^3$ **d** $5^2 \div (5^3 \times 5^1)$

16 Write each expression as a power of *a*.

   a $a^2 \times a^4$ **b** $a^2 \div a^4$ **c** $a^2 \times a^0$ **d** $a^1 \times a^4$ **e** $a^2 \div a^4$

17 Simplify each expression.

   a $\dfrac{4^2 \times 4^4}{4^3}$ **b** $\dfrac{a^2}{a^3 \times a}$ **c** $\dfrac{n^2 \times n^1}{n^2}$

18 Find the value of *n* in each of these equations.

   a $4^n = 1$ **b** $5^n = 0.2$ **c** $n \times n^2 = 343$ **d** $2^4 \div 2^n = 4$

2 Sequences and functions

All children learn to count. They learn this **sequence** of numbers.

1 2 3 4 5 6 7 8 9 10 11 12 13 .....

You can use this sequence to make a new sequence by colouring numbers in equal steps.

Here are three examples:

1 2 3 4 5 6 7 8 9 10 11 12 13 .....

This gives the odd numbers

1 3 5 7 9 11 13 15 17 .....

1 2 3 4 5 6 7 8 9 10 11 12 13 .....

This gives the sequence

2 5 8 11 14 17 20 23 .....

1 2 3 4 5 6 7 8 9 10 11 12 13 14 15 16 17 18 .....

This gives the sequence

2 7 12 17 22 27 32 .....

Can you find the 10th term of each sequence?

You should know how to use a formula for the nth term of a sequence.

Here are the nth terms of the three sequences. They are **not** in the correct order:

$3n - 1$ $5n - 3$ $2n - 1$

Which nth term goes with which sequence?

If you have a formula for the nth term it is easy to find the 10th term of the sequence. Check that you found the 10th term of each of the sequences above correctly.

Using formulas like this is an example of **algebra.**

Al-Khwārizmī

The word algebra comes from the title of a book written by the Persian mathematician Muhammad ibn Mūsā al-Khwārizmī in 820 CE. The book was called *Hisab al-jabr w'al-muqabala*. Can you see a word in the title that looks similar to the word algebra? This was the first book ever written about algebra.

In this chapter you will be studying different sequences and finding a formula for the nth term for some of them.

2.1 Generating sequences

In a **linear sequence** the terms increase (or decrease) by the <u>same</u> amount each time.

In a **non-linear sequence** the terms increase (or decrease) by a <u>different</u> amount each time.

Here is a non-linear sequence of numbers.

     3, 6, 11, 18, 27, ...

Look at the differences between each of the terms.

     $3 + 3 = 6, 6 + 5 = 11, 11 + 7 = 18, 18 + 9 = 27, ...$

Can you see that the differences between the terms are <u>not</u> the same?

The **term-to-term rule** is 'add 3, add 5, add 7, add 9, ...'.

The **position-to-term rule** for this sequence is

'term = position number^2 + 2'.

Check that this rule works by substituting the
position numbers given in the table.

Position number	1	2	3	4	5
Term	3	6	11	18	27

For example: 2nd term $= 2^2 + 2 = 4 + 2 = 6$ ✓   4th term $= 4^2 + 2 = 16 + 2 = 18$ ✓

To find any other term in the sequence, substitute the position number into the rule.

For example: 6th term $= 6^2 + 2 = 36 + 2 = 38$

Worked example 2.1

  a Are these sequences linear or non-linear?   **i** 6, 4, 2, 0, −2, ...   **ii** 8, 5, 1, −4, −10, ...
  b The first term of a non-linear sequence is 4.
     The term-to-term rule is multiply by 2.
     Write down the first four terms of the sequence.
  c The position-to-term rule of a non-linear sequence is: term = 2 × position number^2.
     Work out the first four terms of the sequence.

  a **i** The sequence is linear.   The sequence is decreasing by the same amount (2) each time.
      ii The sequence is non-linear.   The sequence is decreasing by a different amount (3, 4, 5, 6, ...)
                                         each time.
  b First four terms are 4, 8, 16, 32.   Write down the first term, which is 4, then use the
                                        term-to-term rule to work out the next three terms.
                                        Second term = 4 × 2 = 8, third term = 8 × 2 = 16,
                                        fourth term = 16 × 2 = 32.
  c First four terms are 2, 8, 18, 32.   Use the position-to-term rule to work out each term.
                                        First term $= 2 × 1^2 = 2 × 1 = 2$, second term $= 2 × 2^2 = 2 × 4 = 8$,
                                        third term $= 2 × 3^2 = 2 × 9 = 18$, fourth term $= 2 × 4^2 = 2 × 16 = 32$.

◆◆ **Exercise 2.1**

  1 Write down whether each sequence is linear or non-linear.
      Explain your answers.

      a 11, 15, 19, 23, 27, ...   **b** 20, 30, 40, 50, 60, ...   **c** 4, 5, 7, 10, 14, ...
      d 20, 18, 15, 11, 6, ...   **e** 100, 95, 90, 85, 80, ...   **f** 10, 7, 1, −8, −20, ...
      g 0.5, 1, 1.5, 2, 2.5, ...   **h** $3\frac{1}{2}, 5\frac{1}{2}, 9\frac{1}{2}, 17\frac{1}{2}, 33\frac{1}{2}, ...$ **i** 20, 12, 4, −4, −12, ...

2 Write down the first four terms of each sequence.
  a first term is 8   term-to-term rule is 'subtract 5'
  b first term is $2\frac{1}{2}$ term-to-term rule is 'add $1\frac{1}{2}$'
  c first term is 4   term-to-term rule is 'add 1, add 2, add 3, …'
  d first term is 24   term-to-term rule is 'divide by 2'.

3 Zalika is trying to solve this problem.
Work out the answer to the problem.
Explain the method you used to solve
the problem.

> The tenth term of a linear sequence is 18.
> The term-to-term rule is 'subtract 4'.
> Work out the fourth term of the sequence.

4 Shen is trying to solve this problem.
Work out the answer to the problem.
Explain the method you used to solve
the problem.

> The fifth term of a non-linear sequence is 9.
> The term-to-term rule is 'divide by 3'.
> Work out the second term of the sequence.

5 Use the position-to-term rule to work out the first four terms of each sequence.
  a term = position number + 5   **b** term = 3 × position number − 1
  c term = position number^2 + 4   **d** term = 3 × position number^2

6 Use the position-to-term rules to work out:
  i the fifth term   **ii** the 10th term   **iii** the 20th term of each sequence.
  a term = 4 × position number + 1   **b** term = position number^2 − 2

7 The third term of a sequence is 25. The fifth term of the sequence is 73.
Which of these position-to-term rules is the correct one for the sequence?
  A term = position number^2 + 16   **B** term = 5 × position number + 10
  C term = 3 × position number^2 − 2   **D** term = 9 × position number − 2
Show how you worked out your answer.

8 This is Shen's homework. He has spilt tea on some of the questions and answers!

> Question 1   The position-to-term rule of a sequence is:
>   term = 2 × position number +
>
>   Work out the first three terms of the sequence.
>
> Answer   1st term = 9   2nd term =   3rd term =
> Question 2   The position-to-term rule of a sequence is: term =   ×
>   position number^2
>   Work out the first three terms of the sequence.
>
> Answer   1st term =   2nd term = 20   3rd term =

Work out the missing answers for Shen. Explain how you worked them out.

2.2 Finding the *n*th term

A linear sequence may also be called an **arithmetic sequence**.

You can write the position-to-term rule of an arithmetic sequence as an expression called the *n*th term.

For example, the arithmetic sequence   8, 11, 14, 17, ...

has position-to-term rule   term = 3 × position number + 5

which can be written as: *n*th term is $3n + 5$.

But when you look at an arithmetic sequence of numbers, how can you work out the expression for the *n*th term?

Start by writing the sequence in a table like this.

The sequence is increasing by 3 every time, so the *n*th term expression will start with $3n$.

Add a row for $3n$ to the table and work out the values.

Now note that you need to add 5 to every $3n$ term to get the terms in this sequence.

This means the expression for the *n*th term is $3n + 5$.

n	1	2	3	4
terms	8	11	14	17
3n	3×1 3	3×2 6	3×3 9	3×4 12
3n + 5	$3 + 5$ 8	$6 + 5$ 11	$9 + 5$ 14	$12 + 5$ 17

Worked example 2.2

a The *n*th term of a sequence is $6 - 2n$. Work out the first three terms and the 10th term of the sequence.

b Work out the expression for the *n*th term for each sequence.
  i 6, 8, 10, 12, ...   **ii** 10, 7, 4, 1, ...

a   1st term $= 6 - 2 \times 1 = 6 - 2 = 4$ To find the first term substitute $n = 1$ into the expression.
2nd term $= 6 - 2 \times 2 = 6 - 4 = 2$ To find the second term substitute $n = 2$ into the expression.
3rd term $= 6 - 2 \times 3 = 6 - 6 = 0$ To find the third term substitute $n = 3$ into the expression.
10th term $= 6 - 2 \times 10 = 6 - 20 = -14$ To find the tenth term substitute $n = 10$ into the expression.

b i

n	1	2	3	4
terms	6	8	10	12
2n	2	4	6	8
2n + 4	6	8	10	12

*n*th term expression is $2n + 4$.

Start by writing the sequence in a table.
The sequence is increasing by 2 every time, so the *n*th term expression will start with $2n$. Add a row for $2n$ to the table and work out the values.
You can see that you need to add 4 to the $2n$ values to get the terms of the sequence.

ii

n	1	2	3	4
terms	10	7	4	1
−3n	−3	−6	−9	−12
−3n + 13	10	7	4	1

*n*th term expression is $-3n + 13$.
This can be written as $13 - 3n$.

Start by writing the sequence in a table.
The sequence is decreasing by 3 every time, so the *n*th term expression will start with $-3n$. Add a row for $-3n$ to the table and work out the values.
You need to add 13 to the $-3n$ values to get the terms of the sequence.

It is neater to write the expression with the positive term before the negative one.

🔷 Exercise 2.2

1 The *n*th term of a sequence is $3n$. Work out the first three terms and the 10th term of the sequence.

2 The *n*th term of a sequence is $6 - n$. Work out the first three terms and the 20th term of the sequence.

3 The *n*th term of a sequence is $4n + 7$. Work out the first three terms and the 50th term of the sequence.

4 The *n*th term of a sequence is $10n - 8$. Work out the first three terms and the 100th term of the sequence.

5 Match each yellow sequence card with the correct blue *n*th term expression card.

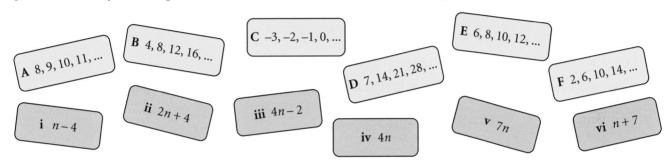

A $8, 9, 10, 11, \ldots$
B $4, 8, 12, 16, \ldots$
C $-3, -2, -1, 0, \ldots$
D $7, 14, 21, 28, \ldots$
E $6, 8, 10, 12, \ldots$
F $2, 6, 10, 14, \ldots$

i $n - 4$
ii $2n + 4$
iii $4n - 2$
iv $4n$
v $7n$
vi $n + 7$

6 Work out an expression for the *n*th term for each sequence.
   a $3, 5, 7, 9, \ldots$ **b** $5, 8, 11, 14, \ldots$ **c** $4, 9, 14, 19, \ldots$
   d $2, 10, 18, 26, \ldots$ **e** $8, 6, 4, 2, \ldots$ **f** $11, 7, 3, -1, \ldots$
   g $-2, -7, -12, -17, \ldots$ **h** $-3, 6, 15, 24, \ldots$ **i** $23, 35, 47, 59, \ldots$

7 Use the *n*th term expression to work out the 100th term of each sequence in question **6**.

8 Tanesha and Jake are looking at the number sequence.

$4, 4\frac{1}{2}, 5, 5\frac{1}{2}, 6, \ldots$

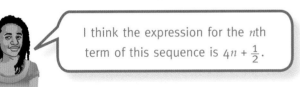

I think the expression for the *n*th term of this sequence is $4n + \frac{1}{2}$.

I think the expression for the *n*th term of this sequence is $\frac{1}{2}n + 4$.

Is either statement correct? Explain your answer.

9 Look at this number sequence. $24, 18, 12, 6, 0, \ldots$

By just looking at the numbers in the sequence, explain why you can tell that the *n*th term expression for this sequence cannot be $6n + 18$.

10 This pattern is made from green squares.

        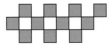   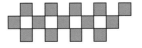

Pattern 1   Pattern 2   Pattern 3   Pattern 4

Razi thinks that the *n*th term for the sequence of numbers of green squares is $3n + 2$.
Is Razi correct? Explain how you worked out your answer.

2.3 Finding the inverse of a function

You can represent a function in three different ways.

① As a function machine   ② As an equation   ③ As a mapping

$x \longrightarrow \boxed{\times 2} \longrightarrow \boxed{+3} \longrightarrow y$ $y = 2x + 3$ $x \rightarrow 2x + 3$

To work out the output values, substitute the input values into the function.

In this function, the missing output values are:

$5 \times 2 + 3 = 13$ and $8 \times 2 + 3 = 19$

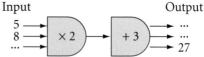

To work out the missing input value you take the output value and reverse the function.

So, in this function, the missing input value is: $\frac{27-3}{2} = 12$

When you reverse the function you are finding the **inverse function**.

You can write an inverse function as a function machine, an equation or a mapping like this.

Function: $x \longrightarrow \boxed{\times 2} \longrightarrow \boxed{+3} \longrightarrow 2x+3$

Inverse: $\frac{x-3}{2} \longleftarrow \boxed{\div 2} \longleftarrow \boxed{-3} \longleftarrow x$

So the inverse function is $y = \frac{x-3}{2}$ or $x \rightarrow \frac{x-3}{2}$.

Worked example 2.3

Work out the inverse function for: **a** $y = x + 5$ **b** $x \rightarrow \frac{x}{2} - 4$.

a

$x \longrightarrow \boxed{+5} \longrightarrow x+5$ Draw the function machine.

$x-5 \longleftarrow \boxed{-5} \longleftarrow x$ Reverse the function machine.

$y = x - 5$ Write the inverse function as an equation.

b

$x \longrightarrow \boxed{\div 2} \longrightarrow \boxed{-4} \longrightarrow \frac{x}{2} - 4$ Draw the function machine.

$2(x+4) \longleftarrow \boxed{\times 2} \longleftarrow \boxed{+4} \longleftarrow x$ Reverse the function machine.

$x \rightarrow 2(x + 4)$ Write the inverse function as a mapping.

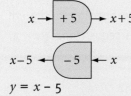 **Exercise 2.3**

1 Work out the inverse function for each equation.
   a $y = x + 9$ **b** $y = x - 1$ **c** $y = 3x$ **d** $y = \frac{x}{6}$

2 Work out the inverse function for each mapping.
  a $x \rightarrow x + 3$ **b** $x \rightarrow x - 8$ **c** $x \rightarrow 4x$ **d** $x \rightarrow \frac{x}{3}$

3 Work out the inverse function for each equation.
  a $y = 2x + 5$ **b** $y = 4x - 7$ **c** $y = \frac{x}{2} + 1$ **d** $y = \frac{x-4}{3}$

4 Work out the inverse function for each mapping.
  a $x \rightarrow 5x + 1$ **b** $x \rightarrow 3x - 7$ **c** $x \rightarrow \frac{x}{5} - 10$ **d** $x \rightarrow \frac{x+9}{4}$

5 This is part of Mia's homework.

Question   What do you notice about the inverse function of $x \rightarrow 2 - x$?

Answer $x \rightarrow 2 - x$ is the same as $x \rightarrow -x + 2$.

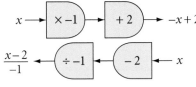

$\dfrac{x-2}{-1}$ is the same as $\dfrac{2-x}{1}$ or $2 - x$.

The inverse function is $x \rightarrow 2 - x$, which is the same as the function.

This function is called a _self-inverse_ function.

  a Use Mia's method to work out the inverse function of each mapping.
    i $x \rightarrow 10 - x$ **ii** $x \rightarrow 1 - 2x$ **iii** $x \rightarrow 4 - x$ **iv** $x \rightarrow 3 - 4x$
  b Which of the functions in part **a** are self-inverse functions?

6 Harsha thought of a number. She added 13 to the number then multiplied the result by 4.
  a Write this as a function as a mapping.
  Harsha's answer was 6.
  b Use inverse functions to work out the number Harsha thought of. Show all your working.

Summary

You should now know that:

★ The word 'algebra' comes from the word _al-jabr_. It was first used by the Persian mathematician Al-Khwārizmī, who wrote the first book on algebra.

★ In a non-linear sequence the terms increase, or decrease, by a different amount each time.

★ You find the inverse of a function by reversing the function.

You should be able to:

★ Use term-to-term and position-to-term rules to generate terms of a sequence.

★ Derive an expression to find the *n*th term of an arithmetic sequence.

★ Find the inverse of a linear function.

End-of-unit review

1 Is the sequence 15, 14, 12, 9, ... linear or non-linear? Explain your answer.

2 The eighth term of a linear sequence is 26. The term-to-term rule is 'add 3'.
Work out the fourth term of the sequence.
Explain the method you used to solve this problem.

3 The fifth term of a non-linear sequence is 324. The term-to-term rule is 'multiply by 3'.
Work out the second term of the sequence.
Explain the method you used to solve this problem.

4 A sequence follows the position-to-term rule: term = $2 \times$ position number$^2 - 2$.
Work out:
i the first four terms   **ii** the 10th term   **iii** the 20th term.

5 Work out an expression for the nth term for each sequence.
a 5, 7, 9, 11, ...   **b** 10, 8, 6, 4, ...   **c** $-8, -5, -2, 1, ...$

6 Look at this number sequence.
Maha thinks that the nth term expression for this sequence
cannot be $10 - 6n$.
Explain why she is correct.

4, 10, 16, 22, ...

7 This pattern is made from pink dots.

Pattern 1   Pattern 2   Pattern 3   Pattern 4

Alicia thinks the expression for the nth term for the sequence of the numbers of pink dots is $4n + 2$.
Anders thinks it is $2n + 2$. Oditi thinks it is $n + 3$.
Who is correct? Explain how you worked out your answer.

8 Work out the inverse function for each equation.
a $y = x - 2$ **b** $y = 8x$ **c** $y = \frac{x}{5} + 2$ **d** $y = \frac{x+1}{2}$

9 Work out the inverse function for each mapping.
a $x \rightarrow x + 1$ **b** $x \rightarrow \frac{x}{4}$ **c** $x \rightarrow 3x - 7$ **d** $x \rightarrow \frac{x+2}{10}$

10 Dakarai thought of a number. He subtracted 11 from the number then divided the result by 4.
a Use a mapping to write this as a function.
Dakarai's answer was -1.2.
b Use inverse functions to work out the number Dakarai thought of. Show all your working.

11 Sasha thought of a number. She added 22.5 to the number then multiplied the result by 2.
a Write this as a function as a mapping.
Sasha's answer was 50.
b Use inverse functions to work out the number Sasha thought of. Show all your working.

3 Place value, ordering and rounding

There are hundreds of different languages in use in the world today.
However, all over the world people write numbers in the same way.
Everyone uses the decimal system to write numbers.
The decimal system is a universal language. Why is that?
One system that was used in the past is Roman numerals.
2000 years ago the Romans used letters to represent numbers.
You can still see them on clock faces and carvings.

Key words

Make sure you learn and understand these key words:

jottings
significant figures
BIDMAS
order of operations

Their use continued in Europe for over 1000 years. Here are some examples.

Roman	III	VII	IX	XX	C	MCMXXX	S
Decimal	3	7	9	20	100	1930	0.5

Here are some calculations, multiplying or dividing by 10 or 100, written with Roman numerals.

III × X = XXX   V × C = D   M ÷ C = X   LV ÷ X = VS

Can you work out what D, M and L represent?
You can see that arithmetic with Roman numerals is very difficult. You keep needing new letters.
The decimal system uses **place value**. That is why it only needs ten symbols: 0, 1, 2, 3, 4, 5, 6, 7, 8 and 9.
The symbols mean different things in different places. It makes arithmetic much easier.
Multiplying or dividing by 10 or 100 becomes very easy. You should be able to do these in your head.

7 × 10 = ...   2.4 × 100 = ...   6.3 ÷ 10 = ...   45 ÷ 100 = ...

You should be able to multiply or divide by 0.1 or 0.01 as well.

7 × 0.1 = ...   2.4 × 0.01 = ...   6.3 ÷ 0.1 = ...   45 ÷ 0.01 = ...

- The decimal system was first developed in India.
- It was adopted by Persian and Arab mathematicians in the 9th century.
- It was introduced into Europe about 1000 years ago.
- At first it was banned in some European cities. People did not understand it and thought they were being cheated.

Check: here are the answers to the questions: 70; 240; 0.63; 0.45; 0.7; 0.024; 63; 4500

In this unit you will learn how to multiply and divide decimals mentally. You will also learn how to multiply and divide numbers by powers of 10, round numbers to a given number of decimal places and significant figures, and make sure you use the correct order of operations.

3.1 Multiplying and dividing decimals mentally

To multiply or divide a number by a decimal number, you need to be able to work out an equivalent calculation that you can do 'in your head', or mentally.

This might be easy for a simple question. For a more difficult question, you can use brief notes to write down some of the steps in the working. These are called **jottings**. They help you remember what you have worked out so far, and what you still need to do.

Here are two reminders to help you check whether your answer could be right or wrong.

- When you <u>multiply</u> any number by a decimal number between 0 and 1, your answer will be <u>smaller</u> than the number you started with.

- When you <u>divide</u> any number by a decimal number between 0 and 1, your answer will be <u>greater</u> than the number you started with.

Worked example 3.1

Work these out mentally.   **a** 12×0.6 **b** 0.3×0.15 **c** $16 \div 0.4$ **d** $8 \div 0.02$ **e** $\dfrac{36 \times 0.5}{0.2 \times 4.5}$

a $12 \times 6 = 72$
   $12 \times 0.6 = 7.2$

Ignore the decimal point and work out $12 \times 6 = 72$ in your head.
The answer 72 is 10 times bigger than the actual answer, because 6 is 10 times bigger than 0.6. Divide the answer 72 by 10 to get 7.2.

b $3 \times 15 = 45$
   $0.3 \times 0.15 = 0.045$

Ignore the decimal points, and work out $3 \times 15 = 45$ in your head.
$3 \times 15 = 45 \rightarrow 0.3 \times 15 = 4.5 \rightarrow 0.3 \times 0.15 = 0.045$.

c $\dfrac{16 \times 10}{0.4 \times 10}$
   $\dfrac{160}{4} = 40$

In your head, think of the division as a fraction, then multiply the top and the bottom of the fraction by 10 to eliminate the decimal from the division.
This makes an equivalent calculation, which is much easier to do.

d $\dfrac{8 \times 100}{0.02 \times 100}$
   $\dfrac{800}{2} = 400$

Again, in your head, think of the division as a fraction, then multiply the top and the bottom of the fraction by 100 to eliminate the decimal.
This again makes an equivalent calculation, which is much easier to do.

e $36 \times 0.5 = 18$

Work out the answer to the numerator first. Since 0.5 is the same as one half, work out $\frac{1}{2} \times 36 = 18$. Jot down the answer 18 so you don't forget it.

   $2 \times 4.5 = 9$
   So $0.2 \times 4.5 = 0.9$
   $\dfrac{36 \times 0.5}{0.2 \times 4.5} = \dfrac{18}{0.9}$

Work out $2 \times 4.5 = 9$ in your head.
2 is 10 times bigger than 0.2, so divide the answer 9 by 10 to get 0.9.

   $\dfrac{18 \times 10}{0.9 \times 10}$
   $\dfrac{180}{9} = 20$

Multiply the top and the bottom of the fraction by 10 to eliminate the decimal.

This makes an equivalent calculation, which is much easier to do.

◆ Exercise 3.1

1 Work these out mentally.
   a 8×0.2 **b** 12×0.3 **c** 8×0.7 **d** 0.6×9 **e** 0.4×15
   f 6×0.05 **g** 18×0.02 **h** 22×0.03 **i** 0.08×30 **j** 0.04×45

2 Work these out mentally.

    a $4 \div 0.2$ **b** $9 \div 0.3$ **c** $25 \div 0.5$ **d** $12 \div 0.4$ **e** $60 \div 0.1$

    f $2 \div 0.05$ **g** $6 \div 0.02$ **h** $28 \div 0.07$ **i** $24 \div 0.12$ **j** $45 \div 0.15$

3 Arrange these cards into groups that have the *same* answer.

A 3×0.05	**B** 30×0.05	**C** 0.3×0.05	**D** 0.005×3

E 500×0.03	**F** 5×0.03	**G** 0.3×5	**H** 0.3×0.5

I 0.003×5	**J** 0.005×30	**K** 0.03×0.5	**L** 0.5×3

4 Which answer is correct, A, B, C or D?

    a $0.8 \div 0.02 =$ **A** 0.04 **B** 0.4 **C** 4 **D** 40

    b $4.5 \div 0.5 =$ **A** 0.9 **B** 9 **C** 90 **D** 900

    c $0.09 \div 0.003 =$ **A** 0.3 **B** 3 **C** 30 **D** 300

    d $3.6 \div 0.006 =$ **A** 0.6 **B** 6 **C** 60 **D** 600

5 Work these out mentally.

    a 0.6×0.2 **b** 4.5×0.3 **c** 0.18×0.4 **d** 0.06×2.5 **e** 0.11×0.5

    f $0.6 \div 0.02$ **g** $2.7 \div 0.3$ **h** $0.45 \div 0.09$ **i** $0.28 \div 0.04$ **j** $3.6 \div 0.09$

6 This is part of Hassan's homework.
He has jotted down some workings to help
him answer the question.
He has made a mistake.
Explain the mistake Hassan has made and
work out the correct answer.

> *Question* Work out mentally $\dfrac{24 \times 0.25}{0.2 \times 0.6}$
>
> *Answer* Top: $\frac{1}{4}$ of $24 = 6$ Bottom: 1.2
> $6 \div 1.2 = 60 \div 12 = 5$

7 Work out the answers mentally. Use jottings to help.

    a $\dfrac{48 \times 0.5}{0.04 \times 3}$ **b** $\dfrac{120 \times 0.3}{0.2 \times 1.5}$ **c** $\dfrac{84 \times 0.25}{35 \times 0.002}$ **d** $\dfrac{120 \times 0.4 \times 0.1}{0.8 \times 0.15}$

8 a Work these out mentally.

    i 8×0.1 **ii** 8×0.2 **iii** 8×0.3 **iv** 8×0.4 **v** 8×0.5 **vi** 8×0.6

  b Use your answers to part **a** to answer this question.
    If you multiply a number by 0.7, would you expect the answer to be larger or smaller than your
    answer when you multiply the same number by 0.6?

9 a Work these out mentally.

    i $12 \div 0.1$ **ii** $12 \div 0.2$ **iii** $12 \div 0.3$ **iv** $12 \div 0.4$ **v** $12 \div 0.5$ **vi** $12 \div 0.6$

  b Use your answers to part **a** to answer this question.
    If you divide a number by 0.7, would you expect your answer to be larger or smaller than when
    you divide the same number by 0.6?

3.2 Multiplying and dividing by powers of 10

Look at this section of the decimal place-value table.

...	Thousands	Hundreds	Tens	Units	•	tenths	hundredths	thousandths	...
...	1000	100	10	1	•	$\frac{1}{10}$	$\frac{1}{100}$	$\frac{1}{1000}$	...

The numbers 10, 100, 1000, ... can be written as powers of 10.

The numbers $\frac{1}{10}, \frac{1}{100}, \frac{1}{1000}$, ... can also can be written as powers of 10.

Look at this pattern of numbers, written as powers of 10. Is there a link between the powers and the value?

..., $1000 = 10^3$, $100 = 10^2$, $10 = 10^1$, $1 = 10^0$, $\frac{1}{10} = 10^{-1}$, $\frac{1}{100} = 10^{-2}$, $\frac{1}{1000} = 10^{-3}$, ...

You should see that the decimal 0.1 can be written as $\frac{1}{10}$ or 10^{-1}.

You can also see that the decimal 0.01 can be written as $\frac{1}{100}$ or 10^{-2}.

This pattern continues as the numbers get bigger and smaller.

For example, $10\,000 = 10^4$ and $\frac{1}{10\,000} = 10^{-4}$, $100\,000 = 10^5$ and $\frac{1}{100\,000} = 10^{-5}$.

It is important to remember these two key points:

① Multiplying a number by $\frac{1}{10}, \frac{1}{100}, \frac{1}{1000}$, ... is the same as dividing the same number by 10, 100, 1000, ...

② Dividing a number by $\frac{1}{10}, \frac{1}{100}, \frac{1}{1000}$, ... is the same as multiplying the same number by 10, 100, 1000, ...

Worked example 3.2

Work these out.　　**a** 2.5×10^3　　**b** 12×10^{-2}　　**c** $365 \div 10^4$　　**d** $0.45 \div 10^{-3}$

a　$10^3 = 1000$　　　　　Start by writing 10^3 as 1000.
　　2.5×1000　　　　Rewrite the multiplication as 2.5×1000.
　　$= 2500$　　　　　　Finally, work out the answer.

b　$10^{-2} = \frac{1}{100}$　　　　Start by writing 10^{-2} as $\frac{1}{100}$.
　　$12 \times \frac{1}{100} = 12 \div 100$　Multiplying 12 by $\frac{1}{100}$ is the same as dividing 12 by 100.
　　　　　$= 0.12$　　Finally, work out the answer.

c　$10^4 = 10\,000$　　　　Start by writing 10^4 as 10 000.
　　$365 \div 10\,000$　　　Rewrite the division as $365 \div 10\,000$.
　　$= 0.0365$　　　　Finally, work out the answer.

d　$10^{-3} = \frac{1}{1000}$　　　Start by writing 10^{-3} as $\frac{1}{1000}$.
　　$0.45 \div \frac{1}{1000} = 0.45 \times 1000$　Dividing 0.45 by $\frac{1}{1000}$ is the same as multiplying 0.45 by 1000.
　　　　　$= 450$　　Finally, work out the answer.

◆ Exercise 3.2

1 Work these out.
   a 13×10^2 **b** 7.8×10^3 **c** 24×10 **d** 8.55×10^4

   e 6.5×10^1 **f** 0.08×10^5 **g** 17×10^0 **h** 8×10^{-1}

   i 8.5×10^{-2} **j** 4500×10^{-4} **k** 32×10^{-3} **l** 125×10^{-2}

> **Remember:**
> $10^0 = 1$
> $10^1 = 10$

2 Work these out.
   a $27 \div 10$ **b** $450 \div 10^3$ **c** $36 \div 10^2$ **d** $170 \div 10^4$

   e $0.8 \div 10^1$ **f** $2480 \div 10^5$ **g** $9 \div 10^0$ **h** $0.25 \div 10^{-1}$

   i $18 \div 10^{-2}$ **j** $4.76 \div 10^{-4}$ **k** $0.07 \div 10^{-3}$ **l** $0.085 \div 10^{-2}$

3 Copy this table, which contains a secret coded message.

					S	!
3 3.3	0.3 3.3 300	300 33 6 6	0.6 0.3 0.33 3.3 0.3 33	300 0.06 33	60 33 0.03 600 33 300	

Work out the answers to the calculations in the code
box on the right.
Find the answer in your secret code table. Write the
letter from the code box above the number in your table.
For example, the first calculation is 0.6×10^2.
$0.6 \times 10^2 = 60$, so write S above 60 in the table.
What is the secret coded message?

$0.6 \times 10^2 = S$	$60 \times 10^{-1} = L$
$0.06 \div 10^{-1} = A$	$600 \div 10^0 = R$
$60 \times 10^{-3} = H$	$33 \div 10^1 = O$
$0.33 \times 10^0 = Y$	$300 \times 10^{-3} = N$
$300 \div 10^4 = C$	$3300 \times 10^{-2} = E$
$0.3 \div 10^{-3} = T$	$300 \div 10^2 = D$

4 Work out the missing power in each of the questions in these spider diagrams.
In each part, all the questions in the outer shapes should give the answer in the centre shape.

a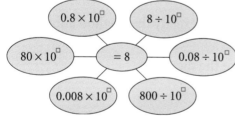

b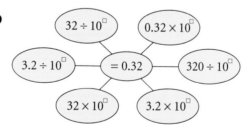

> These are
> called spider
> diagrams
> because they
> have a central
> 'body' with
> several 'legs'.

 5 **a** Work these out.
   i 4×10^2 **ii** 4×10^1 **iii** 4×10^0 **iv** 4×10^{-1} **v** 4×10^{-2} **vi** 4×10^{-3}

   b Use your answers to part **a** to answer this question.
   If you multiply a number by 10^{-4}, would the answer be larger or smaller than when you multiply
   the same number by 10^{-3}?

 6 **a** Work these out.
   i $12 \div 10^2$ **ii** $12 \div 10^1$ **iii** $12 \div 10^0$ **iv** $12 \div 10^{-1}$ **v** $12 \div 10^{-2}$ **vi** $12 \div 10^{-3}$

   b Use your answers to part **a** to answer this question.
   If you divide a number by 10^{-4}, would the answer be larger or smaller than when you divide the
   number by 10^{-3}?

3.3 Rounding

You know how to round decimal numbers to one or two decimal places (d.p.).

You can use exactly the same method to round decimal numbers to more than two decimal places.

> The 'degree of accuracy' is the number of decimal places you are working to.

- Look at the digit in the position of the <u>degree of accuracy</u>.
- If the value of the numeral to the right of this digit is 5 or more, increase the digit by 1.
  If the value is less than 5, leave the digit as it is.

Worked example 3.3a

Round the number 5.376 398 to the given degree of accuracy.
a one decimal place   **b** three decimal places   **c** five decimal places

a 5.376 398 = 5.4 (1 d.p.)	The digit in the first decimal place is 3. The digit to the right of it is 7. 7 is more than 5, so round the 3 up to 4. The letters 'd.p.' stand for 'decimal place'.
b 5.376 398 = 5.376 (3 d.p.)	The digit in the third decimal place is 6. The digit to the right of it is 3. 3 is less than 5 so the 6 stays the same.
c 5.376 398 = 5.376 40 (5 d.p.)	The digit in the fifth decimal place is 9. The digit to the right of it is 8. 8 is more than 5 so round the 9 up to 10. This has the effect of rounding the fourth and fifth digits (39) up to 40. Notice that you <u>must</u> write down the zero at the end, as the number <u>must</u> have five decimal places.

You also need to know how to round numbers to a given number of **significant figures**.

The first significant figure in a number is the first non-zero digit in the number.

For example: 4 is the first significant figure in the number 450
                 8 is the first significant figure in the number 0.008 402.

To round a number to a given number of significant figures follow exactly the method above.

- Look at the digit in the position of the degree of accuracy.
- If the number to the right of this digit is 5 or more, increase the digit by 1.
  If the number is less than 5, leave the digit as it is.

Worked example 3.3b

a   Round 4286 to one significant figure.
b   Round 0.080 69 to three significant figures.

a 4286 = 4000 (1 s.f.)	The first significant figure is 4. The digit to the right of it is 2. 2 is less than 5, so 4 stays the same. Replace the 2, the 8 and the 6 with zeros to keep the size of the number consistent. In this case, rounding to one significant figure is the same as rounding to the nearest 1000. The letters 's.f.' stand for 'significant figure'.
b 0.080 69 = 0.0807 (3 s.f.)	The first significant figure is 8, the second is 0 and the third is 6. The digit to the right of the 6 is 9. 9 is more than 5 so round the 6 up to 7. You must keep the zeros at the start of the number to keep the size of the number consistent. In this case, rounding to 3 s.f. is the same as rounding to 4 d.p.

◆ Exercise 3.3

1 Round each number to the given degree of accuracy.
   a 4.76 (1 decimal place (d.p.))   b 8.792 (2 d.p.)   c 0.4766 (3 d.p.)
   d 0.96552 (2 d.p.)   e 3.599761 (4 d.p.)   f 18.34987 (3 d.p.)

2 Round the number 25.496 723 815 to the stated number of decimal places (d.p.).
   a 3 d.p.   b 1 d.p.   c 5 d.p.   d 4 d.p.   e 2 d.p.   f 7 d.p.

3 Round each number to the stated number of significant figures (s.f.).
   a 135 (1 s.f.)   b 45678 (2 s.f.)   c 18.654 (3 s.f.)
   d 0.0931 (1 s.f.)   e 0.7872 (2 s.f.)   f 1.40948 (3 s.f.)

4 Which answer is correct, A, B, C or D?
   a 2569 rounded to 1 s.f.   A 2   B 3   C 2000   D 3000
   b 47.6821 rounded to 3 s.f.   A 47.6   B 47.682   C 47.7   D 48.0
   c 0.0882 rounded to 2 s.f.   A 0.08   B 0.088   C 0.09   D 0.1
   d 3.089 62 rounded to 4 s.f.   A 3.089   B 3.0896   C 3.09   D 3.090

5 Round the number 4509.0298 to the stated number of significant figures (s.f.).
   a 3 s.f.   b 1 s.f.   c 5 s.f.   d 4 s.f.   e 2 s.f.   f 7 s.f.

6 At a football match there were 63475 Barcelona supporters and 32486
  Arsenal supporters.
  How many supporters were there altogether?
  Give your answer correct to two significant figures.

7 Ahmad has a bag of peanuts that weighs 150 g.
  There are 335 peanuts in the bag.
  Work out the average (mean) mass of a peanut.
  Give your answer correct to one significant figure.

8 The speed of light is approximately 670616629 miles per hour.
  Use the conversion 1 mile ≈ 1.6 km to work out the speed of light
  in metres per second.
  Give your answer correct to three significant figures.

> The symbol ≈ means 'is approximately equal to'.

9 This is part of Jake's homework.
  He works out an estimate by
  rounding each number to one
  significant figure.
  Follow these steps for each of the
  calculations below.
   i Use Jake's method to work
      out an estimate of the answer.
   ii Use a calculator to work out
      the accurate answer. Give this
      answer correct to three
      significant figures.
   iii Compare your estimate

Question a Work out an estimate of $\frac{0.238 \times 576}{39.76}$.
          b Work out the accurate value.
          c Compare your estimate with the
             accurate value.

Answer a 0.238 ≈ 0.2, 576 ≈ 600, 39.76 ≈ 40
             0.2 × 600 = 120, 120 ÷ 40 = 3 *Estimate* = 3
          b 0.238 × 576 = 137.088,
             137.088 ÷ 39.76 = 3.45 (3 s.f.)
             Accurate = 3.45 (3 s.f.)
          c My estimate is close to my accurate
             answer, so my accurate answer is
             probably correct.

  with the accurate answer. Decide if your accurate answer is correct.
   a $\frac{0.3941 \times 196}{4.796}$ b $\frac{4732 + 9176}{19.5166}$ c $\frac{2.764 \times 84.695}{9.687 - 4.19}$ d $\frac{58432 \times 0.08}{0.2 \times 348}$

3.4 Order of operations

When calculations involve more than one operation, such as addition <u>and</u> multiplication, always make sure you do the operations in the correct order.

BIDMAS can help you remember the correct **order of operations**.

BIDMAS stands for Brackets, Indices (powers), Division, Multiplication, Addition and Subtraction.

BIDMAS describes the order in which you must do operations.

Work out Brackets and Indices first, followed by

Divisions and Multiplications, and finally

Additions and Subtractions.

Worked example 3.4

Work these out.　**a** $4 + 2 \times 6$　**b** $6 - 2(3 + 9)$　**c** $\dfrac{4^2}{8}$　**d** $(29 - 5^2)^3$

a $4 + 2 \times 6 = 4 + 12$ 　　 Start by working out the multiplication: $2 \times 6 = 12$.
$\quad\quad\quad\quad = 16$ 　　 Then work out the addition: $4 + 12 = 16$.

b $6 - 2(3 + 9) = 6 - 2 \times 12$ 　 Start by working out the calculation in brackets: $3 + 9 = 12$.
$\quad\quad\quad\quad\quad = 6 - 24$ 　　 Then work out the multiplication: $2 \times 12 = 24$.
$\quad\quad\quad\quad\quad = -18$ 　　 Finally, work out the subtraction: $6 - 24 = -18$.

c $\dfrac{4^2}{8} = \dfrac{16}{8}$ 　　 Start with the index and work out $4^2 = 16$.
$\quad\quad = 2$ 　　 Then work out the division: $16 \div 8 = 2$.

d $(29 - 5^2)^3 = (29 - 25)^3$ 　 Work out the 5^2 before calculating the expression in the brackets: $5^2 = 25$.
$\quad\quad\quad\quad\quad = 4^3$ 　　 Then work out the expression in the brackets: $29 - 25 = 4$.
$\quad\quad\quad\quad\quad = 64$ 　　 Finally, work out $4^3 = 64$.

◆ **Exercise 3.4**

1 Work these out.

　a $8 + 3 \times 4$　　**b** $12 \times 2 - 5$　　**c** $16 - \dfrac{27}{3}$　　**d** $18 - 5 \times 6$　　**e** $4 \times 3 - 7 \times 2$

　f $\dfrac{24}{8} + \dfrac{60}{12}$　　**g** $8(12 - 9)$　　**h** $13 + 2^2$　　**j** $8^2 + 6^2$　　**k** $100 - 2(12 + 13)$

2 Write the correct sign, =, < or >, to go in the box between the expressions.

　a $16 + 2 \times 4 \,\square\, 30 - \dfrac{48}{8}$　　　　**b** $50 - 6^2 \,\square\, 3(26 - 19)$

　c $5^2 + (11 - 6) \,\square\, 41 - 3 \times 4$　　　**d** $\dfrac{60}{4} + \dfrac{51}{3} \,\square\, 7^2 - 0.5 \times 4$

　e $46 - 2(3 + 5) \,\square\, 3(4^2 - 5)$　　　**f** $(12 - 4)^2 \,\square\, 5^2 + \dfrac{72}{2}$

3 Work out if the answers to these calculations are right (✓) or wrong (✗).
　　If the answer is wrong, work out the correct answer.

　a $6 + 3 \times 2 = 18$　　　**b** $3(16 - 3^2) + 9 = 30$　　　**c** $5 - (8 - 6)^3 = 27$

4 This is part of Zalika's homework.

> Question Work out: **a** $27 - 5 \times 2$ **b** $2(14 - 9)^2$ **c** $\frac{18 + 22}{8 - 3}$
>
> Answers **a** $27 - 5 = 22, 22 \times 2 = 44$
> **b** $14 - 9 = 5, 2 \times 5 = 10, 10^2 = 100$
> **c** $18 + 22 = 40, 40 \div 8 = 5, 5 - 3 = 2$

All of her answers are wrong.
For each part:
i explain the mistake that Zalika has made
ii work out the correct answer.

5 Oditi and Shen work out the value of the expression $2(a + 5b)$ when $a = 4$ and $b = 3$.

> I think the value of the expression is 114 because $4 + 53 = 57$, then $2 \times 57 = 114$.

> I think the value of the expression is 54 because $4 + 5 = 9$, $9 \times 3 = 27$, and $2 \times 27 = 54$.

Is either of them correct? Explain your answer.

6 Work out the value of each expression when $x = 6$ and $y = 2$.
  a $3x + y^2$ **b** $2x^2 - 4y$ **c** $(2x - 3y)^2$ **d** $2(3x - 6y)^2$

Summary

You should now know that:

★ When you multiply any number by a decimal number between 0 and 1, the answer is smaller than the number you started with.

★ When you divide any number by a decimal number between 0 and 1, the answer is greater than the number you started with.

★ The decimals 0.1, 0.01, 0.001, … can all be written as negative powers of 10. $0.1 = \frac{1}{10} = 10^{-1}$, $0.01 = \frac{1}{100} = 10^{-2}$, $0.001 = \frac{1}{1000} = 10^{-3}$, …

★ The first significant figure in a number is the first non-zero digit in the number.

★ When you round a number to a given number of significant figures you must keep the value of the rounded answer consistent with the number you are rounding.

★ You can use BIDMAS (Brackets, Indices or powers, Division, Multiplication, Addition, Subtraction) to remember the correct order of operations.

You should be able to:

★ Calculate with decimals mentally, using jottings where appropriate.

★ Multiply by decimals, understanding where to put the decimal point by considering equivalent calculations.

★ Divide by decimals by transforming the calculation to division by an integer.

★ Recognise the effects of multiplying and dividing by numbers between 0 and 1.

★ Recognise the equivalence of 0.1, $\frac{1}{10}$ and 10^{-1}.

★ Multiply and divide numbers by 10 to the power of any positive or negative integer.

★ Round numbers to a given number of decimal places or significant figures; use rounding to give solutions to problems with an appropriate degree of accuracy.

★ Use the order of operations, including brackets and powers.

End-of-unit review

1 Work these out mentally.
  a 7×0.3 **b** 15×0.4 **c** 21×0.03 **d** 0.06×6 **e** 0.05×20
  f $8 \div 0.4$ **g** $49 \div 0.7$ **h** $30 \div 0.1$ **i** $3 \div 0.05$ **j** $55 \div 0.11$

2 Work these out mentally.
  a 0.8×0.2 **b** 1.5×0.3 **c** 0.22×0.4 **d** 0.04×2.5 **e** 0.08×0.02
  f $0.8 \div 0.2$ **g** $0.21 \div 0.3$ **h** $0.32 \div 0.08$ **i** $0.35 \div 0.07$ **j** $2.4 \div 0.03$

3 a Work these out mentally.
  i 4×0.1 **ii** 4×0.2 **iii** 4×0.3 **iv** 4×0.4 **v** 4×0.5
  b Use your answers to part **a** to answer this question.
  If you multiply a number by 0.8, would the answer be larger or smaller than the answer when you multiply the same number by 0.4?

4 a Work these out mentally.
  i $15 \div 0.1$ **ii** $15 \div 0.2$ **iii** $15 \div 0.3$ **iv** $15 \div 0.4$ **v** $15 \div 0.5$
  b Use your answers to part **a** to answer this question.
  If you divide a number by 0.8, would the answer be larger or smaller than the answer when you divide the number by 0.4?

5 Work these out.
  a 9×10^2 **b** 3.7×10^3 **c** 24×10 **d** 5.55×10^0 **e** 7.5×10^{-2}
  f $5340 \div 10$ **g** $2 \div 10^0$ **h** $0.1 \div 10^{-1}$ **i** $62 \div 10^2$ **j** $0.076 \div 10^{-3}$

> **Remember:**
> $10^0 = 1$
> $10^1 = 10$

6 Anders says that if you multiply a number by 10^{-3}, the answer would be smaller than the answer you find when you multiply the number by 10^{-4}.
Is Anders correct? Give an example to show your answer is true.

7 Round each number to the given degree of accuracy.
  a 2.83 (1 d.p.)   **b** 11.859 (2 d.p.)   **c** 0.555 44 (3 d.p.)
  d 0.298 11 (2 d.p.)   **e** 0.123 456 (4 d.p.)   **f** 111.999 99 (3 d.p.)
  g 105.45 (1 s.f.)   **h** 234.511 (2 s.f.)   **i** 0.654 (2 s.f.)
  j 0.018 831 (1 s.f.)   **k** 0.9999 (3 s.f.)   **l** 1.011 (2 s.f.)

> **Remember:**
> s.f. = significant figures
> d.p. = decimal places

8 Round the number 3893.009 561 to the stated degree of accuracy.
  a 1 s.f.   **b** 2 s.f.   **c** 3 s.f.   **d** 4 s.f.   **e** 5 s.f.
  f 1 d.p.   **g** 2 d.p.   **h** 3 d.p.   **i** 4 d.p.   **j** 5 d.p.

9 Work these out.
  a $20 - 4 \times 4$ **b** $10 \times 3 + 3$ **c** $40 - \frac{30}{10}$ **d** $\frac{100}{2} - 6 \times 5$ **e** $6 \times 6 - 5 \times 5$
  f $\frac{40}{8} - \frac{60}{10}$ **g** $5(23 - 21)$ **h** $5 + 3^2$ **j** $3^2 + 4^2$ **k** $10^2 - 2(22 + 28)$

10 Work out the value of each expression when $x = 5$ and $y = 3$.
  a $5x - y^2$ **b** $2y^2 + 4x$ **c** $(x + 2y)^2$ **d** $10(x^2 - 6y)^2$

The Shanghai Lupu Bridge across the Huangpu River is 3.9 km long.
How many metres is that?

This is the Empire State Building in New York. For over 40 years it was the world's tallest building. It is 44 309 cm high. Change this to a more sensible unit of length.

The Bloodhound rocket car is being designed and built in England.
It will travel at 1690 km/h. How far will it travel in one second?
The mass of the Bloodhound, including fuel, is 7786 kg.
How does that compare to an ordinary car?

How much water is in this swimming pool?

500 litres?   5000 litres?   50 000 litres?

What is the area of a football pitch?

700 m^2? 7000 m^2? $70 000 \text{ m}^2$?

In this unit you will solve problems involving measurements and average speed. You will also use compound measures such as metres per second and cents per gram to make comparisons in real-life contexts.

4.1 Solving problems involving measurements

To solve problems involving measurements, you must know how to convert between the metric units. You also need to know how to convert between units of time.

When you are working with measurements, you need to use skills such as finding fractions and percentages of amounts. You should be confident in multiplying and dividing by 10, 100 and 1000.

When you have to solve a problem in mathematics, follow these steps.

- Read the question very carefully.
- Go over it several times if necessary. Make sure you understand what you need to work out, and how you will do it.
- Write down every step of your working. Set out each stage, clearly.
- Check that your answer is reasonable.
- Check your working to make sure you haven't made any mistakes.

Worked example 4.1

a A rose gold necklace weighs 20 g. The necklace is made from 75% gold, 21% copper and 4% silver. What is the mass of copper in the necklace?
b A bottle of medicine holds 0.3 litres.
The instructions on the bottle say: 'Take two 5 ml spoonfuls four times a day.'
How many days will a full bottle of medicine last?

a $21\% \text{ of } 20\,g = \frac{21}{100} \times 20$

$= 4.2\,g$

Check: 10% of 20 g = 2 g
1% of 20 g = 0.2 g
21% of 20 g = 2 + 2 + 0.2 = 4.2 g ✓
Or: 21% is just less than 25%.
25% of 20 g = $\frac{1}{4}$ of 20 g = 5 g
So 4.2 g is a reasonable answer. ✓

First decide what you need to work out. Then write down the calculation that you need to do.
Work it out.
Check your answer is correct by using a different method.

You could also check your answer is reasonable by comparing it with a common amount that is easy to calculate, such as 25%, or $\frac{1}{4}$, in this case.

b Amount of medicine per day = 2 × 5 ml × 4
= 40 ml

0.3 litres = 300 ml
300 ÷ 40 = 7.5 days

Check: 2 × 5 = 10, 10 × 4 = 40 ml per day
7.5 × 40 = 300 ml ✓
Or: In 7 days, total dose = 7 × 40 = 280 ml
In 8 days, total dose = 8 × 40 = 320 ml
So 7.5 days is a reasonable answer. ✓

There are several steps in solving this problem.
Take it one step at a time. Start by using the instructions on the bottle to work out how much medicine is used each day.
Change the litres to millilitres so the units are the same.
Divide by 40 to work out the number of days the medicine will last.
Check by recalculating the amount needed per day.
Use an inverse operation to check the number of days.
You could also check your answer by working out how much medicine would be used for 7 days and 8 days.
This shows that 7.5 is a reasonable answer.

◆ Exercise 4.1 For each question in this exercise, show all your workings and check your answers.

1 A pink gold bracelet weighs 60 g. It is made from 76% gold, 18% copper and 6% aluminium.
  a What is the mass of the gold in the bracelet?
  b What is the mass of the copper in the bracelet?

2 A bottle of medicine holds 0.25 litres.
  The instructions on the bottle of medicine say: 'Take two 5 ml spoonfuls three times a day.'
  How many days will a full bottle of medicine last?

3 Some instructions for the time it takes to roast a turkey are: 'allow 20 minutes for every 450 g'.
  How long will it take to roast a turkey that weighs 6.3 kg?
  Give your answer in hours and minutes.

4 This chart shows the distances, in miles, between some towns in England.

Birmingham					
137	Hull				
93	60	Leeds			
93	95	44	Manchester		
208	148	98	147	Newcastle	
132	41	25	70	90	York

For example, this box shows that the distance between Hull and Newcastle is 148 miles.

Steve drives a delivery van. On Thursday he drives from Manchester to Leeds, then Leeds to York, then York to Hull, then Hull back to Manchester.
Work out the total distance, in kilometres, that he drives on Thursday.

5 Paolo is building a brick wall.
  So far, the wall has five layers of bricks.
  Each brick is 7.5 cm high.
  The layers of mortar between the bricks are 15 mm thick.
  a Work out the total height of the wall, in centimetres.
  b How many more layers of bricks does Paolo need, for the wall to reach a total height of 0.7 m?

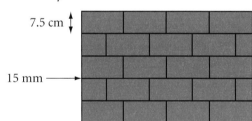

7.5 cm

15 mm

6 Ismail orders some logs for his open fire.
  The mass of one log is 2 kg. There are 5 logs in each bag.
  Ismail orders 150 bags.
  a What is the total mass of the logs Ismail orders?
    Give your answer in tonnes.
  b What is the total amount that Ismail pays for the logs?

Logs
Usual price $3.40 per bag.
Order more than 1.2 tonnes and get 15% off!

7 Henri plans to sell cups of coffee at his school sports event.
  Henri has a hot water container that holds 16 litres.
  He needs about 200 ml of hot water for each cup of coffee.
  a How many cups of coffee can he make from a full bottle of water?
  Henri will charge 80 cents per cup of coffee. He hopes to sell 250 cups of coffee.
  b How many full containers of water will he use?
  c How much money will he make?

4.2 Solving problems involving average speed

If you know the total distance travelled and the total time taken for a journey, you can work out the **average speed** for the journey.

Use the formula: average speed = $\frac{\text{total distance}}{\text{total time}}$

which is usually written as: speed = $\frac{\text{distance}}{\text{time}}$

Two other versions of this formula are:

distance = speed × time   time = $\frac{\text{distance}}{\text{speed}}$

This triangle can help you remember the three formulae.

D represents the distance, **S** the speed and **T** the time.

The triangle shows that: $D = S \times T$ $S = \frac{D}{T}$ $T = \frac{D}{S}$.

The units for speed depend upon the units you are using for distance and time. For example:

> You can only calculate with the average speed, as the actual speed over a journey changes all the time.

> Remember that these formulae are only true when the speed is constant.

- when the distance is measured in <u>kilometres</u> and the time is in <u>hours</u>, the speed is measured in <u>kilometres per hour (km/h)</u>
- when the distance is measured in <u>metres</u> and the time is in <u>seconds</u>, the speed is measured in <u>metres per second (m/s)</u>.

Worked example 4.2

a   It takes Omar $3\frac{1}{4}$ hours to drive a distance of 273 km. Work out his average speed.

b   Kathy is an 800 m runner. She runs at an average speed of 6 metres per second (m/s). How long does it take her to run 800 m at this speed? Give your answer in minutes and seconds.

a $3\frac{1}{4}$ hours = 3.25 hours	First write the number of hours as a decimal.
Speed = $\frac{\text{distance}}{\text{time}}$ = $\frac{273}{3.25}$ = 84 km/h	Write down the formula you need to use. Substitute the values into the formula and work out the answer.
<u>Check:</u> $\frac{270}{3}$ = 90 km/h ✓	Check, using estimation. 90 km/h is close to the answer of 84 km/h, so the answer is probably correct.
b Time = $\frac{\text{distance}}{\text{speed}}$ = $\frac{800}{6}$ = 133.33... seconds = 133 seconds (nearest second)	Write down the formula you need to use. Substitute the values into the formula and work out the answer. Round the answer to a sensible degree of accuracy.
2 minutes = 120 seconds So 133 seconds = 2 minutes 13 seconds	Convert the answer in seconds into minutes and seconds.
<u>Check:</u> 2 minutes 13 seconds = 133 seconds Distance = 133 × 6 = 798 km ✓	Use an inverse calculation to check. 798 km is close to the answer of 800 km, so the answer is probably correct.

◆ **Exercise 4.2**

> For each question in this exercise show all your workings and check your answers.

1   A cyclist travels a distance of 116 km in 4 hours. What is his average speed?

2   A motorist drives at an average speed of 80 km/h. How far does she travel in $3\frac{1}{2}$ hours?

3 How long will it take Seb to run 4000 m at an average speed of 5 m/s?
Give your answer in minutes and seconds.

4 Sundeep travels by train to a meeting in Barcelona.
Barcelona is 270 km from where he lives. He catches the train
at 9:45 a.m. The train travels at an average speed of 120 km/h.
At what time will the train arrive in Barcelona?

5 Steffan cycled 10 km in 45 minutes. He rested for
20 minutes then cycled a further 8 km in 40 minutes.
Work out his average speed for the whole journey.
Give your answer correct to one decimal place.

To change a decimal or fraction of an hour into minutes, multiply by 60, for example:

$\frac{1}{3}$ of an hour → $\frac{1}{3}$ × 60 = 20 minutes

0.2 hours → 0.2 × 60 = 12 minutes

To change minutes back to hours, divide by 60, for example:

72 minutes → 72 ÷ 60 = 1.2 hours

140 minutes → 140 ÷ 60 = $2\frac{1}{3}$ hours

6 Avani runs and walks 10 km from her home to work
and then back again each day.
She runs the first 8 km at a speed of 12 km/h.
She walks the last 2 km at a speed of 5 km/h.
   a Work out the total time it takes her to travel from
   home to work each day. Give your answer in
   hours and minutes.
   b Work out her average speed for the whole journey.
   Avani works Monday to Friday every week.
   c Work out the total time that Avani spends travelling to and from work in one week.

7 Greg lives in the UK. His car shows the speed he
is travelling, in <u>miles per hour</u>.
Greg went on holiday to France. He took his car.
He saw this table that shows information about
the speed limits on the different types of road in
France. The speeds are shown in <u>kilometres per hour.</u>

Type of road	Raining	Not raining
Motorway	110 km/h	130 km/h
Dual carriageway	100 km/h	110 km/h
Open road	80 km/h	90 km/h
Town	50 km/h	50 km/h

   a Work out the speed limit, in miles per hour, when Greg was travelling on:
   i a motorway when it was raining   **ii** an open road when it was not raining
   iii a dual carriageway when it was raining   **iv** a town.
   b On Tuesday it was not raining. Greg drove on the French motorway at 75 miles per hour.
   Was he breaking the speed limit? Explain your answer.
   c On Thursday it was raining. Greg drove on an open road in France at 55 miles per hour.
   Was he breaking the speed limit? Explain your answer.

8 A high-speed train travels at a maximum speed of 320 kilometres
per hour (km/h).
Work out the maximum speed of this train in metres per second (m/s).
Give your answer to the nearest whole number.

9 An aeroplane travels at a cruising speed of 570 miles per hour.
Work out the cruising speed of this aeroplane in metres per second (m/s).
Give your answer to the nearest whole number.

4.3 Using compound measures

Compound measures are measures made up of mixed units. For example, 'kilometres per hour', 'miles per hour' and 'metres per second' are compound measures for speed.

You can use compound measures to make comparisons in real life. For example, you can compare speeds of cars to see which car can travel fastest.

You can also use compound measures, such as 'cents per gram' or 'cents per litre', to compare prices of products. This means you can work out which items are best value for money.

Worked example 4.3

a A train travels 185 km in $1\frac{1}{4}$ hours. A different train travels 500 km in $3\frac{1}{2}$ hours.
Which train travels faster?
b A 250 g jar of coffee costs \$6.75. A 100 g jar of the same coffee costs \$2.68.
Which jar of coffee is better value for money?

a Speed of 1st train = $\frac{185}{1.25}$ Use the formula speed = $\frac{\text{distance}}{\text{time}}$ to work out the speed

     = 148 km/h   of the first train. $1\frac{1}{4}$ hours = 1.25 hours.

Speed of 2nd train = $\frac{500}{3.5}$ Work out the speed of the second train.

     = 142.9 km/h   Round the answer to a suitable degree of accuracy
                     e.g. one decimal place.

The 1st train is faster.   Compare the speeds and write down which is faster.

b \$6.75 ÷ 2.5 = \$2.70   Divide \$6.75 by 2.5 to work out the cost per 100 g of coffee.
1st jar costs \$2.70 per 100 g.   You could compare the costs per gram, per 50 g, per 500 g, etc.
2nd jar costs \$2.68 per 100 g.   It doesn't matter which measure you choose to compare as long as
2nd jar is better value for money.   it is the same for both items.

◆ **Exercise 4.3**   For each question in this exercise show all your working and check your answers.

1 A train travels 420 km in $2\frac{1}{2}$ hours. Another train travels 530 km in $3\frac{1}{4}$ hours.
Which train travels faster?

2 Pierre drove from Paris to Bordeaux. The total distance was 584 km.
He drove the first 242 km in $2\frac{3}{4}$ hours. He drove the rest of the way in $3\frac{3}{4}$ hours.
Was he travelling faster during the first part of the journey or the second?

3 Sally is training for a marathon. She goes for a run every Tuesday and Friday evening.
Last week, on Tuesday she ran 2.4 km in 18 minutes. On Friday she ran 1.8 km in 12 minutes.
  a Work out the speed Sally ran each evening, in <u>kilometres per minute</u>.
  b On which evening did Sally run faster?

4 A pack of four toilet rolls costs \$2.28. A pack of nine of the same toilet rolls costs \$4.95.
  a Work out the cost per roll for each pack.
  b Which pack is the better value for money?

5 A 750 ml bottle of FabCo costs \$1.80. A 1.4 litre bottle of FabCo costs \$3.50.
  a Work out the cost for each bottle, in <u>cents per millilitre</u>.
  b Which bottle is better value for money?

6 A 500 g bag of rice costs $0.64. A 2 kg bag of the same rice costs $2.65. Which bag is better value for money?

7 A 330 ml bottle of mineral water costs $0.42. A 1.5 litre bottle of the same water costs $1.65. Which bottle is better value for money?

8 Marc likes to solve number puzzles. It took him $4\frac{1}{2}$ minutes to complete one puzzle with 18 numbers.

It took him 6 minutes 24 seconds to complete a different puzzle with 32 numbers.
  a For each puzzle work out how many seconds it took Marc to complete one number.
  b Use your answer to part **a** to decide which puzzle Marc completed faster.

9 Ricardo goes on holiday by car. The travel graph shows his car journey. He stopped once for a break.
  a Work out Ricardo's average speed for:
    i the first part of the journey, before he took a break
    ii the second part of the journey, after he took a break.
  b During which part of the journey was Ricardo travelling faster?
  c Work out Ricardo's average speed for the whole journey, including the break.

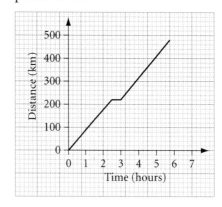

10 Lauren cycled to visit her Aunt. The travel graph shows her journey to and from her Aunt's house.
  She stayed with her Aunt for $1\frac{1}{3}$ hours before returning home.
  a Work out Lauren's average speed for:
    i the journey to her Aunt's house
    ii the journey home from her Aunt's house.
  b During which part of the journey was Lauren travelling fastest?
  c Work out Lauren's average speed for the whole journey.
    Do not include the time she spent at her Aunt's house.

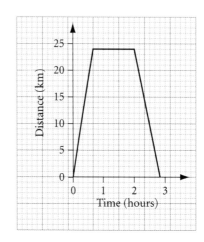

Summary

You should now know that:

★ When you solve problems you should write down every step in your working, check your working is correct and check your answers are reasonable.

★ The three formulae linking distance, speed and time are: ① distance = speed × time

  ② speed = $\frac{distance}{time}$ ③ time = $\frac{distance}{speed}$

★ When you use compound measures to make comparisons, the measures you compare must all be the same, e.g. km/h or $ per 100 g.

You should be able to:

★ Solve problems with measurements in a variety of contexts.

★ Solve problems involving average speed.

★ Use compound measures to make comparisons in real-life contexts, such as travel graphs and value for money.

End-of-unit review

For each question in this exercise show all your working and check your answers.

 1 Dave wants to put a row of tiles in his kitchen.
The row has to be 3 m long.
Each tile is a square, with 25 cm sides.
How many tiles does he need?

 2 Caroline is tiling her bathroom floor.
Each tile is a square, with 25 cm sides.
The bathroom floor is in the shape of a rectangle, 4.5 m by 2 m.
  a How many packs of tiles does Caroline need?
  b What is the total amount that Caroline pays for the tiles?

Tile sale!
Usual price $15 per pack.
10 tiles per pack
Buy more than 10 packs and get 20% off the total price!

 3 A long-distance runner travels a distance of 108 km in 8 hours.
What is his average speed?

 4 Umi walked 8 km in 45 minutes. She rested for 15 minutes then walked a further 6 km in 30 minutes.
Work out her average speed for the whole journey.
Give your answer correct to one decimal place.

 5 The legal maximum speed on UK motorways is 70 miles per hour.
Work out the legal maximum speed on UK motorways in metres per second (m/s).
Give your answer to the nearest whole number.

Remember that 1 mile is about 1.6 km.

 6 Cyclist A travels 55 km in 2 hours and 20 minutes.
Cyclist B travels 135 km in 5 hours and 36 minutes.
Which cyclist is travelling faster?

7 Fiona ran to raise money for charity.
The travel graph shows her journey.
She stopped once for a break.
  a Work out Fiona's average speed for:
    i the first part of the journey before she took a break
    ii the second part of the journey after she took a break.
    Give your answers to the nearest whole number.
  b During which part of the journey was Fiona travelling fastest?
  c Work out Fiona's average speed for the whole journey, including the break.

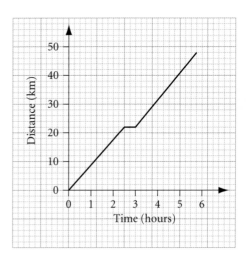

The topic of angles and lines is very important in mathematics. Understanding the basic geometry is essential in many areas, including engineering and architecture.

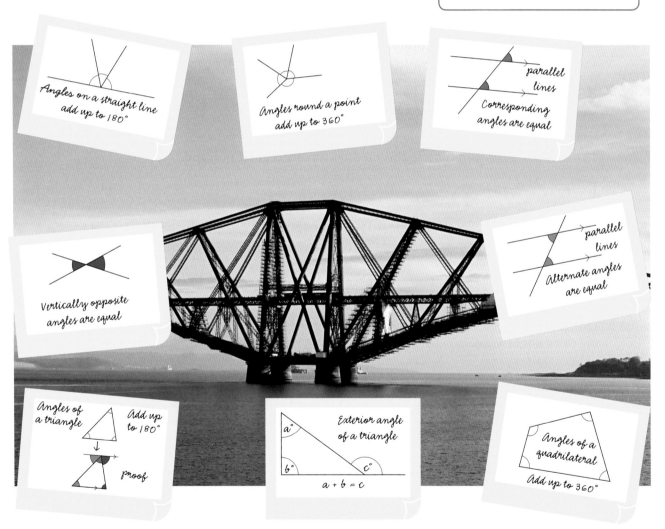

Angles on a straight line add up to 180°

Angles round a point add up to 360°

parallel lines
Corresponding angles are equal

Vertically opposite angles are equal

parallel lines
Alternate angles are equal

Angles of a triangle — Add up to 180°

proof

Exterior angle of a triangle
$a°$ $b°$ $c°$
$a + b = c$

Angles of a quadrilateral
Add up to 360°

In this unit you will learn more about lines and angles in polygons, and how to make mathematical drawings of solid shapes.

5.1 Regular polygons

All the angles of a **regular polygon** are the same size.

All the sides of a regular polygon are the same length.

This is a regular pentagon.

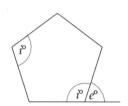

Each **interior angle** of a regular polygon is the same size.

The two angles labelled $i°$ are interior angles of this regular pentagon.

You can extend a side of any polygon to make an **exterior angle**.

The angle labelled $e°$ is an exterior angle of this pentagon.

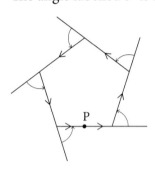

Imagine you could walk anticlockwise along the sides of the pentagon.

Start and finish at P.

At each corner you turn left through $e°$.

After five turns you have turned 360°, so $e = 360 ÷ 5 = 72$.

The exterior angle of the pentagon is 72°.

The interior angle of the pentagon is $180° − 72° = 108°$.

You can use this method for any regular polygon.

> The angle is labelled $e°$, so e is a number, without units. If an angle is labelled e, you must include the degrees sign when you state the size of the angle.

Regular polygon, N sides

Exterior angle $e = 360 ÷ N$ Interior angle $= 180 − e$ or $180 − \dfrac{360}{N}$

> This is a general result.

Diagrams in this excerise are not drawn accurately.

Worked example 5.1

The interior angle of a regular polygon is 140°.
How many sides does the polygon have?

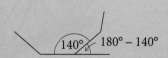

The exterior angle is $180° − 140° = 40°$.
The number of exterior angles is $360° ÷ 40° = 9$.
The regular polygon has nine sides.

Number of angles × 40° = 360°
Nine exterior angles, nine sides

Exercise 5.1

1 a Write down the usual name for:
   i a regular quadrilateral   **ii** a regular triangle.
b Find the interior and exterior angles of:
   i a regular quadrilateral   **ii** a regular triangle.

2 Work out the following angles, giving reasons.
  a the exterior angle of a regular hexagon
  b the interior angle of a regular hexagon

3 Work out the following angles, giving reasons.
   a the exterior angle of a regular octagon
   b the interior angle of a regular octagon

4 A regular polygon has an interior angle of 144°.
   Work out:
   a the exterior angle
   b the number of sides.

5 A regular polygon has an interior angle of 150°.
   How many sides does it have?

6 The diagram shows the exterior angle of a regular polygon.
   How many sides does the polygon have?

7 The diagram shows part of a regular polygon.
   How many sides does the polygon have?

8 Three identical regular polygons are put together at one point.
   There is a gap of 36°.
   What is the name of the polygon?

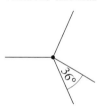

9 Three regular polygons fit together at one point without a gap.
   One is a square and one is a hexagon.
   How many sides does the third shape have?

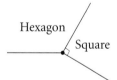

10 Say, and give a reason, whether each angle is the interior angle of a regular polygon.
   If it is, say how many sides the polygon has.
   a 110°   **b** 120°   **c** 130°   **d** 140°   **e** 150°

11 A heptagon has seven sides. How large is each interior angle of a regular heptagon?

12 How many sides does a regular polygon have if it has:
   a an exterior angle of 5°   **b** an interior angle of 178°?

5.2 More polygons

What do you know about the angles of a pentagon that is <u>not</u> regular?

The <u>external</u> angles still add up to 360°, as long as all the interior angles are less than 180°. The explanation is the same as for a regular pentagon.

What about the <u>internal</u> angles?

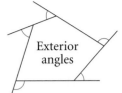

Exterior angles

You can divide any pentagon into three triangles.

The angles of the three triangles make up the five angles of the pentagon.

The sum of the angles of the pentagon is $3 \times 180° = 540°$.

Interior angles

You can use this method for <u>any</u> polygon.

This is a general result.

Polygon, N sides   Sum of exterior angles = 360°   Sum of interior angles = $(N - 2) \times 180°$

Worked example 5.2

One angle of a hexagon is 90°. The other angles are all equal. How big are the other angles?

A hexagon has six angles that add up to 720°. $N = 6$; $(N - 2) \times 180 = 4 \times 180 = 720$
720 − 90 = 630
The other angles are each 630 ÷ 5 = 126°.

Exercise 5.2

1 Work out the sum of the interior angles of:
   a a heptagon (7 sides)   **b** a nonagon (9 sides)   **c** a decagon (10 sides).

2 Five of the interior angles of a hexagon are 90°, 100°, 110°, 120° and 130°.
   a Work out the other interior angle of the hexagon.
   b Calculate the external angles of the hexagon and show that they have the correct total.

3 Four of the interior angles of a hexagon are 128°. The other two angles are equal.
   How large are the other two angles?

4 Xavier has a rectangular piece of card. He cuts off the four corners.
   What do the angles of the remaining shape add up to?

5 Read what Alicia says.

The angles of this pentagon are 100°, 105°, 72°, 126° and 127°.

Explain why she must be wrong.

6 The interior angles of a polygon add up to 1800°.
   How many sides does it have? Give a reason for your answer.

7 **a** Four of the interior angles of a pentagon are 105°. Work out the fifth angle.
   b Can a pentagon have four right angles? Give a reason for your answer.

5.3 Solving angle problems

What do you remember about angles?

- The sum of the angles at a point or on a straight line.
- Angle properties of triangles and special quadrilaterals, such as a parallelogram.
- The sum of the angles of a quadrilateral and other polygons.
- Properties of parallel lines, including corresponding angles and alternate angles.

There is a summary of all these topics on the first page of this unit.

In this section you will practise using the facts you know to solve problems.

As well as finding the answer, you also need to explain your reasoning to show why the answer is correct. You can use words or diagrams to do this.

Diagrams in this exercise are not drawn accurately.

Worked example 5.3

In the diagram, CA is parallel to EF.
a Work out the size of the angle labelled $f°$.
b Work out the value of d.

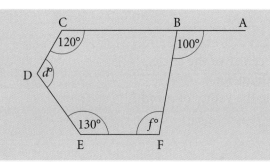

a The angle marked $f°$ is 100°.

CA and EF are parallel so angles ABF (100°) and BFE ($f°$) are alternate angles. They are equal.

b Angle CBF = 80°

Angles on a straight line add up to 180°. Now we know four of the angles of the pentagon.

The angles of a pentagon add up to 540°.
So $d = 540 - (120 + 80 + 100 + 130)$
$\quad = 110$

The sum of the angles of a pentagon is 3 × 180°.
Subtract the other four angles of the pentagon from 540.

> Give reasons for your answers in all the questions in this exercise.

1 ABC is a triangle and DE is parallel to BC.
   a Work out the value of a.
   b Work out the value of b.

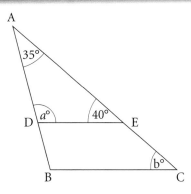

2 PQS and RQT are straight lines.
  a Work out the value of c.
  b Work out the value of d.

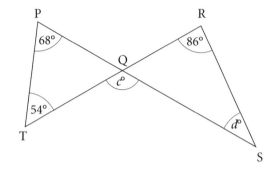

3 ABCD is a square.
  DEF is an equilateral triangle.
  Work the size of the angle labelled d°.

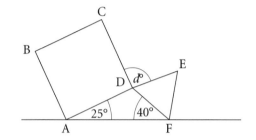

4 O is the centre of the circle.
  AB is a diameter.
  Calculate the values of a and b.

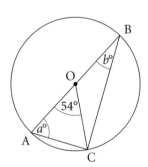

5 This shape has a line of symmetry through W.
  Calculate the value of w.

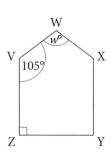

6 PQR is a straight line.
  QRST is a parallelogram.
  a Work out the value of x.
  b Work out the value of y.
  c Work out the value of z.

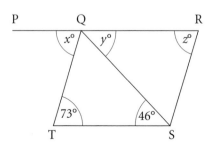

7 A regular hexagon and a regular pentagon have a common edge.
Work out the value of *a*.

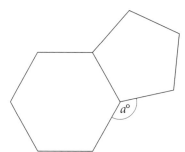

8 This shape is a kite.
Calculate the value of *a*.

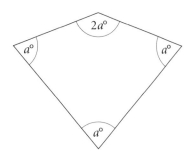

9 XYZV is a straight line.
Calculate the values of *a*, *b* and *c*.

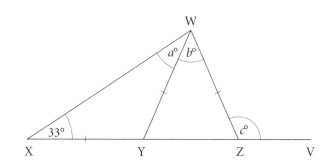

10 ABCD is a trapezium.
AB and DC are parallel sides.
  a Show that *a* + *d* = 180.
  b Show that *b* + *c* = 180.

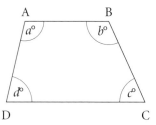

5.4 Isometric drawings

Isometric paper is made with a grid of equilateral triangles.

You can use isometric paper to draw three-dimensional objects.

You can also use triangular dot paper.

This is a sketch of a cuboid.

The sides of the cuboid are 2, 3 and 4 units long.

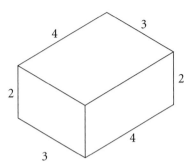

This is the same cuboid drawn on isometric paper.

The sides of the cuboid on the isometric drawing are 2, 3 and 4 units long.

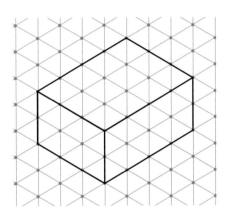

◆ Exercise 5.4

1 Draw these cuboids on isometric paper.

a
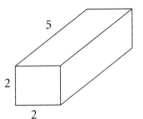

b
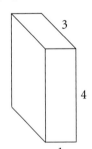

c
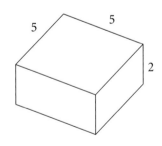

2 Draw on isometric paper:
a a cube with side 2 units long
b a cube with side 3 units long.

3 Here are some scale drawings of cuboids. They are drawn on isometric paper.

a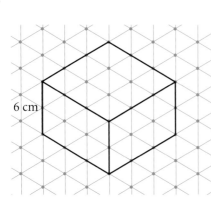

b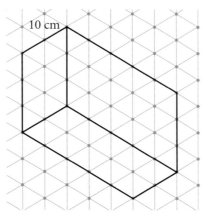

The length of one side of each cuboid is given.
Work out the lengths of the other two sides of each cuboid.

4 Draw, on isometric paper, two different views of a cuboid with sides 2 cm, 2 cm and 4 cm.

5 Three identical cubes are joined together to make a shape.

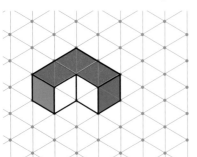
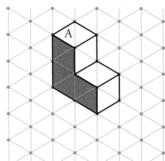
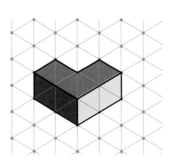

The drawings show three different views of the shape on isometric paper.
a In the diagram, face A has not been coloured. What colour should it be?
b What colour is the rectangular face that is opposite the blue square face?

6 The diagram shows four identical cubes joined together.
Each side of each cube is 2 units long.
Draw the shape on isometric paper.

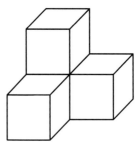

7 The diagram shows a triangular prism.
Each of the triangles in the prism has a right angle.
a What are the dimensions of the rectangle on the bottom of the prism?
b Draw the prism on isometric paper.

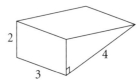

5.5 Plans and elevations

You can use isometric paper to make accurate drawings of three-dimensional shapes.

Another way of drawing or describing three-dimensional shapes is to use plans and elevations.

These can be drawn on squared paper.

Plans and elevations show what a shape looks like from different directions.

An example will make this clear.

This shape is drawn on isometric paper.

A **plan** is the view from overhead, in the direction marked A.

An **elevation** is the view from the front (from direction B) or from the sides (directions C and D) or from the back.

Here is the plan.

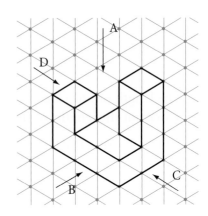

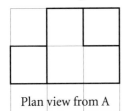

Plan view from A

The lines show where you would see an edge, looking from above.

The column that is three units high in the isometric drawing is shown as a square in the top right-hand corner of the plan.

The column that is two units high on the left of the isometric drawing is show as a square in the bottom left-hand corner of the plan.

Here are three elevations of the same shape.

You can see the columns that are two units high and three units high in each elevation.

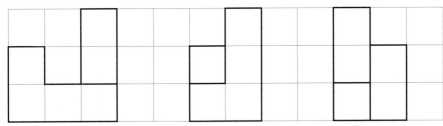

Elevation from B   Elevation from C   Elevation from D

Exercise 5.5

1 These are isometric drawings of four shapes.

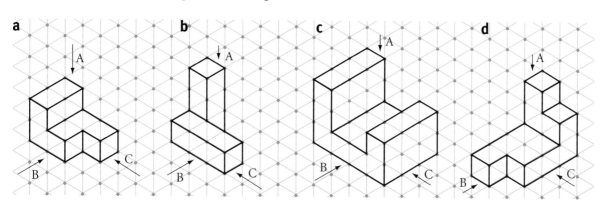

a   b   c   d

For each one, draw the plan (from direction A) and two elevations (from directions B and C).
Use squared paper.

2 The diagram shows the plan and three elevations of a shape.
Draw the shape on isometric paper.

Left elevation   Plan   Right elevation

Front elevation

3 The diagram shows the plan and an
elevation of a shape.
The shape is made from six cubes
joined together.

Plan   Front
elevation

  a Draw the left elevation on
squared paper.
  b Draw the shape on isometric paper.

5.6 Symmetry in three-dimensional shapes

Three-dimensional shapes can be symmetrical.

This chair is symmetrical.

The second picture shows a **plane of symmetry**.

Imagine a mirror on the plane.

One half of the chair is a reflection of the other.

Worked example 5.6

Look at this table.
a How many planes of symmetry does it have?
b Show them on a diagram.

a Two
b

◆ **Exercise 5.6**

1 Each of these shapes has one plane of symmetry. Show them on drawings.

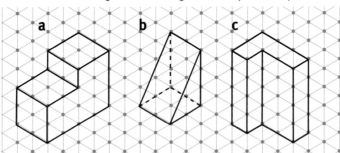

2 **a** has two planes of symmetry and **b** has three. Show them on diagrams.

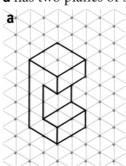

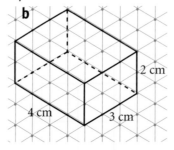

2 cm
4 cm
3 cm

3 The diagram shows an L-shaped prism.
  a How many faces does it have?
  b Draw the object on isometric paper.
  c The prism has a plane of symmetry. Show it on your isometric drawing.

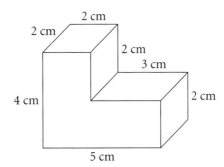

4 a Draw a cube. Show a plane of symmetry that passes through four edges but no vertices.
  b Draw the cube again. Show a plane of symmetry that passes through four vertices of the cube.

5 a Draw a cylinder.
  b Draw a plane of symmetry that passes through the circular ends of the cylinder.
  c Draw a plane of symmetry that does **not** pass through the circular ends of the cylinder.

Summary

You should now know that:

★ The angles of a regular polygon are all the same size and the sides are all the same length.

★ The sum of the interior angles of a polygon with N sides is $(N - 2) \times 180°$.

★ The sum of the exterior angles of a polygon is 360°.

★ The angle properties of parallel lines and polygons can be used to solve problems about angles and explain reasoning.

★ Three-dimensional shapes can be shown as diagrams on isometric paper or by drawing plans and elevations.

★ Three-dimensional shapes can have reflection symmetry.

You should be able to:

★ Calculate the interior and exterior angle of any regular polygon.

★ Prove the formula for the sum of the interior angles of any polygon and that the sum of the exterior angles is 360°.

★ Solve problems by using properties of angles, of parallel and intersecting lines, and of triangles, other polygons and circles, and explain reasoning.

★ Draw 3D shapes on isometric paper.

★ Analyse 3D shapes through plans and elevations.

★ Draw a plane of symmetry on a three-dimensional shape.

 ★ Recognise and use spatial relationships in two dimensions and three dimensions.

 ★ Draw accurate mathematical diagrams.

 ★ Present arguments to justify solutions or generalisations, using symbols and diagrams or graphs and related explanations.

End-of-unit review

1 A regular polygon has 15 sides.
Work out:
a the exterior angle   **b** the interior angle.

2 The diagram shows a regular nonagon. O is the centre of the nonagon.
a Work out the size of the angle labelled $a°$.
b Explain why triangle OPQ is isosceles.
c Calculate the size of the angle labelled $b°$.
d Use the answer to part **c** to explain why the interior angle of a regular nonagon is 140°.

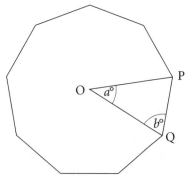

3 The angles of a pentagon are $a°$, $(a + 10)°$, $(a + 20)°$, $(a + 30)°$ and $(a + 40)°$. Work out the size of the largest angle of the pentagon.

4 ABD is a triangle. AB is parallel to EC.
a Work out the size of the angle labelled $a°$. Give a reason for your answer.
b Work out the size of the angle labelled $b°$. Give a reason for your answer.

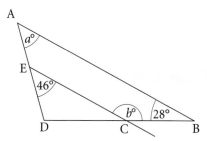

5 PRT is a triangle.
Work out the values of c and d. Give reasons for your answers.

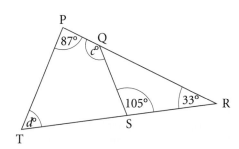

6 A cuboid has sides of length 1 cm, 4 cm and 6 cm.
Draw two different diagrams of the cuboid on isometric paper.

7 This is an isometric drawing of a shape.
Use squared paper to draw:
a a plan view from direction A
b elevations in the directions of B, C and D.

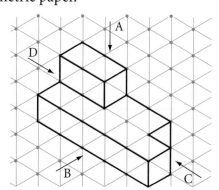

6 Planning and collecting data

What do you remember about planning and collecting data?
Use the summary diagram, below, to remind yourself.

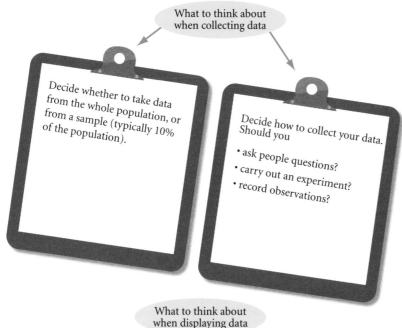

What to think about when collecting data

Decide whether to take data from the whole population, or from a sample (typically 10% of the population).

Decide how to collect your data. Should you

- ask people questions?
- carry out an experiment?
- record observations?

Your Opinion

☐ Strongly agree
☐ Agree
☐ Neither agree nor disagree
☐ Disagree
☐ Strongly disagree

What to think about when displaying data

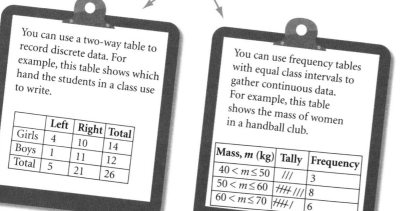

You can use a two-way table to record discrete data. For example, this table shows which hand the students in a class use to write.

	Left	Right	Total
Girls	4	10	14
Boys	1	11	12
Total	5	21	26

You can use frequency tables with equal class intervals to gather continuous data. For example, this table shows the mass of women in a handball club.

Mass, m (kg)	Tally	Frequency
$40 < m \le 50$	///	3
$50 < m \le 60$	卌 ///	8
$60 < m \le 70$	卌 /	6

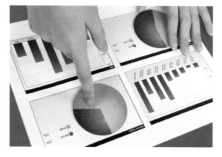

In this unit you will learn more about collecting data. You will design data-collection sheets, identify where and how to get data, and use your data-collection sheets to collect real data.

6.1 Identifying data

When you carry out a statistical investigation, the first thing you need to do is decide on a **hypothesis**.

A hypothesis is a statement that you think may be true. It is not the same as a question.

A hypothesis must be written so that it is either 'true' or 'false'.

Here are some examples of hypothesis statements.

> * Girls take care of their health better than boys do.
>
> * More people go to work by bus than by any other form of transport.
>
> * Using fertiliser on my tomato plants makes them grow bigger.

When you carry out a statistical investigation, you need to plan it first. Here is a suggestion for a plan.

1.	Decide on a hypothesis to test. For example: '13-year-old girls, on average, are taller than 13-year-old boys.'
2.	Decide on the question, or questions, to ask. For example: 'Are you 13 years old?', 'Are you a girl or a boy?' and 'How tall are you?'
3.	Decide what data to collect. For example: The heights of 13-year-old girls and boys.
4.	Decide how to collect the data. For example: Carry out a survey of Stage 9 students.
5.	Decide how big the sample size will be. For example: 10% of the number of Stage 9 students (half boys, half girls).
6.	Decide how accurate the data needs to be. For example: Heights measured to the nearest centimetre.

Worked example 6.1

a Aiden lives in the UK. He is investigating which month of the year is the coldest.
Write a hypothesis for this investigation.
b Fran is investigating who is healthier, the males or the females in her village.
  i Write down examples for each of the six steps suggested above.
  ii What other factors could Fran consider?
  iii Write down some problems Fran might have in collecting her data.

a 'December is the coldest month of the year.'   Aiden could choose any of the winter months, so this
                                would be a suitable hypothesis.

b i 1 Hypothesis: 'Males are healthier than females in my village'.
   2 Questions: 'Are you male or female?', 'What is your height?',
     'How much do you weigh?', 'How many hours of exercise do you do each week?'
   3 Data to collect: Heights and masses of adults so that Body Mass Index can be calculated.
     Amount of exercise adults do so that comparisons can be made.

4 Method of collection: Questionnaire.
5 Sample size: There are 380 adults in my village. 10% of 380 = 38, so 19 males and 19 females.
6 Accuracy of data: Heights measured to the nearest cm, masses to the nearest kg, hours of exercise to the nearest half-hour.

ii She could also collect data on diet, age, blood pressure, cholesterol levels, family history of illness.

iii The adults in her village may not want to give sensitive information such as how much they weigh, their blood pressure, cholesterol level or family history of illness.

◆ Exercise 6.1

1 Write a hypothesis for each of these investigations.
  a Sasha wants to know whether more men than women watch sport on the TV.
  b Anders wants to know if silver is the most popular colour of car that is sold.
  c Oditi wants to know if girls are better than boys at estimating the masses of different objects.
  d Alicia wants to know whether it is true that the more you revise the better your exam result will be.

2 There are 800 students in Dakarai's school.
  He wants to know whether boys or girls are better at maths.
  a Write down examples for each of the six steps for Dakarai to follow.
  b What other factors could Dakarai consider?
  c Write down some problems he might have in collecting his data.

Work in pairs, or groups of three, to answer questions **2** and **3**.

3 Kiera is reading a book that has 120 pages.
  She wants to know whether 'e' is the most commonly used letter in the book.
  a Write down examples for each of the six steps for Kiera to follow.
  b What other factors could Kiera consider?
  c Write down some problems Kiera might have in collecting her data.

 4 Razi is talking to Mia. He wants to know the favourite sport of the students in his school.
  He uses all the students in his class as his sample. There are 15 boys and 3 girls in his class.
  The favourite sport of the students in his class is cricket.

The favourite sport of the students in my school must be cricket.

But you cannot assume cricket is the favourite sport of the students in the whole school, as most of the students in your class are boys. The school has equal numbers of boys and girls so you need to sample equal numbers of boys and girls.

For each part of this question give a reason why the conclusion is not valid and suggest a better sample that they could use.

  a Hassan wants to know who are better at spelling in his school, the boys or the girls. He tests all the students in his top-set maths class. There are 12 boys and 18 girls in his class. Hassan says: 'The boys had better scores than the girls, so the boys in the school are better at spelling than the girls.'

  b Harsha lives in a village 25 km from her school. She catches a bus to school every morning. There are 520 students in her school. Harsha wants to know the most popular method of travelling to school. She asks the 24 students who live in her village. Harsha says: 'Most of the students who I asked travel to school by bus. So, the most popular method of travelling to school, used by all the students in the school, is the bus.'

6.2 Types of data

When you carry out a statistical investigation, you need to know where to collect or find your data. There are two types of data.

Primary data is data that you collect yourself. You can carry out an experiment, or you can do a survey and ask people questions.

Secondary data is data that has already been collected by someone else. You can look, for example, in books, newspapers, magazines or on the internet to find this data.

Worked example 6.2

a Shen is investigating the hypothesis: 'Eight-year-old boys are taller than eight-year-old girls in the village school.' Should he use primary or secondary data?
b Tanesha is investigating the hypothesis: 'In June, Madrid has more hours of sunshine than Milan does.' Should she use primary or secondary data?

a	Primary data	Shen should carry out a survey in his village school. It wouldn't take him long to measure the heights of eight-year-old children and record the information.
b	Secondary data	Tanesha would have to get this information from weather records. She could use the internet to look for weather records for Europe. She may also be able to get this information from travel brochures.

◆ Exercise 6.2

1 Decide whether primary or secondary data should be used in each of these investigations. Give a reason for each answer.
   a Sasha is investigating whether children are taller now than they were 50 years ago.
   b Anders is investigating whether boys prefer to eat an apple, an orange or a banana.
   c Oditi is investigating whether there is more rainfall in India than there was 10 years ago.
   d Ahmad is investigating the most popular brand of TV sold in his country.
   e Alicia is investigating the average salary earned by government employees.
   f Jake is investigating the favourite sport of 15-year-old children.
   g Zalika is investigating the most popular size of shoes sold in her country.
   h Xavier is investigating the number of visits people make to a dentist each year.

2 Hassan wants to find out the most popular colour of car that is sold in the USA. He finds data that shows the most popular colour of car that is sold in Europe is silver.

> Work in pairs, or groups of three, to answer question **2**.

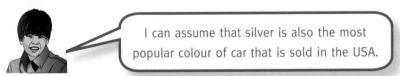

I can assume that silver is also the most popular colour of car that is sold in the USA.

   a Give a reason why Hassan could be right to make this assumption.
   b Give a reason why Hassan could be wrong to make this assumption.

6.3 Designing data-collection sheets

When you collect primary data you need to make sure it is easy to read and understand.

A **data-collection sheet** is a frequency table that you fill in as people give you the answers to your questions. It has three columns, one for listing the different categories or answers, one for tally marks and one for the total number of tallies, or frequency.

> A frequency table is a table that shows how frequently – or how often – something occurs.

When you design a data-collection sheet, make sure that:

- it includes all possible answers
- each possible answer is only available in one tally box
- all the answers can be easily and quickly tallied.

Worked example 6.3

a Mrs Patel is organising an outing for her youth club. She asks each student whether they would like to go to the beach, a theme park, an activity centre or an art gallery.
Design a suitable data-collection sheet for her.

b Mrs Jones is doing an investigation into the ages of the mothers of the students in her school. She asks 20 students from each year group, from Stage 7 to Stage 11, to mark the age group into which their mother falls.

This is the data-collection sheet she designs.

Age (years)	25–30	30–35	35–40	40–45	45–50	Total
Stage 7						
Stage 8						
Stage 9						
Stage 10						
Stage 11						
Total						

i Give two reasons why her data-collection sheet is not suitable.

ii Design a better data-collection sheet.

a

Trip destination	Tally	Frequency
Beach		
Theme Park		
Activity centre		
Art gallery		
Total		

This data-collection sheet includes all the possible answers. It has a tally column and a frequency column. It also has a total box, for the total of all the frequencies. This enables Mrs Patel to check that all the tallies add up to the number of students asked.

b i 1 There is no tally box for mothers under 25 or over 50.
    2 The age groups overlap. A mother aged 30 could be entered in the 25–30 box or the 30–35 box.

ii

Age (years)	< 25	25–29	30–34	35–39	40–44	45–49	> 49	Total
Stage 7								
Stage 8								
Stage 9								
Stage 10								
Stage 11								
Total								

The ages no longer overlap and there are separate columns for the under 25s and the over 49s.

◆ Exercise 6.3

1 Harsha carries out an experiment with a spinner.
The sections of the spinner are coloured red, yellow, blue and green, as shown.
She spins the spinner 100 times and records the colour the spinner lands
on each time.
Design a suitable data-collection sheet for her.

2 Razi does a survey on the make of cars that pass his house one Saturday.
He records the makes 'BMW', 'Ford', 'Nissan', 'Toyota', 'Vauxhall' and 'Other'.
Design a suitable data-collection sheet for him.

3 Mia asks 100 students in her school how many times they have been to a foreign country.
Design a suitable data-collection sheet for her. (The highest number of times is six.)

4 Dakarai has two tetrahedral dice, numbered 1 to 4.
He rolls the dice together and adds the numbers they show
to get a score.
He decides to do this 150 times and record each score he gets.
a Design a data-collection sheet for Dakarai.
b Compare your data-collection sheet with a partner's, in your class.
   i Are your data-collection sheets the same or similar?
   ii Could you improve your data-collection sheet? If so, explain how you would do it.

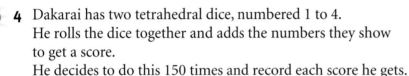

5 Shen investigates the favourite flavour of ice-cream of the students in his school.
He asks 30 students from each stage, from 7 to 11, to take part. He asks them to choose their
favourite flavour from vanilla, strawberry, chocolate, raspberry ripple, mint choc-chip or 'other'.
a Design a data-collection sheet for Shen.
b Compare your data-collection sheet with a partner's, in your class.
   i Are your data-collection sheets the same or similar?
   ii Could you improve your data-collection sheet? If so, explain how you would do it.

> For questions **6** and **7**, work in groups of two or three. Discuss the answers to each question and then write down your answers. Compare your answers with other groups.

6 Tanesha is investigating the age of the workers in a factory.
She uses this data-collection sheet.
She asks 100 workers to say which age group they are in.
a Give two reasons why her data-collection sheet is
not suitable.
b Design a better data-collection sheet.

Age (years)	Tally	Frequency
20–30		
30–40		
40–50		
Total		

7 Zalika is comparing the fitness of men and women.
She asks 50 men and 50 women how many times
they exercise each week.
She records the information on this data-collection sheet.
a Give three reasons why her data-collection sheet is
not suitable.
b Design a better data-collection sheet.

Number of times	Tally	Frequency
1–2		
2–4		
4–6		

6.4 Collecting data

You can use a frequency table or data-collection sheet to record grouped or ungrouped discrete data and grouped continuous data. If you are grouping data, it is helpful to use **equal class intervals**.

If, for example, you were collecting data about the number of goals scored per match by a football team, your data-collection sheet may look like this. The data values are only likely to vary between 0 goals and maybe 4 goals, so there is no need to group this data.

Goals scored	Tally	Frequency
0		
1		
2		
3		
4		

If you were collecting data about the number of points scored per game by a netball team, your data-collection sheet may look more like this.

Goals scored	Tally	Frequency
0–9		
10–19		
20–29		
30–39		
40–49		

This time, the data values are likely to vary between 0 goals and perhaps 50 goals, so you <u>would</u> group this data.

Always look at all the values the data can take, then decide whether you need to group the data.

Worked example 6.4

Here are the heights of 20 teachers, measured to the nearest centimetre.

1.71 m 1.66 m 1.82 m 1.74 m 1.62 m 1.76 m 1.57 m 1.79 m 1.75 m 1.69 m
1.65 m 1.77 m 1.80 m 1.52 m 1.75 m 1.60 m 1.72 m 1.85 m 1.59 m 1.88 m

a Put these heights into a grouped frequency table.
b Write down one conclusion that you can draw from the results on your data-collection sheet.

a
Height, h (m)	Tally	Frequency
$1.50 \leq h < 1.60$	///	3
$1.60 \leq h < 1.70$	/////	5
$1.70 \leq h < 1.80$	//// ///	8
$1.80 \leq h < 1.90$	////	4
	TOTAL	20

The shortest teacher is 1.52 m and the tallest is 1.88 m, so the values of the groups can range between 1.50 m and 1.90 m. A range of 10 cm per group is the best option, as the table is easy to fill in and there are enough groups to be able to compare the data.
Note that: ≤ means 'less than or equal to'
< means 'less than'.

b The group $1.70 \leq h < 1.80$ has the highest frequency.

Look at the frequency column and make a comment about the group with the highest or lowest frequency.

Exercise 6.4

1 Xavier rolls a dice 30 times. These are the numbers he scores.

1 6 4 6 1 6 4 2 6 1 4 6 3 4 1
3 2 1 5 2 4 6 5 3 6 2 4 1 6 4

a Record this information on a data-collection sheet.
b Write down one conclusion that you can draw from the results on your data-collection sheet.

2 These are the points scored by a basketball team in 20 matches.

42 54 32 46 62 52 48 28 56 68
34 65 45 55 44 26 35 58 49 38

a Record this information on a data-collection sheet.
b Write down one conclusion that you can make from the results on your data-collection sheet.

3 These are the masses, to the nearest kilogram, of 24 members of an athletics club.

66	72	88	52	64	85	68	86	75	82	56	61
78	58	62	75	84	62	81	55	95	67	74	63

    a Record this information on a data-collection sheet.

    b Write down one conclusion that you can make from the results on your data-collection sheet.

> For questions **4** and **5,** work in groups of three or four.

4 Choose a topic and carry out a survey of the students in your class.
Make sure the topic of your survey does not refer to something that you need to measure (continuous data). For example, you could ask how students travel to school, the colour of their eyes, their favourite drink or what football team they support.

    a Write down the question you will ask the students in your class.

    b Design a data-collection sheet for your survey.

    c Carry out the survey and complete your data-collection sheet.

    d Write down one conclusion that you can make from the results of your survey.

5 Choose a topic and carry out a survey of the students in your class.
Make sure the topic of your survey does refer to something that you need to measure (continuous data). For example, you might investigate students' heights, how far they can reach in a standing jump, how far up a wall they can reach, the masses of their bags or the time it takes for them to write out the 8-times table.

    a Write down the question you are going to ask the students in your class.

    b Design a data-collection sheet for your survey.

    c Carry out the survey and complete your data-collection sheet.

    d Write down one conclusion that you can make from the results of your survey.

Summary

You should now know that:

★ When you carry out a statistical investigation, the first thing to do is decide on a hypothesis. A hypothesis is a statement that you think may be true.

★ Primary data is data that you collect yourself.

★ Secondary data is data that has already been collected by someone else.

★ A data-collection sheet usually has three columns, one for listing the different categories, one for tally marks and one for the total number of tallies. This is the frequency.

★ When you are grouping data you should use equal class intervals. Look at all the values the data can take before you decide whether to group the data.

You should be able to:

★ Suggest a question to explore, using statistical methods; identify the sets of data needed, how to collect them, sample sizes and degree of accuracy.

★ Identify primary or secondary sources of suitable data.

★ Design, trial and refine data-collection sheets.

★ Collect and make a table of discrete and continuous data, choosing suitable equal class intervals where appropriate.

End-of-unit review

1. Hassan is investigating whether good basketball players are also good at rugby.
Write a hypothesis for his investigation.

2. When carrying out a statistical investigation, Maha follows these steps.
   ① Choose a hypothesis to test.
   ② Decide on the question, or questions, to ask.
   ③ Decide what data to collect.
   ④ Decide how to collect the data.
   ⑤ Decide on the sample size.
   ⑥ Decide how accurate the data needs to be.

   There are 30 students in Maha's class.
   Maha wants to know whether boys or girls eat more chocolate.
   a Write down examples for each of the six steps that Maha will follow.
   b What other factors should Maha consider?
   c Write down some problems Maha may have in collecting her data.

3. Sasha wants to investigate the average number of pairs of shoes owned by Canadian women.
She finds data that shows the average number of pairs of shoes owned by American women is 19.

> I can assume that the average number of pairs of shoes owned by Canadian women is 19.

   a Explain why it might be reasonable for Sasha to make this assumption.
   b Explain why it might <u>not</u> be reasonable for Sasha to make this assumption.

4. Maha wants to find out the average salary of a shop assistant in the UK.
She finds data that shows that the average salary of a shop assistant in five cities in the UK is £15 000.

> I can assume that the average salary of a shop assistant in the UK is £15 000.

   a Give a reason why Maha could be right to make this assumption.
   b Give a reason why Maha could be wrong to make this assumption.

5. Harsha is investigating the film-watching habits of men and women.
She asks 30 men and 50 women how many films they watched last week.
She records the information on a data-collection sheet similar to this one.

Number of films	Tally	Frequency
1		
2–4		
4–6		

   a Give four reasons why her data-collection sheet is not suitable.
   b Design a better data-collection sheet.

6. These are the numbers of goals scored by a football team in the 20 matches they played.
   | 0 | 2 | 2 | 0 | 0 | 0 | 1 | 3 | 2 | 0 |
   | 1 | 1 | 3 | 1 | 0 | 2 | 3 | 6 | 0 | 1 |

   0 2 2 0 0 0 1 3 2 0
   1 1 3 1 0 2 3 6 0 1

   a Record this information onto a data-collection sheet.
   b Write down one conclusion that you can make from the results on your data-collection sheet.

7 Fractions

This is a well-known puzzle.

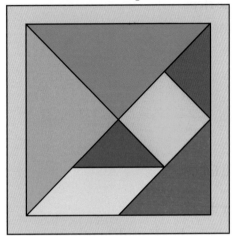

It is called a **tangram**.

There are seven parts. They can be used to make different shapes.

Which parts have the same area?

> Suppose the **whole shape** has area 1.
>
> Find the area of each part. Write the answers as fractions.
>
> You should find that each area is $\frac{1}{4}$, $\frac{1}{8}$ or $\frac{1}{16}$.
>
> Check that the areas add up to 1.

Here is another way to divide a square.

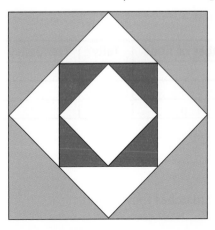

In this unit you will continue work on simplifying fractions as well as adding, subtracting, multiplying and dividing fractions using both written and mental methods.

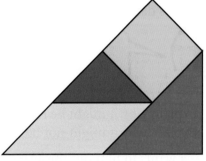

Find the area of this shape.

Can you explain your answer in different ways?

By addition? By subtraction?

What fraction of the square is green?

What fraction is red?

Try to explain your answers in different ways.

Can you see why the red fraction is $\frac{1}{4}$ of the green fraction?

Key words

Make sure you learn and understand these key words:

simplify

simplest form

highest common factor (HCF)

lowest common denominator

cancelling common factors

invert and multiply

7.1 Writing a fraction in its simplest form

To **simplify** a fraction, you divide the numerator and the denominator by a common factor.

You simplify a fraction into its **simplest form**, or lowest terms, by dividing the numerator and the denominator by the **highest common factor (HCF)**.

If you do not find the highest common factor straight away, just cancel by one factor at a time until you cannot cancel any further.

Worked example 7.1

Write the fraction $\frac{60}{72}$ in its simplest form.

HCF of 60 and 72 is 12.

The highest common factor of 60 and 72 is 12.
Divide the numerator and the denominator by 12.

$\frac{60}{72}$ cancels to $\frac{5}{6}$. Notice that you could have cancelled one factor at a time like

this: $\frac{60}{72} = \frac{30}{36} = \frac{15}{18} = \frac{5}{6}$. You still reach the same result.

◆ **Exercise 7.1**

1 Write each fraction in its simplest form.

   a $\frac{4}{6}$ **b** $\frac{20}{25}$ **c** $\frac{21}{35}$ **d** $\frac{12}{15}$ **e** $\frac{26}{39}$ **f** $\frac{18}{21}$

2 Write each fraction in its lowest terms.

   a $\frac{8}{24}$ **b** $\frac{12}{30}$ **c** $\frac{30}{45}$ **d** $\frac{24}{32}$ **e** $\frac{27}{45}$ **f** $\frac{36}{60}$

3 This is part of Razi's homework.
He has used inverse operations to check his answers but he has spilt tomato sauce over the last two checks!
Check his answers to parts **b** and **c** for him.
If he has made a mistake, work out the correct answer.

Write each fraction in its lowest terms.
Check your answers.

  a $\frac{15}{25} = \frac{15 \div 5}{25 \div 5} = \frac{3}{5}$ *Check:* $\frac{3}{5} = \frac{3 \times 5}{5 \times 5} = \frac{15}{25}$ ✓

  b $\frac{156}{216} = \frac{156 \div 12}{216 \div 12} = \frac{13}{19}$ *Check:*

  c $\frac{315}{342} = \frac{315 \div 9}{342 \div 9} = \frac{34}{37}$ *Check:*

4 Write each fraction in its lowest terms. Check your answers.

   a $\frac{81}{126}$ **b** $\frac{78}{108}$ **c** $\frac{121}{231}$ **d** $\frac{104}{120}$ **e** $\frac{105}{165}$ **f** $\frac{54}{90}$

7.2 Adding and subtracting fractions

Before you can add or subtract fractions, make sure they have the <u>same denominator</u>.

If the denominators are <u>different</u>, you must find equivalent fractions with a <u>common denominator</u>, then add or subtract the numerators. It makes the calculation simpler if you use the **lowest common denominator**.

You can also add and subtract mixed numbers.

Here is a method for <u>adding</u> mixed numbers. There are other methods, as well.

> Remember to write your answer in its simplest form.

① Add the whole-number parts.
② Add the fractional parts and cancel this answer to its simplest form.
   If this answer is an improper fraction, write it as a mixed number.
③ Add your answers to steps ① and ②.

Here is a method for <u>subtracting</u> mixed numbers.

> You can use this method for addition, too. Try it out.

① Change both mixed numbers into improper fractions.
② Subtract the improper fractions and cancel this answer to its simplest form.
③ If the answer is an improper fraction, change it back to a mixed number.

Worked example 7.2

a Work these out.　　**i** $\frac{4}{7}+\frac{3}{4}$　　**ii** $1\frac{1}{4}+2\frac{5}{6}$　　**iii** $6\frac{1}{3}-2\frac{4}{9}$

b Read what Dakarai says. Use a counter-example to show that he is wrong.

> If I add together two different fractions, my answer will always be greater than 1.

a i　$\frac{4}{7}+\frac{3}{4}=\frac{16}{28}+\frac{21}{28}$　　　Rewrite each fraction with the lowest common denominator before adding.

　　　$=\frac{37}{28}=1\frac{9}{28}$　　　The answer is an improper fraction, so change to a mixed number.

ii　① $1+2=3$　　　Add the whole-number parts.

　　② $\frac{1}{4}+\frac{5}{6}=\frac{3}{12}+\frac{10}{12}=\frac{13}{12}$　　Add the fractional parts, using the lowest common denominator of 12.

　　　$\frac{13}{12}=1\frac{1}{12}$　　　The answer is an improper fraction, so change it to a mixed number.

　　③ $3+1\frac{1}{12}=4\frac{1}{12}$　　　Add the two parts together to get the final answer.

iii　① $6\frac{1}{3}=\frac{19}{3}$ and $2\frac{4}{9}=\frac{22}{9}$　　Change both the mixed numbers into improper fractions.

　　② $\frac{19}{3}-\frac{22}{9}=\frac{57}{9}-\frac{22}{9}=\frac{35}{9}$　　Subtract the fractions, using the lowest common denominator of 9.

　　③ $\frac{35}{9}=3\frac{8}{9}$　　　The answer is an improper fraction so change it back to a mixed number.

b　$\frac{1}{2}+\frac{1}{6}=\frac{3}{6}+\frac{1}{6}=\frac{4}{6}$　　　You only need one example (a counter-example), to show that he is wrong.

　　$\frac{4}{6}=\frac{2}{3}$ and $\frac{2}{3}<1$, so the statement is not true.

Exercise 7.2

1 Work out these additions and subtractions.
Write each answer in its simplest form and as a mixed number when appropriate.

a $\frac{1}{3}+\frac{2}{9}$ **b** $\frac{2}{5}+\frac{3}{10}$ **c** $\frac{2}{7}+\frac{5}{14}$ **d** $\frac{7}{9}-\frac{1}{3}$ **e** $\frac{4}{5}-\frac{2}{15}$ **f** $\frac{7}{8}-\frac{1}{4}$

g $\frac{2}{3}+\frac{4}{5}$ **h** $\frac{7}{9}+\frac{1}{2}$ **i** $\frac{5}{6}+\frac{3}{4}$ **j** $\frac{9}{10}-\frac{3}{4}$ **k** $\frac{4}{5}-\frac{2}{3}$ **l** $\frac{13}{20}-\frac{3}{8}$

2 Copy and complete these.

a $5\frac{2}{3}+3\frac{4}{5}$ ① $5+3=8$ ② $\frac{2}{3}+\frac{4}{5}=\frac{\square}{15}+\frac{\square}{15}=\frac{\square}{15}, \frac{\square}{15}=1\frac{\square}{15}$ ③ $8+1\frac{\square}{15}=9\frac{\square}{15}$

b $5\frac{3}{4}-3\frac{5}{6}$ ① $\frac{23}{4}-\frac{23}{6}$ ② $\frac{23}{4}-\frac{23}{6}=\frac{\square}{12}-\frac{\square}{12}=\frac{\square}{12}$ ③ $\frac{\square}{12}=1\frac{\square}{12}$

3 Work out these additions and subtractions.
Write each answer in its simplest form and as a mixed number when appropriate.
Show all the steps in your working.

a $2\frac{3}{4}+\frac{3}{8}$ **b** $3\frac{1}{5}+2\frac{4}{15}$ **c** $2\frac{7}{9}+2\frac{31}{36}$

d $4\frac{3}{4}+\frac{5}{7}$ **e** $15\frac{3}{8}+2\frac{7}{10}$ **f** $4\frac{5}{6}+5\frac{3}{5}$

g $3\frac{4}{5}-\frac{9}{10}$ **h** $2\frac{1}{6}-\frac{23}{24}$ **i** $3\frac{3}{14}-1\frac{4}{7}$

j $7\frac{1}{3}-2\frac{7}{12}$ **k** $8\frac{2}{3}-4\frac{1}{4}$ **l** $6\frac{7}{12}-4\frac{17}{18}$

4 Read what Zalika says.

> If I add together two fractions that are the same, my answer will always be greater than 1.

Use at least two counter-examples
to show that this statement is not true.

5 Kwan is making a shelf from two pieces of wood.
The first piece is $1\frac{1}{4}$ m long; the second is $1\frac{4}{5}$ m long.
He fixes them on a wall, as shown in the diagram.
a What is the total length of the shelf?
b Show how to check your answer is correct.

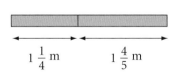

$1\frac{1}{4}$ m $1\frac{4}{5}$ m

6 Yun has a piece of silk $3\frac{3}{8}$ m long.

She cuts a piece of silk $\frac{3}{4}$ m long from the piece she has, to
give to her aunt.
Then she cuts a piece $1\frac{2}{3}$ m long from the piece she has left over,
to give to her sister.
a How long is the piece of silk that Yun has left?
b Show how to check your answer is correct.

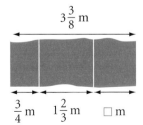

$3\frac{3}{8}$ m

$\frac{3}{4}$ m $1\frac{2}{3}$ m $\square$ m

7.3 Multiplying fractions

You already know how to multiply an integer by a fraction and multiply a fraction by a fraction.
You can complete multiplications more easily by **cancelling common factors** before you multiply.

Worked example 7.3

Work out: **a** $\frac{2}{3} \times 18$ **b** $\frac{3}{4} \times 26$ **c** $\frac{5}{7} \times \frac{4}{9}$ **d** $\frac{2}{7} \times \frac{14}{15}$ **e** $\frac{4}{5} \times \frac{15}{22}$

a $\frac{2}{{}_1\cancel{3}} \times \cancel{18}^{6}$ Divide 3 and 18 by 3. The 3 cancels to 1 and the 18 cancels to 6.

$= 2 \times 6 = 12$ $\frac{2}{1}$ is the same as 2, so just work out 2×6. $2 \times 6 = 12$.

b $\frac{3}{{}_2\cancel{4}} \times \cancel{26}^{13}$ 4 won't divide into 26, but 4 and 26 can both be divided by 2 to give 2 and 13.

$= \frac{3}{2} \times 13 = \frac{39}{2}$ $3 \times 13 = 39$, so the answer is $\frac{39}{2}$.

$= 19\frac{1}{2}$ This is an improper fraction, so change it to a mixed number.

c $\frac{5}{7} \times \frac{4}{9} = \frac{5 \times 4}{7 \times 9}$ There are no common factors between the numbers in the numerators and denominators, so simply multiply 5 by 4 and 7 by 9.

$= \frac{20}{63}$ $\frac{20}{63}$ cannot be cancelled further and is a proper fraction.

d $\frac{2}{{}_1\cancel{7}} \times \frac{\cancel{14}^{2}}{15}$ 7 divides into 7 and 14 to give 1 and 2. There are no other common factors.

$\frac{2}{1} \times \frac{2}{15} = \frac{2 \times 2}{1 \times 15}$ Now multiply 2 by 2 and 1 by 15.

$= \frac{4}{15}$ $\frac{4}{15}$ cannot be cancelled further and is a proper fraction.

e $\frac{{}^2\cancel{4}}{{}_1\cancel{5}} \times \frac{\cancel{15}^{3}}{\cancel{22}_{11}}$ 5 divides into 5 and 15 to give 1 and 3, 4 and 22 can be divided by 2 to give 2 and 11.

$\frac{2}{1} \times \frac{3}{11} = \frac{2 \times 3}{1 \times 11}$ Now multiply 2 by 3 and 1 by 11.

$= \frac{6}{11}$ $\frac{6}{11}$ cannot be cancelled further and is a proper fraction.

◆ Exercise 7.3

1 Work out these multiplications. Cancel common factors before multiplying.

   a $\frac{3}{4} \times 12$ **b** $\frac{5}{7} \times 28$ **c** $\frac{4}{5} \times 45$ **d** $\frac{3}{8} \times 72$ **e** $\frac{7}{11} \times 132$ **f** $\frac{7}{9} \times 180$

2 Work out these multiplications. Cancel common factors before mutliplying.
Write each answer as a mixed number in its simplest form.

   a $\frac{3}{8} \times 36$ **b** $\frac{4}{9} \times 39$ **c** $\frac{5}{6} \times 8$ **d** $\frac{7}{10} \times 45$ **e** $\frac{1}{12} \times 30$ **f** $\frac{9}{14} \times 35$

3 Work out these multiplications. Cancel common factors before multiplying when possible.
Write each answer in its lowest terms.

   a $\frac{3}{4} \times \frac{5}{7}$ **b** $\frac{4}{5} \times \frac{3}{8}$ **c** $\frac{9}{11} \times \frac{2}{5}$ **d** $\frac{6}{7} \times \frac{5}{9}$ **e** $\frac{3}{8} \times \frac{5}{6}$ **f** $\frac{8}{9} \times \frac{3}{13}$

   g $\frac{4}{5} \times \frac{5}{12}$ **h** $\frac{3}{4} \times \frac{8}{9}$ **i** $\frac{2}{5} \times \frac{15}{16}$ **j** $\frac{5}{9} \times \frac{6}{25}$ **k** $\frac{4}{9} \times \frac{15}{22}$ **l** $\frac{8}{21} \times \frac{9}{20}$

4 This is part of Mia's homework. Use Mia's method to work out these multiplications. Write each answer as a mixed number in its simplest form.

> *Question* Work out $2\frac{1}{2} \times 2\frac{4}{15}$
>
> *Answer*   ① *Change to improper fractions:* $\frac{5}{2} \times \frac{34}{15}$
>
>   ② *Cancel common factors:* $\frac{{}^{1}\cancel{5}}{{}_{1}\cancel{2}} \times \frac{\cancel{34}{}^{17}}{\cancel{15}{}_{3}}$
>
>   ③ *Multiply:* $\frac{1}{1} \times \frac{17}{3} = \frac{17}{3}$
>
>   ④ *Change to a mixed number:* $\frac{17}{3} = 5\frac{2}{3}$

a $1\frac{1}{2} \times 3\frac{3}{5}$ **b** $2\frac{1}{4} \times 3\frac{2}{3}$

c $1\frac{1}{8} \times 3\frac{1}{6}$ **d** $3\frac{2}{3} \times 1\frac{5}{22}$

e $3\frac{3}{4} \times 4\frac{3}{5}$ **f** $4\frac{4}{7} \times 2\frac{5}{16}$

g $8\frac{2}{9} \times \frac{5}{37}$ **h** $\frac{3}{5} \times 6\frac{4}{11}$

5 Read what Xavier says.

> If I multiply a fraction by itself, my answer will always be smaller than the fraction I started with.

Use at least two counter-examples to show that this statement is not true.

6 This is part of Razi's homework.

> *Question*   I eat $\frac{1}{4}$ of a pizza. My brother eats $\frac{2}{3}$ of what is left.
>   What fraction of the pizza does my brother eat?
>
> *Answer* $\frac{3}{4}$ is left, $\frac{3}{4} \times \frac{2}{3} = \frac{{}^{1}\cancel{3}}{{}_{2}\cancel{4}} \times \frac{\cancel{2}{}^{1}}{\cancel{3}{}_{1}}$
>
> $= \frac{1}{2} \times \frac{1}{1}$
>
> $= \frac{1}{2}$
>
> *Check* $\frac{3}{4} \times \frac{2}{3} = \frac{\cancel{6}{}^{1}}{\cancel{12}{}_{2}} = \frac{1}{2}$ ✓

Razi works out the answer to the question by cancelling common factors <u>before</u> multiplying. He checks his answer is correct by cancelling common factors <u>after</u> multiplying. Use Razi's method to work out and check the answer to these questions.

a The guests at a party eat $\frac{5}{8}$ of a cake. Sam eats $\frac{1}{4}$ of what is left. What fraction of the cake does Sam eat?

b The guests at a party eat $\frac{7}{10}$ of the rolls. Ed eats $\frac{5}{6}$ of what is left. What fraction of the rolls does Ed eat?

7.4 Dividing fractions

In Stage 8 you learned how to divide an integer by a fraction and also a fraction by a fraction.

In both cases you start by turning the fraction you are dividing by upside down, and then multiplying instead.

This is called **invert and multiply**. Remember to cancel common factors before you multiply, and write each answer in its simplest form and as a mixed number when appropriate.

Worked example 7.4

Work out: **a** $18 \div \frac{2}{3}$ **b** $26 \div \frac{3}{4}$ **c** $\frac{5}{7} \div \frac{4}{9}$ **d** $\frac{1}{7} \div \frac{5}{21}$ **e** $\frac{4}{5} \div \frac{6}{25}$

a $18 \div \frac{2}{3} = 18 \times \frac{3}{2}$

$^9\cancel{18} \times \frac{3}{\cancel{2}_1} = 9 \times \frac{3}{1}$

$= 9 \times 3 = 27$

Start by turning the fraction upside down and multiplying.

2 divides into 2 and 18, so the 2 cancels to 1 and the 18 cancels to 9.

$\frac{3}{1}$ is the same as 3, so just work out 9 × 3.

b $26 \div \frac{3}{4} = 26 \times \frac{4}{3}$

$= \frac{26 \times 4}{3} = \frac{104}{3}$

$= 34\frac{2}{3}$

Start by turning the fraction upside down and multiplying.

There are no common factors to cancel, so multiply 26 by 4.

Change $\frac{104}{3}$ to a mixed number.

c $\frac{5}{7} \div \frac{4}{9} = \frac{5}{7} \times \frac{9}{4}$

$= \frac{5 \times 9}{7 \times 4} = \frac{45}{28}$

$= 1\frac{17}{28}$

Start by turning $\frac{4}{9}$ upside down and multiplying.

There are no common factors to cancel, so multiply 5 by 9 and 7 by 4.

Change $\frac{45}{28}$ to a mixed number.

d $\frac{1}{7} \div \frac{5}{21} = \frac{1}{7} \times \frac{21}{5}$

$\frac{1}{_1\cancel{7}} \times \frac{\cancel{21}^3}{5} = \frac{1}{1} \times \frac{3}{5}$

$= \frac{1 \times 3}{1 \times 5} = \frac{3}{5}$

Start by turning $\frac{5}{21}$ upside down and multiplying.

7 divides into 7 and 21, so the 7 cancels to 1 and the 21 cancels to 3.

Multiply 1 by 3 and 1 by 5. The answer is a proper fraction, so leave it as it is.

e $\frac{4}{5} \div \frac{6}{25} = \frac{4}{5} \times \frac{25}{6}$

$\frac{^2\cancel{4}}{_1\cancel{5}} \times \frac{\cancel{25}^5}{\cancel{6}_3} = \frac{2}{1} \times \frac{5}{3}$

$= \frac{2 \times 5}{1 \times 3} = \frac{10}{3}$

$= 3\frac{1}{3}$

Start by turning $\frac{6}{25}$ upside down and multiplying.

2 divides into 4 and 6 to give 2 and 3. 5 divides into 5 and 25 to give 1 and 5.

Multiply 2 by 5 and 1 by 3.

Change $\frac{10}{3}$ to a mixed number.

◆ **Exercise 7.4**

1 Work out these divisions.
Write each answer in its simplest form and as a mixed number when appropriate.

a $16 \div \frac{4}{7}$ **b** $21 \div \frac{3}{5}$ **c** $14 \div \frac{2}{9}$ **d** $8 \div \frac{4}{11}$ **e** $22 \div \frac{2}{3}$ **f** $25 \div \frac{5}{8}$

g $18 \div \frac{4}{5}$ **h** $26 \div \frac{6}{7}$ **i** $6 \div \frac{4}{9}$ **j** $25 \div \frac{10}{11}$ **k** $32 \div \frac{6}{13}$ **l** $42 \div \frac{4}{7}$

2 Work out these divisions.
Write each answer in its lowest terms and as a mixed number when appropriate.

a $\frac{3}{4} \div \frac{5}{7}$ b $\frac{7}{9} \div \frac{2}{5}$ c $\frac{11}{12} \div \frac{3}{5}$ d $\frac{4}{5} \div \frac{2}{3}$ e $\frac{8}{9} \div \frac{4}{7}$ f $\frac{7}{8} \div \frac{3}{4}$

g $\frac{6}{7} \div \frac{3}{14}$ h $\frac{5}{6} \div \frac{15}{24}$ i $\frac{25}{32} \div \frac{5}{8}$ j $\frac{6}{7} \div \frac{9}{10}$ k $\frac{8}{15} \div \frac{12}{25}$ l $\frac{9}{28} \div \frac{15}{42}$

3 This is part of Jake's homework.
Use Jake's method to work out
these divisions. Write your
answer in its simplest form
and as a mixed number
when appropriate.

a $1\frac{1}{2} \div 1\frac{4}{5}$ b $2\frac{1}{4} \div 1\frac{2}{3}$

c $4\frac{1}{8} \div 5\frac{1}{6}$ d $2\frac{2}{3} \div 3\frac{1}{4}$

e $5\frac{1}{2} \div 2\frac{3}{4}$ f $4\frac{4}{5} \div 2\frac{3}{8}$

g $1\frac{1}{4} \div \frac{10}{11}$ h $\frac{3}{5} \div 2\frac{1}{10}$

> _Question_ _Work out $2\frac{1}{2} \div 3\frac{4}{7}$_
>
> _Answer_   ① _Change to improper fractions:_ $\frac{5}{2} \div \frac{25}{7}$
>
> ② _Invert and multiply:_ $\frac{5}{2} \times \frac{7}{25}$
>
> ③ _Cancel common factors::_ $\frac{{}^{1}\cancel{5}}{2} \times \frac{7}{\cancel{25}_{5}}$
>
> ④ _Multiply:_ $\frac{1}{2} \times \frac{7}{5} = \frac{7}{10}$

4 Read what Tanesha says.

> If I divide a mixed number by a different mixed number, my answer will always be a mixed number.

Use at least two counter-examples to show that this statement is not true.

5 This is part of Harsha's homework. She uses
an inverse operation to check her answer
is correct.
Work out the answer to these divisions.
Use Harsha's method to check your answers
are correct.

a $\frac{2}{5} \div \frac{3}{7}$ b $\frac{4}{7} \div \frac{1}{5}$

c $\frac{6}{7} \div \frac{3}{4}$ d $\frac{8}{9} \div \frac{4}{5}$

e $\frac{2}{9} \div \frac{6}{11}$ f $\frac{10}{11} \div \frac{5}{6}$

> _Question_ _Work out $\frac{3}{4} \div \frac{2}{3}$_
>
> _Answer_ $\frac{3}{4} \div \frac{2}{3} = \frac{3}{4} \times \frac{3}{2}$
>
> $= \frac{9}{8}$
>
> $= 1\frac{1}{8}$
>
> _Check_ $1\frac{1}{8} = \frac{9}{8}, \frac{9}{8} \times \frac{2}{3} = \frac{18}{24}$
>
> $\frac{18}{24} = \frac{18 \div 6}{24 \div 6}$
>
> $= \frac{3}{4} \checkmark$

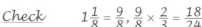

7.5 Working with fractions mentally

You need to be able to work with fractions mentally. This means that you should be able to do simple additions, subtractions, multiplications and divisions 'in your head'. You should also be able to solve word problems mentally. This section will help you practise the skills you need.

For complicated or difficult questions, it may help if you write down some of the steps in the working. These workings, or jottings, will help you remember what you have worked out so far, and what you still need to do.

Worked example 7.5

Work these out mentally.　　**a** $\frac{3}{4}+\frac{3}{8}$　　**b** $\frac{4}{5}-\frac{3}{4}$　　**c** $\frac{2}{5}\times 20$　　**d** $\frac{2}{3}\times\frac{6}{7}$　　**e** $\frac{4}{7}\div\frac{8}{9}$

a $\frac{6}{8}+\frac{3}{8}=\frac{9}{8}=1\frac{1}{8}$ 　　In your head, change $\frac{3}{4}$ to $\frac{6}{8}$ so you can add it to $\frac{3}{8}$.

b $\frac{4\times4-3\times5}{20}$ 　　The lowest common denominator is $5\times4=20$.

$=\frac{16-15}{20}=\frac{1}{20}$ 　　In your head, work out $4\times4-3\times5$ to give a numerator of 1.

c $20\div5=4,\ 4\times2=8$ 　　Divide 20 by the denominator 5, then multiply the result by 2.

d $\frac{2}{{}_1\cancel{3}}\times\frac{\cancel{6}^{\,2}}{7}=\frac{2\times2}{1\times7}$ 　　In your head divide the 3 and 6 by 3 to cancel before multiplying.

$=\frac{4}{7}$ 　　Multiply the numerators and the denominators to work out the answer.

e $\frac{{}^1\cancel{4}}{7}\times\frac{9}{\cancel{8}_2}=\frac{1\times9}{7\times2}$ 　　In your head invert and multiply the second fraction, then divide the 4 and 8 by 4.

$=\frac{9}{14}$ 　　Multiply. Use jottings to help if you need to, as there is a lot of work to do here in your head.

Exercise 7.5

> In this exercise, write each answer in its simplest form and as a mixed number when appropriate.

1 Work out these additions mentally.

　a $\frac{1}{3}+\frac{1}{6}$ 　**b** $\frac{3}{4}+\frac{1}{8}$ 　**c** $\frac{3}{5}+\frac{1}{10}$ 　**d** $\frac{1}{2}+\frac{3}{8}$ 　**e** $\frac{3}{4}+\frac{5}{12}$ 　**f** $\frac{7}{15}+\frac{4}{5}$

　g $\frac{1}{3}+\frac{1}{5}$ 　**h** $\frac{1}{4}+\frac{1}{7}$ 　**i** $\frac{2}{9}+\frac{1}{5}$ 　**j** $\frac{3}{4}+\frac{2}{3}$ 　**k** $\frac{5}{8}+\frac{1}{5}$ 　**l** $\frac{1}{4}+\frac{5}{6}$

2 Work out these subtractions mentally.

　a $\frac{1}{3}-\frac{1}{9}$ 　**b** $\frac{1}{4}-\frac{1}{8}$ 　**c** $\frac{1}{5}-\frac{1}{15}$ 　**d** $\frac{2}{3}-\frac{1}{6}$ 　**e** $\frac{4}{5}-\frac{1}{10}$ 　**f** $\frac{11}{20}-\frac{2}{5}$

　g $\frac{1}{2}-\frac{1}{3}$ 　**h** $\frac{4}{5}-\frac{1}{4}$ 　**i** $\frac{5}{7}-\frac{1}{2}$ 　**j** $\frac{3}{4}-\frac{2}{7}$ 　**k** $\frac{7}{12}-\frac{3}{8}$ 　**l** $\frac{8}{9}-\frac{3}{4}$

3 Work out these multiplications mentally. Use jottings to help if you need to.

　a $\frac{1}{3}\times\frac{1}{5}$ 　**b** $\frac{2}{7}\times\frac{1}{3}$ 　**c** $\frac{3}{4}\times\frac{3}{5}$ 　**d** $\frac{8}{9}\times\frac{2}{7}$ 　**e** $\frac{4}{5}\times\frac{2}{9}$ 　**f** $\frac{6}{13}\times\frac{4}{5}$

　g $\frac{2}{3}\times\frac{1}{4}$ 　**h** $\frac{3}{5}\times\frac{1}{9}$ 　**i** $\frac{4}{5}\times\frac{10}{11}$ 　**j** $\frac{5}{6}\times\frac{8}{9}$ 　**k** $\frac{2}{3}\times\frac{9}{10}$ 　**l** $\frac{4}{5}\times\frac{15}{22}$

4 Work out these divisions mentally. Use jottings to help if you need to.

a $\frac{1}{6} \div \frac{1}{3}$ **b** $\frac{1}{12} \div \frac{1}{4}$ **c** $\frac{2}{7} \div \frac{2}{5}$ **d** $\frac{3}{8} \div \frac{3}{5}$ **e** $\frac{4}{5} \div \frac{4}{9}$ **f** $\frac{7}{8} \div \frac{7}{12}$

g $\frac{2}{3} \div \frac{4}{5}$ **h** $\frac{6}{7} \div \frac{3}{5}$ **i** $\frac{3}{4} \div \frac{6}{7}$ **j** $\frac{8}{9} \div \frac{4}{5}$ **k** $\frac{5}{6} \div \frac{10}{13}$ **l** $\frac{5}{6} \div \frac{15}{16}$

> Work out the answers to questions **5** to **8** mentally. Use jottings to help if you need to.

5 In a UK hockey squad, $\frac{1}{3}$ of the players are English, $\frac{1}{4}$ of the players are Scottish and the rest are Welsh.
What fraction of the squad are Welsh?

6 In a packet of biscuits, $\frac{2}{5}$ are chocolate, $\frac{1}{6}$ are shortbread and the rest are coconut.
What fraction of the biscuits in the packet are coconut?

7 In a cinema $\frac{3}{5}$ of the people watching the film are children.
$\frac{3}{4}$ of the children are girls.
  a What fraction of the people watching the film are girls?
  b What fraction of the people watching the film are boys?

8 At a cricket match $\frac{4}{9}$ of the supporters are supporting the home team.
The rest are supporting the away team. $\frac{3}{5}$ of the away team supporters are male.
  a What fraction of all the supporters are male and supporting the away team?
  b What fraction of all the supporters are female and supporting the away team?

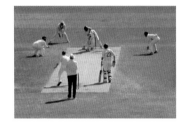

Summary

You should now know that:

★ You simplify a fraction into its simplest form, or lowest terms, by dividing the numerator and the denominator by the highest common factor (HCF).

★ You can only add or subtract fractions when the denominators are the same. If they are different, write them as equivalent fractions with a common denominator, then add or subtract the numerators.

★ When you multiply fractions you should cancel common factors before multiplying.

★ When you divide by a fraction you turn this fraction upside down and multiply instead. This is called 'invert and multiply'.

You should be able to:

★ Write a fraction in its simplest form by cancelling common factors.

★ Add, subtract, multiply and divide fractions, interpreting division as a multiplicative inverse, and cancel common factors before multiplying and dividing.

★ Work with fractions mentally, using jottings where appropriate.

★ Solve word problems mentally.

End-of-unit review

1 Write each fraction in its simplest form.

    a $\dfrac{5}{15}$ **b** $\dfrac{16}{20}$ **c** $\dfrac{24}{32}$ **d** $\dfrac{22}{55}$ **e** $\dfrac{250}{350}$ **f** $\dfrac{21}{27}$

2 Write the fraction $\dfrac{84}{108}$ in its lowest terms.

    Show how you check your answer.

3 Work out these additions and subtractions.

    Write each answer in its simplest form and as a mixed number when appropriate.

    Show all the steps in your working.

    a $\dfrac{1}{4} + \dfrac{3}{8}$ **b** $\dfrac{7}{12} - \dfrac{1}{4}$ **c** $\dfrac{2}{5} + \dfrac{5}{6}$ **d** $4\dfrac{3}{8} + \dfrac{2}{3}$ **e** $3\dfrac{1}{5} - \dfrac{7}{15}$ **f** $7\dfrac{7}{8} - 4\dfrac{1}{12}$

4 Keith is a plumber. He has a 5 m length of pipe.

    He cuts off two pieces of pipe.

    The first piece is $2\dfrac{1}{4}$ m long, the second is $1\dfrac{2}{5}$ m long.

    a How long is the piece of pipe that Keith has left?

    b Show how to check your answer is correct.

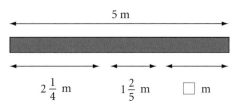

5 Work out these multiplications.

    Cancel common factors before multiplying.

    Write each answer as a mixed number in its simplest form.

    a $\dfrac{3}{5} \times 15$ **b** $\dfrac{2}{9} \times 810$ **c** $\dfrac{5}{9} \times 7$ **d** $\dfrac{2}{5} \times \dfrac{4}{9}$ **e** $\dfrac{3}{4} \times \dfrac{8}{9}$ **f** $\dfrac{4}{9} \times \dfrac{9}{16}$

6 a The guests at a party eat $\dfrac{7}{8}$ of a cake. Tom eats $\dfrac{1}{2}$ of what is left.

      What fraction of the cake does Tom eat?

    b At the party $\dfrac{3}{5}$ of a pie are eaten. Jo eats $\dfrac{4}{5}$ of what is left.

      What fraction of the pie does Jo eat?

7 Work out these divisions.

    Write each answer in its simplest form and as a mixed number when appropriate.

    a $12 \div \dfrac{4}{5}$ **b** $21 \div \dfrac{6}{7}$ **c** $25 \div \dfrac{2}{5}$ **d** $\dfrac{3}{5} \div \dfrac{4}{9}$ **e** $\dfrac{3}{7} \div \dfrac{12}{33}$ **f** $\dfrac{9}{11} \div \dfrac{15}{22}$

8 Read what Dakarai says.

> If I divide an improper fraction by a different improper fraction, my answer will always be an improper fraction.

    Use a counter-example to show that this statement is not true.

Here are some reminders about the work you have already done on shapes and geometric reasoning.

Key words

Make sure you learn and understand these key words:

inscribed
Pythagoras' theorem

Perpendicular lines meet at a right angle (90°). You show that lines are perpendicular with a symbol that looks like the corner of a square (⌐).

To draw a regular polygon, you need to know the lengths of the sides <u>and</u> the size of the internal angles.

— internal angle

Remember that in a regular polygon all the sides are the same length and all the internal angles are the same size.

The perpendicular bisector of the the line segment AB is the line that passes through the midpoint of AB at right angles to AB.

perpendicular bisector of AB

A   B

The angle bisector of angle ABC is the line that cuts the angle exactly in half.
You can draw an angle bisector using only a straight edge and compasses.

A   angle bisector

B   C   these two angles are the same size

In this chapter you will learn about Pythagoras' theorem.

Look at these diagrams.

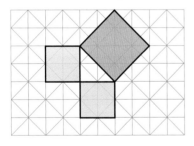
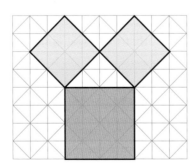
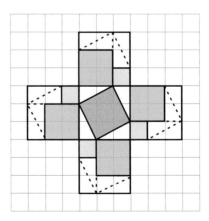

Each diagram illustrates Pythagoras' theorem. Look back at this page when you have finished the chapter and see if you can explain how they do that.

In this unit you will learn how to draw perpendicular lines from a point to a line and from a point on a line. You will also learn how to draw shapes inside circles and use Pythagoras' theorem to solve two-dimensional problems.

8.1 Constructing perpendicular lines

You need to be able to construct the perpendicular from a point on a line, and the perpendicular from a point to a line, using only a straight edge and compasses. You can use a ruler as the straight edge, but you must not use a protractor to do these constructions.

> The term 'straight edge' is used when you are not allowed to use a ruler to measure lengths. You still need to draw straight lines, though.

Worked example 8.1

a A is a point on a line.
  Construct the perpendicular at A.

b P is a point above the line.
  Construct the perpendicular from P to the line.

---

a

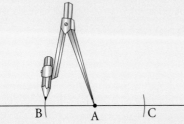

Step 1 Start by putting your compass point on A. Open your compasses and draw arcs both sides of A that cross the line. Label the points where the arcs cross the line as B and C.

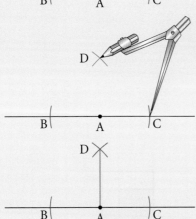

Step 2 Open you compasses a little wider than in Step 1. Put your compass point on points B and C, in turn, and draw arcs that cross above the line. These two arcs must have the same radius. Label the point where the arcs cross as D.

Step 3 Draw a straight line from D to A. This is the perpendicular at A. You can use a protractor to check that the angle is 90°.

b

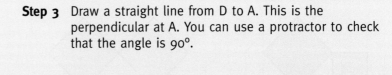

Step 1 Start by putting your compass point on P. Open your compasses a little wider than the distance from P to the line. Draw an arc that crosses the line both sides of P. Label the points where the arcs cross the line as Q and R.

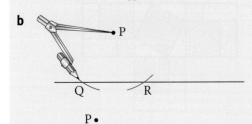

Step 2 Put your compass point on points Q and R, in turn, and draw arcs that cross below the line. These two arcs must have the same radius, but it does not need to be the same as the one you used in Step 1. Label the point where the arcs cross as S.

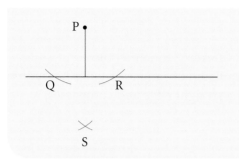

Step 3 Place your straight edge through P and S and draw a straight line from P to the original line. This is the perpendicular from P to the line. You can use a protractor to check that the angle is 90°.

◆ Exercise 8.1

 1 Draw a line PQ 8 cm long. Mark the points R and S on the line, 3 cm from each end of the line.
Construct the perpendicular at R and the perpendicular at S, as shown in the diagram.

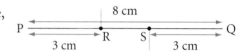

2 Construct a square of side length 4 cm. Do not use a protractor.

3 Anders draws the line EF, 6 cm long at an angle of 30° to a horizontal line. He constructs the perpendicular at F, which meets the horizontal line at G, as shown in the diagram.

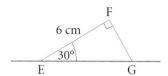

   a Draw an accurate copy of the diagram. You may use a protractor to draw the 30° angle, but not the perpendicular line.
Anders says that angle EGF is 60°.
   b Show that he is correct by:
     i measuring angle EGF with a protractor
     ii calculating angle EGF, using the facts that you know about the sum of the angles in a triangle.

4 Copy each diagram. Construct the perpendiculars from the points P and Q to the line.

   a    **b**

> In questions like these, always draw your lines long enough to add the arcs you will need during the construction.

5 Construct rectangle ABCD with sides AB = 8 cm and BC = 5 cm. Draw diagonal AC. Construct perpendiculars from B and D to AC.

 6 Alicia draws a horizontal line.
She marks the points A and B at different heights above the line. She constructs the perpendiculars from A to the line and from B to the line and labels the points where they meet the line as C and D. Alicia completes the quadrilateral ABCD, as shown in the diagram.

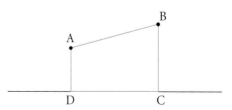

   a Make a copy of the diagram.
Ellie says that the total size of angles ABC and BAD is 180°.
   b Show that she is correct by measuring angles ABC and BAD with a protractor and working out

8.2 Inscribing shapes in circles

An **inscribed** shape is one that fits inside a circle with all its vertices (corners) touching the circumference of the circle. You must be able to inscribe squares, equilateral triangles, regular hexagons and octagons by constructing equal divisions of a circle, using only a straight edge and compasses.

Worked example 8.2

Draw a circle with a radius of 4 cm. Using a straight edge and compasses, construct an inscribed:
a square **b** regular octagon **c** equilateral triangle **d** regular hexagon.

a

Step 1 Start by drawing a circle with radius 4 cm. Mark the centre of the circle with a small dot.

Step 2 Draw a diameter of the circle on the diagram.

Step 3 Using compasses, construct the perpendicular bisector of the diameter. Extend it to form a second diameter.

Step 4 Join the ends of the two diameters, in order, to form a square.

b

Step 1 Start by drawing a circle with radius 4 cm. Mark the centre of the circle with a small dot.

Step 2 Draw a diameter of the circle on the diagram.

Step 3 Using compasses, construct the perpendicular bisector of the diameter. Extend it to form a second diameter.

Step 4 Construct the angle bisector of one of the right angles (90°) at the centre of the circle and extend it to form a third diameter.

Step 5 Construct the angle bisector of one of the other right angles at the centre of the circle and extend it to form a fourth diameter.

Step 6 Join the ends of the four diameters, in order, to form a regular octagon.

c

4 cm

Step 1 Start by drawing a circle with radius 4 cm. Mark the centre of the circle with a small dot.

Step 2 Make a mark at any point on the circumference of the circle.

Step 3 Check that the compasses are still set to 4 cm (radius of the circle). Put the point on the mark you have just made and draw an arc on the circumference of the circle.

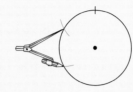

Step 4 Move your compasses to the first arc (made in the previous step) and draw a second arc on the circumference.

Step 5 Repeat step 4 until you have drawn five arcs.

Step 6 Join the original mark to the second arc, then this arc to the fourth, then this arc to the original mark, to form an equilateral triangle.

d Repeat steps 1–5 of part **c**.

Step 6 Join the original mark to the first arc, then continue to join the arcs, in order. Join the last arc to the first mark, to form a regular hexagon.

◆ Exercise 8.2

1 For each part of this question, start by drawing a circle with radius 5 cm. Use a straight edge and compasses to construct an inscribed:

   a square   **b** regular octagon
   c equilateral triangle   **d** regular hexagon.

2 The diagram shows a square inscribed in a circle of radius 6 cm.

   a Draw an accurate copy of the diagram.
   b Measure the length of the side of the square, which is marked x in the diagram.
      Write your measurement to the nearest millimetre.
   c Copy and complete the workings below to calculate the area of the shaded region in the diagram. Use $\pi = 3.14$.

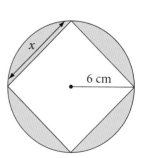

   Area of circle: $\pi \times r^2 = \pi \times 6^2$
                    $= \square$ cm²
   Area of square: $x \times x = \square \times \square$
                    $= \square$ cm²
   Shaded area: area of circle − area of square $= \square - \square$
                                      $= \square$ cm²

3 Shen wants to estimate the area of a hexagon inscribed in a circle of radius 6 cm.
He takes these steps.

Step 1 Draw a circle of radius 6 cm.

Step 2 Construct an inscribed hexagon.

Step 3 Draw a circle inside the hexagon so that it touches all the sides of the hexagon.

Step 4 Measure the radius of the smaller circle.

Step 5 Area of large circle = Π × 6² = 113.04 cm²

Area of small circle = Π × 5.2² = 84.91 cm²

The area of the hexagon must be bigger than 84.91 cm² but smaller than 113.04 cm².

Halfway between 84.91 and 113.04 is $\frac{84.91 + 113.04}{2} = 98.975$

I estimate the area of the hexagon to be 99 cm².

(diagram: 5.2 cm, 6 cm)

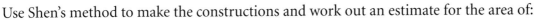

Use Shen's method to make the constructions and work out an estimate for the area of:
a a hexagon inscribed in a circle of radius 7 cm
b an octagon inscribed in a circle of radius 6 cm
c an octagon inscribed in a circle of radius 7 cm.

4 Anders inscribes an octagon in a circle of radius 4.5 cm.
Harsha inscribes an octagon in a circle of radius 9 cm.

> I estimate the area of my inscribed octagon to be about 60 cm².

> That means that the area of my inscribed octagon must be about 120 cm², as my radius is double your radius.

a Draw an accurate diagram and make appropriate calculations to show that Anders has made a correct estimate.
b Without drawing a diagram, how can you tell that Harsha's statement is false?
c Draw an accurate diagram and make appropriate calculations to show that Harsha is wrong.

8.3 Using Pythagoras' theorem

The longest side of a right-angled triangle is called the hypotenuse.

The hypotenuse is the side that is opposite the right angle.

Now look at this triangle. The length of the hypotenuse is labelled a and the lengths of the other two sides are b and c.

Pythagoras' theorem states that in any right-angled triangle, the square of the hypotenuse is equal to the sum of the squares of the other two sides.

For this triangle: $a^2 = b^2 + c^2$

You can use this formula to solve problems involving right-angled triangles.

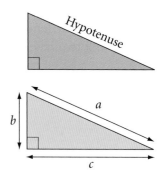

Worked example 8.3

a A right-angled triangle has a base length of 1.2 m and a perpendicular height of 0.9 m.
What is the length of the hypotenuse of the triangle?

b A ladder is 5 m long. Dave rests the ladder against a vertical brick wall. The foot of the ladder is 1.5 m horizontally from the base of the wall. How far up the wall does the ladder reach?

a

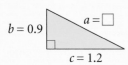

0.9 m

1.2 m

Start by drawing a triangle to represent the problem. Write the dimensions that you know on the triangle.

$b = 0.9$ $a = \square$
$c = 1.2$

Label the sides of the triangle a, b and c. Label the hypotenuse a and the other two sides b and c. It doesn't matter which is which.

$a^2 = b^2 + c^2$
$a^2 = 0.9^2 + 1.2^2$
$a^2 = 0.81 + 1.44$
$a^2 = 2.25$

Write down the formula, then substitute in the numbers that you know.
Solve the equation to work out the value of a. Take it one step at a time.

$a = \sqrt{2.25}$
$a = 1.5\,\text{m}$

Use your calculator to work out the square root.
Remember to write the correct units (metres) with your answer.

b

$a = 5\,\text{m}$ $b = \square$
$c = 1.5\,\text{m}$

Start by drawing a triangle to represent the problem. Write the dimensions that you know on the triangle.
Label the sides of the triangle a, b and c.

$a^2 = b^2 + c^2$
$5^2 = b^2 + 1.5^2$
$25 = b^2 + 2.25$
$b^2 = 25 - 2.25$
$b^2 = 22.75$

Write down the formula, then substitute in the numbers that you know.
Solve the equation to work out the value of b. Take it one step at a time.

$b = \sqrt{22.75}$

Use your calculator to work out the square root.

$b = 4.77\,\text{m}$ (2 d.p.)

If your answer isn't exact, round it to two decimal places. Put the units in your answer.

◆ Exercise 8.3

1 Work out the length of the hypotenuse in each triangle.
The first two have been started for you.

a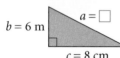

$$a^2 = b^2 + c^2$$
$$a^2 = 6^2 + 8^2$$
$$a^2 = 36 + 64$$

b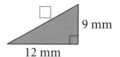

$$a^2 = b^2 + c^2$$
$$a^2 = 9^2 + 12^2$$

c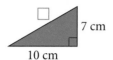

d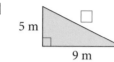

2 Work out the lengths of the sides marked ☐ in each triangle.
The first two have been started for you.

a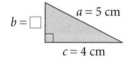

$$a^2 = b^2 + c^2$$
$$5^2 = b^2 + 4^2$$
$$25 = b^2 + 16$$
$$b^2 = 25 - 16$$

b

$$a^2 = b^2 + c^2$$
$$2.6^2 = 1^2 + c^2$$

c

d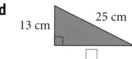

 3 A rectangle is 12 cm long and 5 cm wide.
Work out the length of a diagonal of the rectangle.

> Draw diagrams to help you solve these problems.

 4 Isaac walks 8 km north and then 12 km east.
How far is Isaac from his starting point?

5 The diagram shows a triangle inside a circle with centre O.
The lengths of the shorter sides of the triangle are 12 cm and 16 cm.
Work out the area of the circle.

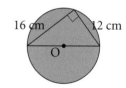

Summary

You should now know that:

★ An inscribed shape fits inside a circle with all its vertices (corners) on the circumference of the circle.

★ Pythagoras' theorem can only be used to solve problems in right-angled triangles. The theorem states that: $a^2 = b^2 + c^2$, where a is the hypotenuse and b and c are the two shorter sides.

You should be able to:

★ Use a straight edge and compasses to construct the perpendicular from a point on a line and the perpendicular from a point to the line.

★ Use a straight edge and compasses to inscribe squares, equilateral triangles and regular hexagons and octagons by constructing equal divisions of a circle.

★ Know and use Pythagoras' theorem to solve two-dimensional problems involving right-angled triangles.

End-of-unit review

1 Draw a line AB 8 cm long.
Mark the point X on the line, 3 cm from A.
Construct the perpendicular at X, as shown in the diagram.

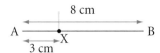

2 Jake draws a line QR, 8 cm long, at an angle of 40° to a horizontal
line through R.
He constructs the perpendicular to QR at Q. It meets the horizontal
line at P, as shown in the diagram.

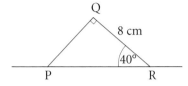

a Draw an accurate copy of the diagram. You may use a protractor to
draw the 40° angle, but not for the perpendicular line.

Jake says that angle QPR is 50°.

b Show that he is correct by:

   i   measuring angle QPR with a protractor

   ii calculating angle QPR, using the facts that you know about the sum of the angles in a triangle.

3 Copy the diagram and construct a perpendicular from the point A to the line.

A •

4 Draw a circle with a radius of 5 cm.
Using a straight edge and compasses, construct an inscribed square.

5 Draw a circle with a radius of 5 cm.
Using a straight edge and compasses, inside the same circle construct an inscribed equilateral
triangle <u>and</u> an inscribed regular hexagon.

6 Work out the length of the hypotenuse marked ☐ in this triangle.

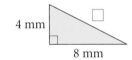

7 Work out the length of the side marked ☐ in this triangle.

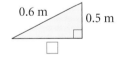

8 Work out the length of the diagonal marked ☐ in this rectangle.

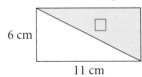

9 A rectangle has a length of 12 cm and a diagonal of 13 cm.
Work out the area of the rectangle.

> Draw a diagram to help you solve this problem.

a

The length of the red line is *a* units.

c

The length of the blue line is *c* units.

What does 4*a* represent?
What does *a* + *c* represent?
What does *ac* represent?

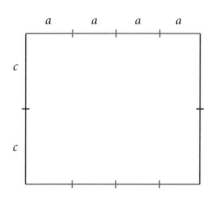

Here is a rectangle.
Which of these is a formula for the length of the perimeter?

$2(4a + 2c)$ $4c + 8a$

$4a + 2c + 4a + 2c$ $4(2a + c)$

Which of these is a formula for the area of the rectangle?

$4a \times 2c$ $2c \times 4a$

$8ac$ $8ca$

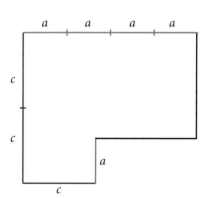

Can you find expressions for the lengths of each of the two black lines in this diagram?

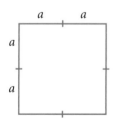

Can you find an expression for the area of this square?

In this unit you will transform algebraic expressions using the laws of indices and factorisation. You will also add and subtract algebraic fractions as well as substituting into formulae and expressions.

9.1 Simplifying algebraic expressions

You already know how to use the laws of indices for multiplication and division of numbers.
You can also use these rules with algebraic expressions.

When you <u>multiply</u> powers of the same variable, you <u>add</u> the indices. $x^a \times x^b = x^{a+b}$

When you <u>divide</u> powers of the same variable, you <u>subtract</u> the indices. $x^a \div x^b = x^{a-b}$

Worked example 9.1

Simplify each expression.   **a** $x^2 \times x^3$ **b** $y^7 \div y^4$ **c** $2m^3 \times 8m^3$ **d** $\frac{12b^9}{6b^8}$

a $x^2 \times x^3 = x^{2+3}$
$\qquad = x^5$

To multiply, add the indices.
2 + 3 = 5, so the answer is x^5.

b $y^7 \div y^4 = y^{7-4}$
$\qquad = y^3$

To divide, subtract the indices.
7 − 4 = 3, so the answer is y^3.

c $2m^3 \times 8m^3 = 2 \times 8 \times m^{3+3}$
$\qquad = 16m^6$

Multiply the 2 by the 8, to simplify the numbers, and add the indices as normal. 2 × 8 = 16, 3 + 3 = 6, so the answer is $16m^6$.

d $\frac{12b^9}{6b^8} = \frac{12}{6} \times b^{9-8}$
$\qquad = 2b$

Divide the 12 by the 6, to simplify the numbers, and subtract the indices as normal.
12 ÷ 6 = 2, 9 − 8 = 1, so the answer is $2b^1$. Write this as $2b$.

Exercise 9.1

1 Simplify each expression.
a $x^4 \times x^5$ **b** $y^2 \times y^4$ **c** $z^7 \times z^3$ **d** $m^8 \times m^6$ **e** $n^9 \times n^3$ **f** $p^6 \times p$
g $q^9 \div q^4$ **h** $r^6 \div r^3$ **i** $t^7 \div t^2$ **j** $u^8 \div u^6$ **k** $v^8 \div v^7$ **l** $w^8 \div w$

2 Simplify each expression.
a $3x^2 \times 2x^3$ **b** $4y^4 \times 3y^5$ **c** $6z^2 \times 5z^5$ **d** $2m^4 \times 2m^3$ **e** $4n^6 \times n^7$ **f** $p^2 \times 8p$
g $6q^{10} \div 2q^6$ **h** $9r^9 \div 3r^5$ **i** $15t^7 \div 5t^3$ **j** $\frac{8u^7}{4u^2}$ **k** $\frac{2v^6}{v^2}$ **l** $\frac{5w^7}{w^6}$

3 Which answer is correct, A, B, C or D?
a Simplify $2e^4 \times 3e^2$.   **A** $5e^6$ **B** $6e^8$ **C** $5e^8$ **D** $6e^6$
b Simplify $3g^6 \times 5g$.   **A** $15g^6$ **B** $15g^7$ **C** $8g^6$ **D** $8g^7$
c Simplify $10k^8 \div 5k^2$.   **A** $5k^6$ **B** $5k^4$ **C** $2k^6$ **D** $2k^4$
d Simplify $\frac{8m^2}{2m}$.   **A** $6m^2$ **B** $6m$ **C** $4m^2$ **D** $4m$

4 Here are some algebra cards.

$4x^5 \times 2x^4$
$2x^3 \times 3x^3$
$8x^6 \times x^3$
$6x^3 \times 2x^3$
$12x^{10} \div 2x$
$12x^8 \div x^2$
$3x^2 \times 4x^3$

a Separate the cards into two groups. Explain how you decided which group to put them in.
b Which card does not fit into either of the groups? Explain why this is.

9.2 Constructing algebraic expressions

In algebraic expressions, letters represent unknown numbers.

You often need to construct algebraic expressions to help you solve problems.

Suppose you want to work out the price of tickets for a day out. You might choose to let a represent the price of an adult's ticket and c represent the price of a child's ticket.

You can write the total price for an adult's ticket and a child's ticket as $a + c$.

You can write the difference between the price of an adult's ticket and a child's ticket as $a - c$.

You can write the total price of tickets for 2 adults and 2 children as $2(a + c)$ or $2a + 2c$.

These expressions are written **in terms of** a and c.

Worked example 9.2

a Ahmad thinks of a number, n. Write down an expression, in terms of n, for the number Ahmad gets when he:
   i doubles the number then adds 5
   ii divides the number by 3 then subtracts 6
   iii adds 3 to the number then multiplies the result by 4
   iv multiplies the number by itself then halves the result.
b Write an expression in terms of x and y for:
   i the perimeter   **ii** the area of this rectangle.
   Write each expression in its simplest form.

a i $2n + 5$ Multiply n by 2, then add 5. Write $2 \times n$ as $2n$.
   ii $\frac{n}{3} - 6$ Divide n by 3 then subtract 2. Write $n \div 3$ as $\frac{n}{3}$.

  iii $4(n + 3)$ Add 3 to n, then multiply the result by 4. Write $n + 3$ inside a pair of brackets to show this must be done before multiplying by 4.
  iv $\frac{n^2}{2}$ Multiply n by itself, to give $n \times n$, and write it as n^2. Write $n^2 \div 2$ as $\frac{n^2}{2}$.

b i Perimeter $= 5x + 2y + 5x + 2y$ Add together the lengths of the four sides to work out the perimeter.
              $= 10x + 4y$ Simplify the expression by collecting like terms.
  ii Area $= 5x \times 2y$ Multiply the length by the width to work out the area.
          $= 10xy$ Simplify the expression by multiplying the numbers and the letters together.

◆ Exercise 9.2

1 Xavier thinks of a number, n.
   Write an expression, in terms of n, for the number Xavier gets when he:
   a multiplies the number by 7   **b** adds 12 to the number
   c subtracts 2 from the number   **d** subtracts the number from 20
   e multiplies the number by 2 then adds 9   **f** divides the number by 2
   g divides the number by 6 then subtracts 4   **h** multiplies the number by itself
   i divides 100 by the number   **j** multiplies the number by 2 then subtracts 1
   k adds 2 to the number then multiplies   **l** subtracts 7 from the number then multiplies
       the result by 5   the result by 8

2 Write an expression for **i** the perimeter **ii** the area of each rectangle.
Write each expression in its simplest form.

a
    x
    y

b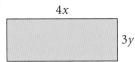
    4*x*
    3*y*

c
    x
    x

d
    2*y*
    2*y*

3 This is part of Mia's homework.

> *Question*   Write an expression for the perimeter and area of this rectangle.
> Write each answer in its simplest form.
>
>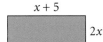
> $x + 5$
> $2x$
>
> *Answer*   Perimeter = $x + 5 + 2x + x + 5 + 2x$ Area = $2x(x + 5)$
>   = $6x + 10$ = $2x^2 + 10x$

To simplify the expression for the area of the rectangle, Mia has expanded the brackets.
Write an expression for the perimeter and area of each of these rectangles.
Write each answer in its simplest form.

a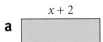
    $x + 2$
    3

b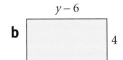
    $y - 6$
    4

c
    $n + 4$
    n

d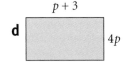
    $p + 3$
    $4p$

4 Alicia and Razi have rods of four different colours.
The blue rods have a length of $x + 1$.
The red rods have a length of $x + 2$.
The green rods have a length of $2x + 1$.
The yellow rods have a length of $3x$.
Alicia shows Razi that the total
length of 3 red rods and 5 yellow
rods is the same as 6 green rods
and 2 yellow rods, like this.

    $x + 1$
    $x + 2$
    $2x + 1$
    $3x$

> 3 red + 5 yellow   6 green + 2 yellow
> = $3(x + 2) + 5(3x)$ = $6(2x + 1) + 2(3x)$
> = $3x + 6 + 15x$ = $12x + 6 + 6x$
> = $18x + 6$ = $18x + 6$

a Show that: **i**   the total
length of 2
red rods and 2 yellow rods is the same as 4 green rods
     ii   the total length of 3 red rods and 3 yellow rods is the same as 6 green rods
     iii   the total length of 4 red rods and 4 yellow rods is the same as 8 green rods.

b What do your answers to part **a** tell you about the connection between the number of red and yellow rods and green rods?

c Show that: **i**   the total length of 3 red rods and 1 yellow rod is the same as 6 blue rods
     ii   the total length of 6 red rods and 2 yellow rods is the same as 12 blue rods
     iii   the total length of 9 red rods and 3 yellow rods is the same as 18 blue rods.

d What do your answers to part **c** tell you about the connection between the number of red and yellow rods and blue rods?

9.3 Substituting into expressions

When you substitute numbers into expressions, remember BIDMAS.

You must work out Brackets and Indices before Divisions and Multiplications.

You always work out Additions and Subtractions last.

> Examples of indices are.
> 4^2, 7^3, $(-2)^2$ and $(-3)^3$

Worked example 9.3

a Work out the value of the expression $5a - 6b$ when $a = 4$ and $b = -3$.
b Work out the value of the expression $3x^2 - 2y^3$ when $x = -5$ and $y = 2$.
c Work out the value of the expression $p(5 - \frac{4q}{p})$ when $p = 2$ and $q = -3$.

a $\begin{aligned} 5a - 6b &= 5 \times 4 - 6 \times -3 \\ &= 20 - -18 \\ &= 20 + 18 \\ &= 38 \end{aligned}$	Substitute $a = 4$ and $b = -3$ into the expression. Work out the multiplications first; $5 \times 4 = 20$ and $6 \times -3 = -18$ Subtracting -18 is the same as adding 18.
b $\begin{aligned} 3x^2 - 2y^3 &= 3 \times (-5)^2 - 2 \times 2^3 \\ &= 3 \times 25 - 2 \times 8 \\ &= 75 - 16 \\ &= 59 \end{aligned}$	Substitute $x = -5$ and $y = 2$ into the expression. Work out the indices first; $(-5)^2 = -5 \times -5 = 25$ and $2^3 = 2 \times 2 \times 2 = 8$. Then work out the multiplications; $3 \times 25 = 75$ and $2 \times 8 = 16$. Finally work out the subtraction.
c $\begin{aligned} p(5 - \tfrac{4q}{p}) &= 2(5 - \tfrac{4 \times -3}{2}) \\ &= 2(5 - -6) \\ &= 2 \times (5 + 6) \\ &= 2 \times 11 \\ &= 22 \end{aligned}$	Substitute $p = 2$ and $q = -3$ into the expression. Work out the term in brackets first. Start with the fraction. $4 \times -3 = -12$; $-12 \div 2 = -6$. Subtracting -6 is the same as adding 6. Finally, multiply the value of the term in brackets by 2; $2 \times 11 = 22$.

◆ Exercise 9.3

1 Work out the value of each expression when $a = -2$, $b = 3$, $c = -4$ and $d = 6$.

  a $b + d$ **b** $a + 2b$ **c** $2d - b$ **d** $a - c$

  e $4b + 2a$ **f** $3d - 6b$ **g** $bd - 10$ **h** $d^2 + ab$

  i $\frac{d}{2} - a$ **j** $20 + b^3$ **k** $ab + cd$ **l** $\frac{bc}{d} + a$

2 Work out the value of each expression when $w = 5$, $x = 2$, $y = -8$ and $z = -1$.

  a $3(w + x)$ **b** $x(2w - y)$ **c** $x + yz$ **d** $3w - z^3$

  e $x^2 + y^2$ **f** $(2x)^3$ **g** $\frac{x}{2} - \frac{y}{4}$ **h** $\frac{wx}{z} + y$

  i $2(x^3 - z^2)$ **j** $25 - 2w^2$ **k** $w + z(2x - y)$ **l** $2(w + x) - 3(w - x)$

3 This is part of Dakarai's homework. Use a counter-example to show that these statements are <u>not</u> always true.

  a $3x^2 = (3x)^2$

  b $(-y)^2 = -y^2$

  c $2(a + b) = 2a + b$

> _Question_   Use a counter-example to show that the statement $2x^2 = (2x)^2$ is <u>not</u> always true.
>
> _Answer_   Let $x = 3$, so $2x^2 = 2 \times 3^2 = 2 \times 9 = 18$ and $(2x)^2 = (2 \times 3)^2 = 6^2 = 36$
>
> $18 \neq 36$, so $2x^2 \neq (2x)^2$

9.4 Deriving and using formulae

A formula is a mathematical rule that shows the relationship between two or more variables.

For example, a formula that is often used in physics is: $v = u + at$.

In this formula, v is the **subject of the formula**. It is written on its own, on the left-hand side.

Depending on the information you are given and the variable that you want to find, you may need to rearrange the formula. This is called **changing the subject** of the formula.

For example, if you know the values of v, a and t in the formula above and you want to work out the value of u, you would rearrange the equation like this.

This makes u the subject of the formula.

$$v = u + at$$
$$u + at = v$$
$$u = v - at$$

If you know the values of v, u and a in the formula above and you want to work out the value of t, you would rearrange the equation like this.

This makes t the subject of the formula.

$$v = u + at$$
$$u + at = v$$
$$at = v - u$$
$$t = \frac{v - u}{a}$$

Worked example 9.4

a Write a formula for the total pay, P dollars, Li earns when he works H hours at R dollars per hour.
b Use the formula in part **a** to work out P when $H = 8\frac{1}{4}$ hours and $R = \$7.80$ an hour.
c Rearrange the formula in part **a** to make H the subject.
d Use the formula in part **c** to work out H when $P = \$81.70$ and $R = \$8.60$ per hour.

a	$P = HR$	Pay (P) = number of hours (H) × rate of pay (R). Remember to write $H \times R$ as HR.
b	$P = 8.25 \times 7.80$	Substitute $H = 8.25$ and $R = 7.80$ into the formula.
	$= \$64.35$	Work out the answer and remember the units ($).
c	$\frac{P}{R} = \frac{H\cancel{R}}{\cancel{R}}$	To make H the subject, divide both sides of the formula by R.
	$H = \frac{P}{R}$	Now rewrite the formula with H as the subject.
d	$H = \frac{81.70}{8.60}$	Substitute $P = 81.70$ and $R = 8.60$ into the formula.
	$= 9.5$ hours	Work out the answer and remember the units (hours).

Exercise 9.4

1 a Write a formula for the number of seconds, S, in any number of minutes, M.
   b Use your formula in part **a** to work out S when $M = 15$.
   c Rearrange your formula in part **a** to make M the subject.
   d Use you formula in part **c** to work out M when $S = 1350$.

2 Use the formula $F = ma$ to work out the value of:
   a F when $m = 12$ and $a = 5$ **b** F when $m = 26$ and $a = -3$
   c m when $F = 30$ and $a = 2.5$ **d** a when $F = -14$ and $m = 8$.

> In parts **c** and **d** you must start by changing the subject of the formula.

3 Use the formula $v = u + at$ to work out the value of:

    a v when $u = 7$, $a = 10$, $t = 8$ **b** v when $u = 0$, $a = 5$, $t = 25$ **c** u when $v = 75$, $a = 4$, $t = 12$

    d u when $v = 97$, $a = 6$, $t = 8.5$ **e** t when $v = 80$, $u = 20$, $a = 6$ **f** a when $v = 72$, $u = 34$, $t = 19$.

4 Amy is x years old. Tom is 2 years <u>older than</u> Amy.

    a Write an expression for Tom's age in terms of x.

    b Write a formula for the total age, T, of Amy and Tom.

    c Use your formula in part **b** to work out T when $x = 19$.

    d Rearrange your formula in part **b** to make x the subject.

    e Use you formula in part **d** to work out x when $T = 48$.

5 Adrian buys and sells paintings.
He uses the formula on the right to work
out the percentage profit he makes.
Work out Adrian's percentage profit on
each of these paintings.

> Percentage profit $= \dfrac{\text{selling price} - \text{cost price}}{\text{cost price}} \times 100$

    a Cost price \$250, selling price \$300

    b Cost price \$120, selling price \$192

    c Cost price \$480, selling price \$1080

6 In some countries the mass of a person is measured in stones (S) and pounds (P).
The formula to convert a mass from stones and
pounds into kilograms is shown opposite.
Work out the mass, in kilograms, of a person
with a mass of:

> $K = \dfrac{5(14S + P)}{11}$ where: K is the number of kilograms
> S is the number of stones
> P is the number of pounds.

    a 10 stones and 3 pounds

    b 7 stones and 10 pounds

    c 15 stones and 1 pound

    d 9 stones

> 9 stones exactly means 9 stones and 0 pounds

7 Sasha uses the relationship shown to change between temperatures in degrees Fahrenheit (°F) and
temperatures in degrees
Celsius (°C).
Sasha thinks that 30 °C is
higher than 82 °F.
Is she correct? Show how you worked out your answer.

> $5F = 9C + 160$ where: F is the temperature in degrees Fahrenheit (°F)
> C is the temperature in degrees Celsius (°C)

8 A doctor uses the formula in the box to calculate
patients' body mass index (BMI).
A patient is described as underweight if their BMI is
below 18.5.

> BMI $= \dfrac{m}{h^2}$ where: m is the mass in kilograms
> h is the height in metres.

    a Tina's mass is 48.8 kg and her height is 1.56 m. Is she underweight? Explain your answer.

    b Stephen's height is 1.80 m and his mass is 68.5 kg. He wants to have a BMI of 20.
How many kilograms must he lose to reach a BMI of 20? Show your working.

9.5 Factorising

To expand a term with brackets, you multiply each term inside the brackets by the term outside the brackets.

When you **factorise** an expression you do the opposite.

You take the <u>highest common factor</u> and put it outside the brackets.

$$4(x + 3) = 4x + 12$$

$$4x + 12 = 4(x + 3)$$

Worked example 9.5

Factorise these expressions. **a** $2x + 10$ **b** $8 - 12y$ **c** $4a + 8ab$ **d** $x^2 - 5x$

a $2x + 10 = 2(x + 5)$ — The highest common factor of $2x$ and 10 is 2, so put the 2 outside the brackets. Divide both terms by 2 and put the result inside the brackets. Check the answer by expanding: $2 \times x = 2x$ and $2 \times 5 = 10$.

b $8 - 12y = 4(2 - 3y)$ — The highest common factor of 8 and $12y$ is 4, so put the 4 outside the brackets. Divide both terms by 4 and put the result inside the brackets. Check the answer by expanding: $4 \times 2 = 8$ and $4 \times -3y = -12y$.

c $4a + 8ab = 4a(1 + 2b)$ — The highest common factor of $4a$ and $8ab$ is $4a$, so put the $4a$ outside the brackets. Divide both terms by $4a$ and put the result inside the brackets. Check the answer: $4a \times 1 = 4a$ and $4a \times 2b = 8ab$.

d $x^2 - 5x = x(x - 5)$ — The highest common factor of x^2 and $5x$ is x, so put the x outside the brackets. Divide both terms by x and put the result inside the brackets. Check the answer: $x \times x = x^2$ and $x \times -5 = -5x$.

Exercise 9.5

1 Copy and complete these factorisations.
   a $3x + 6 = 3(x + \square)$ **b** $10y - 15 = 5(2y - \square)$ **c** $6xy + 12y = 6y(x + \square)$
   d $4x^2 + x = x(4x + \square)$ **e** $9 - 12y = 3(\square - \square)$ **f** $2y^2 - 7y = y(\square - \square)$

2 Factorise each of these expressions.
   a $2x + 4$ **b** $3y - 18$ **c** $10z + 5$ **d** $8a - 4$ **e** $4b + 6$ **f** $16n - 20$
   g $10 - 5x$ **h** $14 + 21x$ **i** $8 - 10y$ **j** $18 + 24z$ **k** $9 + 15m$ **l** $30 - 20k$

3 Factorise each of these expressions.
   a $3x^2 + x$ **b** $6y^2 - 12y$ **c** $z^2 + 4z$ **d** $4a - 2a^2$ **e** $3b + 9b^2$ **f** $12n - 15n^2$
   g $18y - 9x$ **h** $12y + 9x$ **i** $8xy - 4y$ **j** $15z + 10yz$ **k** $14m + 6mn$ **l** $26k - 13kp$

4 Copy and complete these factorisations.
   a $2x + 6y + 8 = 2(x + 3y + \square)$ **b** $4y - 8 + 4x = 4(y - \square + x)$ **c** $9xy + 12y - 15 = 3(3xy + \square - 5)$
   d $5x^2 + 2x + xy = x(5x + \square + \square)$ **e** $9y - y^2 - xy = y(\square - \square - \square)$ **f** $3y^2 - 9y + 6xy = 3y(\square - \square + \square)$

5 Read what Tanesha says. Show that she is right.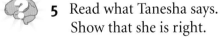

> When I expand $5(2x + 6) + 2(3x - 5)$, then collect like terms and finally factorise the result, I get the expression $4(4x + 5)$.

6 Read what Shen says. Show that he is wrong. Explain the mistake he has made.

> When I expand $6(3y + 2) - 4(y - 2)$, then collect like terms and finally factorise the result, I get the expression $2(7y + 2)$.

9.6 Adding and subtracting algebraic fractions

An **algebraic fraction** is a fraction that contains an unknown variable, or letter.

For example, $\frac{x}{4}$, $\frac{y}{2}$, $\frac{z}{8}$, $\frac{2a}{3}$ and $\frac{4b}{5}$ are all algebraic fractions.

You can write the fraction $\frac{x}{4}$ (say as 'x over 4') as $\frac{1}{4}x$ (say as 'one-quarter of x').

You can write the fraction $\frac{2a}{3}$ (say as '$2a$ over 3') as $\frac{2}{3}a$ (say as 'two-thirds of a').

To add and subtract algebraic fractions, you use the same method as for normal fractions.

- If the denominators are the same, simply add or subtract the numerators.
- If the denominators are different, write the fractions as equivalent fractions with the same denominator, then add or subtract the numerators.
- Cancel your answer to its simplest form.

Worked example 9.6

Simplify these expressions.   **a** $\frac{x}{6}+\frac{x}{6}$ **b** $\frac{y}{3}-\frac{y}{9}$ **c** $\frac{4n}{5}+\frac{2n}{3}$ **d** $\frac{a}{8}+\frac{b}{4}$ **e** $\frac{5p}{6}-\frac{q}{4}$

a $\frac{x}{6}+\frac{x}{6}=\frac{x+x}{6}$ The denominators are the same, so add the numerators.

$\quad\ =\frac{2x}{6}$ Cancel the fraction to its simplest form.

$\quad\ =\frac{x}{3}$ Write $\frac{1x}{3}$ as simply $\frac{x}{3}$.

b $\frac{y}{3}-\frac{y}{9}=\frac{3y}{9}-\frac{y}{9}$ The denominators are different, so change $\frac{y}{3}$ into $\frac{3y}{9}$.

$\quad\ =\frac{3y-y}{9}$ The denominators are now the same, so subtract the numerators.

$\quad\ =\frac{2y}{9}$

c $\frac{4n}{5}+\frac{2n}{3}=\frac{12n}{15}+\frac{10n}{15}$ The denominators are different, so change $\frac{4n}{5}$ into $\frac{12n}{15}$ and $\frac{2n}{3}$ into $\frac{10n}{15}$.

$\quad\ =\frac{12n+10n}{15}$ The denominators are now the same, so add the numerators.

$\quad\ =\frac{22n}{15}$ Leave as an improper fraction in its simplest form.

d $\frac{a}{8}+\frac{b}{4}=\frac{a}{8}+\frac{2b}{8}$ The denominators are different, so change $\frac{b}{4}$ into $\frac{2b}{8}$.

$\quad\ =\frac{a+2b}{8}$ Now add the numerators. You cannot simplify any further as a and $2b$ are not like terms.

e $\frac{5p}{6}-\frac{q}{4}=\frac{10p}{12}-\frac{3q}{12}$ The denominators are different, so change $\frac{5p}{6}$ into $\frac{10p}{12}$ and $\frac{q}{4}$ into $\frac{3q}{12}$.

$\quad\ =\frac{10p-3q}{12}$ Now subtract the numerators. You cannot simplify any further as $10p$ and $3q$ are not like terms.

◆ **Exercise 9.6**

Throughout this exercise give each answer as a fraction in its simplest form.

1 Simplify these expressions.

a $\dfrac{x}{5} + \dfrac{x}{5}$ b $\dfrac{x}{7} + \dfrac{3x}{7}$ c $\dfrac{x}{8} + \dfrac{x}{8}$ d $\dfrac{2x}{3} - \dfrac{x}{3}$ e $\dfrac{7x}{15} - \dfrac{x}{15}$ f $\dfrac{8x}{9} - \dfrac{2x}{9}$

g $\dfrac{y}{2} + \dfrac{y}{4}$ h $\dfrac{2y}{3} + \dfrac{y}{9}$ i $\dfrac{2y}{5} + \dfrac{3y}{10}$ j $\dfrac{y}{2} - \dfrac{y}{8}$ k $\dfrac{2y}{5} - \dfrac{y}{25}$ l $\dfrac{4y}{7} - \dfrac{5y}{14}$

2 Copy and complete these calculations.

a $\dfrac{a}{2} + \dfrac{a}{5} = \dfrac{5a}{10} + \dfrac{\square a}{10}$

$= \dfrac{5a + \square a}{10}$

$= \dfrac{\square a}{10}$

b $\dfrac{b}{4} + \dfrac{b}{3} = \dfrac{3b}{12} + \dfrac{\square b}{12}$

$= \dfrac{3b + \square b}{12}$

$= \dfrac{\square b}{12}$

c $\dfrac{5c}{7} - \dfrac{2c}{5} = \dfrac{25c}{35} - \dfrac{\square c}{35}$

$= \dfrac{25c - \square c}{35}$

$= \dfrac{\square c}{35}$

d $\dfrac{5d}{6} + \dfrac{3d}{5} = \dfrac{\square d}{30} + \dfrac{\square d}{30}$

$= \dfrac{\square d + \square d}{30}$

$= \dfrac{\square d}{30}$

e $\dfrac{5e}{8} + \dfrac{2e}{3} = \dfrac{\square e}{24} + \dfrac{\square e}{24}$

$= \dfrac{\square e + \square e}{24}$

$= \dfrac{\square e}{24}$

f $\dfrac{9f}{10} + \dfrac{3f}{4} = \dfrac{\square}{20} + \dfrac{\square}{20}$

$= \dfrac{\square + \square}{20}$

$= \dfrac{\square}{20}$

3 Simplify these expressions.

a $\dfrac{x}{5} + \dfrac{y}{5}$ b $\dfrac{x}{2} + \dfrac{y}{6}$ c $\dfrac{2x}{3} + \dfrac{y}{9}$ d $\dfrac{2x}{5} - \dfrac{y}{10}$ e $\dfrac{11x}{14} - \dfrac{2y}{7}$ f $\dfrac{9x}{20} - \dfrac{2y}{5}$

g $\dfrac{a}{4} + \dfrac{b}{3}$ h $\dfrac{2a}{5} + \dfrac{b}{6}$ i $\dfrac{5a}{12} + \dfrac{3b}{8}$ j $\dfrac{a}{5} - \dfrac{b}{8}$ k $\dfrac{3a}{10} - \dfrac{b}{15}$ l $\dfrac{4a}{9} - \dfrac{3b}{5}$

4 Here are some algebraic fraction cards.
The red cards are question cards. The blue cards are answer cards.

A $\dfrac{9x}{10} - \dfrac{13x}{20}$ C $\dfrac{2x}{7} + \dfrac{3x}{14}$ E $\dfrac{7x}{9} - \dfrac{5x}{18}$ F $\dfrac{x}{12} + \dfrac{x}{6}$ i $\dfrac{x}{4}$

B $\dfrac{x}{6} + \dfrac{x}{3}$ D $\dfrac{11x}{18} - \dfrac{13x}{36}$ G $\dfrac{x}{30} + \dfrac{3x}{10}$ ii $\dfrac{x}{2}$

a Which question cards match answer card **i**? Show your working.
b Which question cards match answer card **ii**? Show your working.
c Which question card does not match either of the answer cards?
Explain your answer.
d Explain how you can use normal fractions rather than algebraic fractions to work out the answers to parts **a**, **b** and **c**.

9.7 Expanding the product of two linear expressions

When you multiply two expressions in brackets together, you must multiply each term in the first pair of brackets by each term in the second pair of brackets.

> **Worked example 9.7**
>
> Expand and simplify these expressions. **a** $(x + 2)(x + 3)$ **b** $(y + 8)(y - 4)$
>
> **a** $(x + 2)(x + 3)$ First, multiply the x in the first brackets by the x in the second brackets to give x^2.
> Then, multiply the x in the first brackets by the 3 in the second brackets to give $3x$.
> Then, multiply the 2 in the first brackets by the x in the second brackets to give $2x$.
> Finally, multiply the 2 in the first brackets by the 3 in the second brackets to give 6.
> $= x^2 + 3x + 2x + 6$ Write each term down as you work it out.
> $= x^2 + 5x + 6$ Collect together like terms, $3x + 2x = 5x$, to simplify your answer.
>
> **b** $(y + 8)(y - 4)$ First, multiply the y in the first brackets by the y in the second brackets to give y^2.
> Then, multiply the y in the first brackets by the -4 in the second brackets to give $-4y$.
> Then, multiply the 8 in the first brackets by the y in the second brackets to give $8y$.
> Finally, multiply the 8 in the first brackets by the -4 in the second brackets to give -32.
> $= y^2 - 4y + 8y - 32$ Write each term down as you work it out.
> $= y^2 + 4y - 32$ Collect like terms, $-4y + 8y = 4y$, to simplify your answer.

◆ Exercise 9.7

1 Copy and complete these multiplications.

a 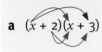 $(x + 4)(x + 1)$ $= x^2 + 1x + \square x + \square$
  $= x^2 + \square x + \square$

b $(x - 3)(x + 6)$ $= x^2 + 6x - \square x - \square$
  $= x^2 + \square x - \square$

c $(x + 2)(x - 8)$ $= x^2 - \square x + \square x - \square$
  $= x^2 - \square x - \square$

d $(x - 4)(x - 1)$ $= x^2 - \square x - \square x + \square$
  $= x^2 - \square x + \square$

2 Expand and simplify.
  a $(x + 3)(x + 7)$ **b** $(x + 1)(x + 10)$ **c** $(x + 5)(x - 3)$
  d $(x - 4)(x + 8)$ **e** $(x - 7)(x - 2)$ **f** $(x - 12)(x - 2)$

3 Expand and simplify.
  a $(y + 2)(y + 4)$ **b** $(z + 6)(z + 8)$ **c** $(m + 4)(m - 3)$
  d $(a - 9)(a + 2)$ **e** $(p - 6)(p - 5)$ **f** $(n - 10)(n - 20)$

4 Which is the correct expansion of the expression, A, B or C?
  a $(w + 9)(w + 3) =$ **A** $w^2 + 6w + 27$ **B** $w^2 + 12w + 12$ **C** $w^2 + 12w + 27$
  b $(x + 1)(x - 5) =$ **A** $x^2 - 6x - 5$ **B** $x^2 - 4x - 5$ **C** $x^2 + 4x - 5$
  c $(y - 8)(y + 6) =$ **A** $y^2 - 2y - 48$ **B** $y^2 - 2y - 14$ **C** $y^2 + 2y - 48$
  d $(z - 4)(z - 5) =$ **A** $z^2 - z + 9$ **B** $z^2 - 9z - 20$ **C** $z^2 - 9z + 20$

5 Copy and complete each expansion.
  a $(x + 2)^2 = (x + 2)(x + 2)$
    $= x^2 + 2x + \square x + \square$
    $= x^2 + \square x + \square$

  b $(x - 3)^2 = (x - 3)(x - 3)$
    $= x^2 - 3x - \square x + \square$
    $= x^2 - \square x + \square$

6 Expand and simplify each expression.
  a $(y+5)^2$ **b** $(z+1)^2$ **c** $(m+8)^2$
  d $(a-2)^2$ **e** $(p-4)^2$ **f** $(n-9)^2$

7 a Expand and simplify each expression.
   i $(x+2)(x-2)$ **ii** $(x-5)(x+5)$ **iii** $(x+7)(x-7)$
  b What do you notice about your answers in part **a**?
  c Write down the simplified expansion of $(x-10)(x+10)$.
  d Write down the simplified expansion of $(x-y)(x+y)$.

8 Here is part of a number grid.
  Look at the **red** block of four squares, and follow these steps.
  ① Multiply the number in the bottom left square by the number
     in the top right square: $9 \times 5 = 45$
  ② Multiply the number in the top left square by the number
     in the bottom right square: $4 \times 10 = 40.$
  ③ Subtract the second answer from the first: $45 - 40 = 5.$
  a Repeat these three steps with the **blue** block of four squares.
  b Repeat these three steps with the **green** block of four squares.
  c What do you notice about your answers to **a** and **b**?
  d Here is a block of four squares from the same number grid.
     Copy the block of four squares and write an expression, in terms of n, in
     each of the other squares to represent the missing numbers.
  e Repeat the three steps above with the block of four squares in part **d**.
     What do you notice about your answer?

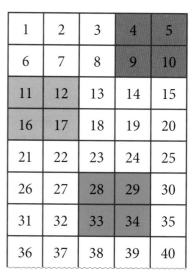

1	2	3	4	5
6	7	8	9	10
11	12	13	14	15
16	17	18	19	20
21	22	23	24	25
26	27	28	29	30
31	32	33	34	35
36	37	38	39	40

n	

Summary

You should now know that:

★ To multiply powers of the same variable, add the indices. $x^a \times x^b = x^{a+b}$

★ To divide powers of the same variable, subtract the indices. $x^a \div x^b = x^{a-b}$

★ The letter that is on its own in a formula is called the subject of the formula.

★ Depending on the information you are given and the variable that you want to find, you may need to rearrange a formula. This is called changing the subject of the formula.

★ When you factorise an expression you take the highest common factor and put it outside the brackets.

★ To add and subtract algebraic fractions, you use the same method that you use to add normal fractions.

★ When you multiply two expressions in brackets together, you must multiply each term in the first brackets by each term in the second brackets.

You should be able to:

★ Use index notation for positive integer powers; apply the index laws for multiplication and division to simple algebraic expressions.

★ Construct algebraic expressions.

★ Substitute positive and negative numbers into expressions and formulae.

★ Derive formulae and, in simple cases, change the subject; use formulae from mathematics and other subjects.

★ Simplify or transform expressions by taking out single-term common factors.

★ Expand the product of two linear expressions and simplify the resulting expression.

End-of-unit review

1 Simplify each expression.

    a $x^2 \times x^3$ **b** $y^8 \times y^4$ **c** $z^9 \times z$ **d** $3m^7 \times 5m^2$ **e** $6n^8 \times n^3$ **f** $2p^6 \times 3p$

    g $q^8 \div q^2$ **h** $r^7 \div r^4$ **i** $t^{10} \div t^5$ **j** $\dfrac{12u^5}{6u^3}$ **k** $\dfrac{18v^9}{6v^3}$ **l** $\dfrac{7w^9}{w^8}$

2 Write an expression for the perimeter of each shape.
Write each expression in its simplest form.

    a   **b**   **c** 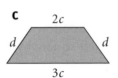   **d**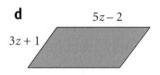

3 Write an expression for the area of each shape.
Write each expression in its simplest form.

    a   **b**    **c**   **d**

4 Work out the value of each expression when $a = -4$, $b = 5$, $c = -2$ and $d = 8$.

    a $b + d$ **b** $3d - b$ **c** $5b + 3a$ **d** $d^2 + bc$

    e $\dfrac{a}{2} + b$ **f** $ac + bd$ **g** $\dfrac{bd}{a} - c$ **h** $7(d - b)$

    i $b^2 + d^2$ **j** $\dfrac{c}{2} - \dfrac{a}{4}$ **k** $100 - 4c^2$ **l** $d + b(3c + a)$

5 Use the formula $x = y + 5z$ to work out the value of:

    a x when $y = 4$ and $z = 3$ **b** x when $y = 16$ and $z = -4$ **c** y when $x = 100$ and $z = 7$

    d y when $x = 20$ and $z = -8$ **e** z when $x = 40$ and $y = 30$ **f** z when $x = 25$ and $y = -5$.

6 Factorise each expression.

    a $2x + 6$ **b** $4y - 12$ **c** $9a - 3$ **d** $20 - 10x$ **e** $24 + 30z$ **f** $50 - 30b$

    g $5x^2 + x$ **h** $3a - 5a^2$ **i** $32y - 8x$ **j** $6xy - 3y$ **k** $18m + 8mn$ **l** $24n - 27n^2$

7 Simplify each expression.
Give each answer as a fraction in its simplest form.

    a $\dfrac{x}{3} + \dfrac{x}{3}$ **b** $\dfrac{x}{5} + \dfrac{2x}{5}$ **c** $\dfrac{4x}{7} - \dfrac{x}{7}$ **d** $\dfrac{y}{5} - \dfrac{y}{15}$ **e** $\dfrac{3y}{4} + \dfrac{9y}{8}$ **f** $\dfrac{4y}{9} - \dfrac{5y}{18}$

    g $\dfrac{x}{4} + \dfrac{y}{4}$ **h** $\dfrac{3x}{5} - \dfrac{y}{20}$ **i** $\dfrac{a}{3} + \dfrac{b}{5}$ **j** $\dfrac{3a}{4} + \dfrac{2b}{5}$ **k** $\dfrac{5a}{6} - \dfrac{b}{8}$ **l** $\dfrac{4a}{7} - \dfrac{2b}{3}$

8 Expand and simplify each expression.

    a $(x + 2)(x + 5)$ **b** $(x - 3)(x + 4)$ **c** $(x + 6)(x - 9)$

    d $(x - 10)(x - 4)$ **e** $(x - 8)(x + 8)$ **f** $(x - 6)^2$

 9 Read what Hassan says.
Show that he is correct.

> When I expand $4(2x + 5) + 3(8x - 4)$, then collect like terms and finally factorise the result, I get the expression $8(4x + 1)$.

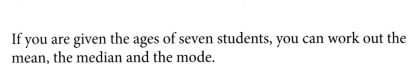

If you are given the ages of seven students, you can work out the mean, the median and the mode.

Can you do it the other way round?

Seven students have a mean age of 12 years, a median of 13 and a mode of 14.

What could the ages be? Is there more than one answer?

The statistic you choose to represent a set of data is important.

In the **Olympics** a medal table is produced.

Usually countries are ranked according to the number of **gold medals** they win.

The first table below shows the top eight countries in the 2012 Olympics.

In the USA they usually use a table based on the **total** number of medals. The results are in the second table below.

Country	Gold medals
USA	46
China	38
UK	29
Russia	24
South Korea	13
Germany	11
France	11
Italy	8

Country	Total medals
USA	104
China	88
Russia	82
UK	65
Germany	44
Japan	38
Australia	35
France	34

You can see that the results are different.

Which do you think is the better way to compare countries?

In this unit you will review and extend what you have already learnt about processing and presenting data.

10.1 Calculating statistics

You can use statistics to <u>summarise</u> sets of data. You can also use them to <u>compare</u> different sets of data.

You should already be able to calculate three different averages: the mode, the median and the mean.

Remember that the range is not an average. It measures how spread out a set of values or numbers is.

For a large set of data, it is not practical to list every number separately. Instead, you can record the data in a frequency table.

The <u>mode</u> is the most common value or number.

The <u>median</u> is the middle value, when they are listed in order.

The <u>mean</u> is the sum of all the values divided by the number of values.

The <u>range</u> is the largest value <u>minus</u> the smallest.

A frequency table is any table that records how often (frequently) data values occur.

Worked example 10.1

The table shows the number of beads on 200 necklaces.
a Find the mode.
b Find the mean.
c Find the range.

Number of beads	25	30	35	40	45	50
Frequency	34	48	61	30	15	12

a The mode is 35. The mode is the number with the highest frequency.

b $6900 \div 200 = 34.5$ $(25 \times 34 + 30 \times 48 + 35 \times 61 + 40 \times 30 + 45 \times 15 + 50 \times 12) \div$ the sum of all the frequencies. This is a reasonable answer because it is near the middle of all the possible number of beads.

c $50 - 25 = 25$ This is the difference between the largest and smallest number of beads.

Exercise 10.1

1 These are the times (in minutes) that eight students took to walk to school.
   a Calculate: i the median time ii the mean time iii the range.

   10, 12, 15, 18, 24, 25, 30, 35

   There is an error in the times given in part **a**. The 35 should be 53.
   b Correct the values for: i the median time   ii the mean time   iii the range.

2 Find the modal age for each set of data.
   a The ages of the members of a fitness class

   57, 56, 51, 59, 51, 56, 58, 58, 51, 53, 50, 51, 54, 51

   b The ages of a group of children

Age (years)	10	11	12	13	14
Frequency	5	12	13	17	20

3 Find the median age for each group in question **2**.

4 Find the mean age for each group in question **2**.

5 Find the range of the ages for each group in question **2**.

6 This table shows the daily pay for a group of workers.

Pay (dollars)	40–59	60–79	80–99	100–119
Frequency	15	58	27	22

For grouped data, the modal class is the class with the highest frequency. Also the range is an <u>estimate</u> because the table does not list the exact values.

a What is the modal class?
b Why can you not find the exact value for the mean pay?
c Xavier is trying to find the range of the data.
Is he correct? Give a reason for your answer.

The range is 53 dollars.

7 Oditi records the midday temperature (to the nearest degree) in the school field every day for one month.

Temperature (°C)	−10 to −6	−5 to −1	0 to 4	5 to 9
Frequency	3	8	16	4

a What can you say about the median temperature?
b Estimate the range.

8 Ahmad has three test marks.
The lowest mark is 52.
The range is 37 marks.
The mean is 66.
What are the three marks?

9 These are the ages of a family of four children and their mother.
Work out:

3, 5, 8, 12, 39

a the mean age of the children
b the median age of the children.
If the age of the mother is included, what effect does this have on:
c the mean age   **d** the median age?

10 Here are some statistics about the masses of a group of 40 children.

Mean = 12.5 kg   Median = 11.7 kg   Range = 6.1 kg

a If the mass of every child increases by 1.4 kg, what are the new statistics?
b If the mass of every child doubles, what are the new statistics?

11 Here is some data about a group of boys and a group of girls.

<u>Boys:</u> number: 20   mean height: 1.55 m   range of heights: 0.42 m
<u>Girls:</u> number: 10   mean height: 1.40 m   range of heights: 0.36 m

For the combined group of boys and girls, work out, if possible:
a the number of children   **b** the mean height   **c** the range of heights.

10.2 Using statistics

Now you can work out several different statistical measures.

In a real situation, you need to decide which one to use.

If you want to measure how spread out a set of measurements is, the range is the most useful statistic.

If you want to find a representative measurement, you need an average. Should it be the mode, the median or the mean? That depends on the particular situation.

Here is a summary to help you decide which average to choose.

- Choose the <u>mode</u> if you want to know which is the most commonly occurring number.
- The <u>median</u> is the middle value, when the data values are put in order. Half the numbers are greater than the median and half the numbers are less than the median.
- The <u>mean</u> depends on every value. If you change one number you change the mean.

Worked example 10.2

Here are the ages, in years, of the players in a football team. Work out the average age. Give a reason for your choice of average.	16, 17, 18, 18, 19, 20, 20, 21, 21, 32, 41
The mode is not a good choice.	There are three modes. Each has a frequency of only 2.
The mean will be affected by the two oldest people.	They are much older and will distort the value. In fact the mean is 22.1 and nine people are younger than this; only two are older.
The median is 20 and this is the best average to use in this case.	Five players are younger than the median and five are older.

Exercise 10.2

1 Maha records the time she waits in line for lunch each day for 20 days. Here are the times, in minutes. Work out Maha's average waiting time.

```
2  5  3  8  5  2  10 7  8  8
4  7  2  2  3  6  10 3  4  7
```

2 The table shows the number of days of rain in the first week of May in a town over 30 years. Work out the average number of days of rain in the first week of May over the 30 years.

Days of rain	0	1	2	3	4	5	6	7
Frequency	11	8	4	1	2	3	0	1

3 a Here are the scores in the football matches in League One on Saturday 17 March. Work out the average number of goals per match.

```
1–1  1–4  1–1  1–1  1–2  0–0
2–0  1–2  3–2  1–1  1–1  2–1
```

b Here are the results for League Two on the same day. Which league has more variation in the number of goals scored in a match? Give a reason for your answer.

```
2–1  1–0  0–2  1–0  1–4
0–3  3–2  2–0  2–0  2–3  2–1
```

4 Belts are sold in different lengths.
This table shows the number of men's belts
sold in a shop during one month.

Length (cm)	32	34	36	38	40	42	44	46
Frequency	6	16	28	41	17	18	10	13

Use an appropriate average to decide which size of belt the shop owner should
always try to keep in stock.

5 These are the annual salaries (to the nearest thousand
dollars) of each employee of a small company.
Work out the average annual salary for the company.

23 000 26 000 26 000 29 000 29 000
30 000 30 000 32 000 46 000 59 000

6 This table shows the lengths of 58 new movies.

Length (minutes)	80–	90–	100–	110–	120–	130–	140–150
Frequency	3	10	12	26	2	4	1

Work out the average length of a new movie.

7 These are the numbers of breakdowns on a motorway
on 12 different days in the summer.
These are the numbers for 10 days in the winter.
Compare the number of breakdowns in summer and
winter. Calculate any statistics you need.

2 5 8 6 4 9 6 3 6 4 7 4

10 13 6 14 7 19 7 15 16 7

8 Three runners each take part in a number of
half marathons in one year. Here are their
times, to the nearest minute.
a Who is the fastest runner?
b Who is the most consistent runner?
Find statistics to support your answers.

Andi	91	83	90	86	88	88		
Bart	90	96	96	77	99	78	88	95
Chris	89	91	92	92	91			

9 Here are the lengths of text messages that Obi and Darth sent during one month from their mobiles.

Characters	1–20	21–40	41–60	61–80	81–100	101–120
Obi	6	32	51	27	11	7
Darth	21	42	16	5	0	0

Compare Obi's and Darth's phone use. Work out any statistics you need.

Summary

You should now know that:

★ The mean, the median and the mode are three
different types of average.

★ The range is a statistic that measures the spread
of a set of data.

★ The average is a representative value and you
can use this fact to check for possible errors in
calculation.

You should be able to:

★ Calculate statistics, including the mean, the
median, the mode and the range.

★ Select the most appropriate statistics for a
particular problem.

★ Decide how to check results by considering
whether the answer is reasonable in the context of
the problem.

End-of-unit review

1 Anders spins a coin until he gets a head, then writes down the number of spins he tried. He does this 24 times. His results are shown on the right.

2	2	2	1	3	1	1	1	2	2	1	2
5	1	1	1	1	1	2	3	2	1	3	1

Work out:

a the modal number of spins   **b** the median   **c** the mean   **d** the range.

2 Sasha uses a spreadsheet to simulate the coin-spinning activity described in question **1**. She records her results in a table.

Spins to get a head	1	2	3	4	5	6	7	8	9
Frequency	160	75	44	18	10	5	2	0	1

Work out: **a** the modal number of spins   **b** the median   **c** the mean   **d** the range.

3 Here are the ages of children in a kindergarden. Work out:

a the median age of the girls
b the mean age of the boys
c the modal age of all the children.

Age	3	4	5	6
Girls	6	14	16	2
Boys	1	13	6	4

4 A group of children and a group of adults estimate the number of sweets in a jar.

Number of sweets	60–64	65–69	70–74	75–79	80–84	85–89
Children	6	13	21	15	5	0
Adults	2	8	19	31	20	20

There are 73 sweets in the jar. Who are the best estimators, children or adults?
Use the appropriate statistics to justify your answer.

5 A snack bar sells two different cold drinks, Coola and Freezy.
Here are the sales each day for a week.

Day	Monday	Tuesday	Wednesday	Thursday	Friday	Saturday	Sunday
Coola	42	58	63	39	74	75	38
Freezy	81	75	63	42	55	25	89

Work out statistics to compare the sales of each drink.

6 When you play darts, you throw three darts at the board and add the scores.
Bristoe and Clancey are practising. Here are their scores for a number of turns.

Bristoe	18, 32, 26, 53, 5, 29, 41, 15, 85, 9, 44, 28, 100, 37, 55
Clancey	41, 26, 33, 51, 26, 29, 60, 45, 60, 19, 42, 36

a Who has the better average score? Give a reason for your answer.
b Who has the more varied scores? Give a reason for your answer.

11 Percentages

Two scientists measure the area covered by weed on a lake. It covers $10 \, \text{m}^2$.

They measure it one week later and it covers $14 \, \text{m}^2$. Each scientist makes a hypothesis.

Scientist X says the increase is $4 \, \text{m}^2$. He thinks it will increase by $4 \, \text{m}^2$ every week.

After two weeks there will be $18 \, \text{m}^2$. After three weeks there will be $22 \, \text{m}^2$. After four weeks there will be $26 \, \text{m}^2$.

Scientist Y says the increase is 40%.

This is because $\frac{4}{10} \times 100 = 40\%$.

She thinks the weed will increase by 40% each week.

After two weeks the area will be
$14 + 40\%$ of $14 = 14 + 5.6 = 19.6 \, \text{m}^2$.

After three weeks the area will be
$19.6 + 40\%$ of $19.6 = 19.6 + 7.84 = 27.44 \, \text{m}^2$.

This graph shows their predictions.

How can they decide who is right?

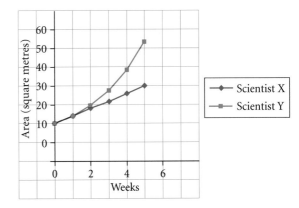

In this unit you will learn more about using percentages.

Make sure you can remember the equivalences between simple fractions, decimals and percentages.

Fraction	1	$\frac{1}{2}$	$\frac{1}{4}$	$\frac{3}{4}$	$\frac{1}{5}$	$\frac{1}{10}$	$\frac{1}{100}$	$\frac{1}{3}$	$\frac{2}{3}$
Decimal	1	0.5	0.25	0.75	0.2	0.1	0.01	0.33...	0.66...
Percentage	100%	50%	25%	75%	20%	10%	1%	$33\frac{1}{3}\%$	$66\frac{2}{3}\%$

11.1 Using mental methods

Some percentages are easy to find because they are simple fractions. There are examples of these on the first page of this unit.

You can use the easy ones to work out more complicated percentages.

You can often do this quite easily. You do not always need a calculator.

> If you know 10%, you can find any multiple of 10%.

Worked example 11.1

There are 4600 people in a stadium. 58% are males. How many is that?

100% = 4600
58% = 50% + 10% − 2%
50% = 2300
10% = 460
1% = 46
58% = 2300 + 460 − (2 × 46) = 2668

These are all easy percentages to find.
50% = $\frac{1}{2}$
$\frac{1}{10}$ is easy. Just divide by 10.
Divide 10% by 10 to find 1%.
Do this sum in your head or on paper.

> You could have found 50% + 5% + 3%. Is that easier?

Exercise 11.1

> Do not use a calculator in this exercise

1 Work out:
   a 35% of 84   **b** 49% of 230   **c** 77% of 4400   **d** 99% of 7900   **e** 45% of 56 000.

2 Look at Alicia's method for finding 85%.
   a Find a better way to work out 85%.
   b Work out 85% of:

   > 85% = 50% + (3 × 10%) + (5 × 1%)

   i 7200 g   **ii** $64   **iii** 3.6 m   **iv** 1800 ml   **v** 85 seconds.

3 Work out:
   a 12.5% of 80   **b** 0.5% of 7000   **c** 150% of 62   **d** 125% of 260   **e** 110% of 36.

4 | 26% of 78 = 20.28 |

   > You can have more than 100%.

   Use this fact to find:
   a 52% of $78   **b** 13% of 78 kg   **c** 65% of 78 km   **d** 104% of 78 million.

5 | 19% of 256 = 48.64 |

   Use this fact to find:
   a 19% of 128   **b** 9.5% of 256   **c** 19% of 512   **d** 9.5% of 512.

6 **a** Show that 30% of 65 is the same as 65% of 30.
   b Show that 20% of 45 is the same as 45% of 20.
   c Now try to generalise this result.

7 Copy and complete this table.

Percentage	5%	20%	40%	60%	80%	120%
Amount ($)			72			

11.2 Comparing different quantities

You will often need to compare groups that are different sizes.

Suppose that, in one school, 85 students took an exam and 59 passed.

In another school, 237 students took an exam and 147 passed.

Which school did better? It is hard to say because each school had a different number of students.

The worked example shows how to use percentages to help to answer questions like this.

Worked example 11.2

In school A, 85 students took a mathematics exam and 59 passed.
In school B, 237 students took a mathematics exam and 147 passed.
Which school had a better pass rate?

59 out of 85 = 59 ÷ 85 = 69%

147 out of 237 = 147 ÷ 237 = 62%

The pass rate in school B is better by seven percentage points.

59 ÷ 85 = 0.694... = 69% to the nearest whole number.

147 ÷ 237 = 0.620... = 62% to the nearest whole number.

The difference between 62% and 69% is given in 'percentage points'.

Exercise 11.2

1   There were 270 people in a cinema. There were 168 women and 102 men.
    There were 152 people in a theatre. There were 78 women and 74 men.
    a Work out the percentage of women in each venue.
    b Work out the percentage of men in each venue.

> The venue is the place where something happens. In this case it is the cinema or the theatre.

2   There are 425 girls and 381 boys in a school. 31 girls and 48 boys are overweight.
    a Work out the percentage of the girls that are overweight.
    b Work out the percentage of the boys that are overweight.
    c Work out the percentage of all the students that are overweight.

3   In Alphatown there are 5400 young people aged 18 or less. There are 9300 aged over 18.
    In Betatown there are 9300 young people aged 18 or less. There are 21 600 aged over 18.
    a Calculate the percentage of young people in each town.
    b Which town has the greater proportion of young people?

4   This table shows the results of a survey in a factory.
    a What percentage of men are smokers?
    b Compare the percentages of men and women who are non-smokers.

	Smoker	Non-smoker	Total
Men	12	64	76
Women	9	32	41

5   This table shows the ages of cars owned by two groups of people.
    Use percentages to compare the ages of cars owned by engineers and by accountants.

Age of car	Less than 5 years	5 years or more
Engineers	34	53
Accountants	41	102

11.3 Percentage changes

You can use percentages to describe a change in a quantity. It could be an **increase** or a **decrease**.

A percentage change is always calculated as a percentage of the initial value.

The initial value is 100%. It is important to choose the correct value to be 100%.

Worked example 11.3

In May 800 people visited a museum. In June 900 people visited. In July, the number was 800 again.
Work out:
a the percentage increase from May to June   **b** the percentage decrease from June to July.

a 100% = 800   The initial value in May.
   The increase is 100.   900 − 800

   The percentage increase is $\frac{100}{800} \times 100 = 12.5\%$.   The fraction $\frac{100}{800}$ simplifies to $\frac{1}{8}$.

b 100% = 900   The initial value is 900 this time.
   The decrease is 100.   A decrease from 900 to 800

   The percentage decrease is $\frac{100}{900} \times 100 = 11.1\%$.   The fraction $\frac{100}{900}$ simplifies to $\frac{1}{9}$.

> The percentages are <u>not</u> the same.

Exercise 11.3

1 Here are the prices of three items in Alain's shop.
   Game $40   Phone $120   Computer $500
   Alain increases all the prices by $10. Find the percentage increase for each item.

2 These are the masses of three children one April.
   Luke 6 kg   Bridget 14 kg   Tomas 25 kg
   Over a year, the mass of each of them increased by 10%. Work out the new mass of each child.

3 **a** One week the height of a plant increased from 30 cm to 35 cm. Work out the percentage increase.
   b The following week the height increased by 12%. Work out the new height.

4 Tebor weighed 84 kg. He went running every day and began to lose mass.
   After one month his mass was 78 kg. What was the percentage decrease?

5 **a** The speed of a car increased from 90 km/h to 120 km/h. What is the percentage increase?
   b Here are some more changes of speed. Write each one as a percentage.
      i from 40 km/h to 55 km/h   **ii** from 55 km/h to 70 km/h   **iii** from 70 km/h to 40 km/h.

6 The price of a car was $20 000. In a sale, the price decreased
   by 4%. After the sale it increased by 4%.
   a What mistake has Ahmad made?
   b What is the correct price after the sale?

> The price after the sale is $20 000 again.

7 A statistician noted the population of her country in three different years.
   1900: 4.6 million   1950: 7.2 million   2000: 13.8 million
   Find the percentage increase:
   a from 1900 to 1950   **b**   from 1950 to 2000   **c**   from 1900 to 2000.

11.4 Practical examples

Here are some real-life examples of uses of percentages.

> Profit = sell for <u>more</u> than you buy.
> Loss = sell for <u>less</u> than you buy.

- If you buy something and sell it, the difference between the two prices is a **profit** or a **loss**.
  It is given as a percentage of the buying price.
  If you buy something for $20 and sell it for $15 you make a loss of $5 or 25%.
- When you buy something you may be offered a **discount**.
  This is a reduction in the price. It is usually given as a percentage.
  If the price is normally $20 and you get a 10% discount, you only pay $18.
- If a bank helps you to buy an item, you may have to pay back more than you borrow. This is the **interest** that the bank charges. It is given as a percentage of the cost. If a car costs $20 000 and the rate of interest is 3%, you will pay $20 600.

> 3% of $20 000 is $600

- If you buy something the price may include a **tax**. This is called a <u>purchase tax</u>. When you earn money you may have to pay tax on what you earn. This is called <u>income tax</u>.

Worked example 11.4

A man earns $45 000 in a year.
He can earn $16 000 without paying any tax. He pays 24% tax on anything above $16 000.
a Work out how much tax he pays.
b What percentage of his income does he pay in income tax?

a $45 000 - 16 000 = 29 000$
  24% of $29 000 = 6960$
  He pays $6960.

This is his taxable income. He pays tax on this amount.
That is $0.24 \times 29 000$

b $\frac{6960}{45 000} \times 100 = 15.5\%$

$45 000 = 100\%$. The answer is rounded to one decimal place.

◆ Exercise 11.4

1 A woman bought an old chair for $240. She sold it for $300.
  Work out the percentage profit.

> The percentage profit is a percentage of 240.

2 A man bought a car for $15 900. He sold it for $9500.
  Work out the percentage loss.

3 A trader buys some goods for $820. When he sells them he makes a profit of 35%.
  a Work out the profit, in dollars.
  b Work out how much he sells them for.

4 A bottle of grape juice costs $6.50.
  If you buy six bottles you can get 10% discount.
  Work out how much you save if you buy six bottles.

5 A restaurant must add 15% tax to the price of a meal.
  a Here are some bill totals <u>before</u> tax is added. Work out the bill <u>after</u> tax is added.
    i $42.20   **ii** $19.50   **iii** $64.80
  b The tax rate is increased to 17%. Work out how much <u>extra</u> tax must be paid in each case.

6 A man invests $4500 in a bank. The bank pays 8% interest.
   a Work out the interest, in dollars.
   b Work out the total.

7 A woman deposited $560 in a bank.
   a The bank decided to give all its customers 4.5% interest. Calculate how much she received in interest.
   b The next year she had $720 in the bank and received $27.36 interest. What was the percentage interest rate?

8 Barry lends Cara $6400.
   Cara agrees to give Barry 5.5% interest every year for four years.
   Work out how much interest Cara will pay altogether.

9 Sam earns $54 275 in a year.
   He pays no income tax on the first $8200.
   He pays 18% income tax on everything he earns over $8200.
   a Work out how much income tax he pays.
   b Work out what percentage of his income he pays in tax.
   c If the income tax rate is increased to 21%, how much <u>more</u> tax will Sam pay?

10 The price of a second-hand car is $6975.
   Which of the three offers on the right is the best offer?
   Give a reason for your answer.

$900 reduction	15% discount

Pay just seven-eighths

11 Kate bought 12 bottles of perfume for $145 altogether and sold them all at $18.50 each.
   Work out her profit or loss. Give your answer as a percentage.

12 An antiques dealer bought three items and then sold them.
   The prices are shown in the table.
   a Work out the percentage profit or loss for each item.
   b Work out the overall percentage profit or loss for all three items together.

Item	Clock	Necklace	Picture
Buying price	$120	$42	$890
Selling price	$205	$95	$725

Summary

You should now know that:
* ★ Percentages can be written as fractions or decimals. This is be useful when making mental calculations.
* ★ Fractions and percentages are a good way to compare different quantities.
* ★ You can solve problems involving percentage changes.
* ★ You can solve problems involving profit and loss, interest, discount, interest and income tax.
* ★ You can solve problems involving percentages, either mentally or with a calculator.

You should be able to:
* ★ Extend mental methods of calculation, working with decimals, fractions, percentages and factors, using jottings where appropriate.
* ★ Recognise when you need to use fractions or percentages to compare different quantities.
* ★ Solve problems involving percentage changes, choosing the correct number to take as 100% or as a whole, including simple problems involving personal and household finance, for example, simple interest, discount, profit, loss and tax.
* ★ Calculate accurately, choosing operations and mental or written methods appropriate to the numbers and context.

End-of-unit review

1 Work out these percentages. Do not use a calculator.
   a 60% of 84   **b** 90% of 320   **c** 15% of 42.6   **d** 31% of 630

2 Without using a calculator, work out:
   a 35% of 2000 mm   **b** 40% of 960 kg   **c** 120% of 760 hours.

3 27% of 430 = 116.1

   Use this fact to work out:
   a 27% of 860   **b** 2.7% of 430   **c** 54% of 215   **d** 13.5% of 4300.

4 This table shows how many men and women in a company cycle to work.

	Cycle to work	Do not cycle	Total
Men	15	41	56
Women	38	82	120

   a Work out the percentage of men who cycle to work.
   b Work out the percentage of women who do not cycle to work.
   c Read what Dakarai is saying. Do the numbers in the table support this statement? Give a reason for your answer.

Men are more likely to cycle to work.

5 One year, in school A, 162 students leave and 109 go to university.
   In school B, 75 students leave and 68 go to university.
   Compare the percentages of students going to university from each school.

6 Work out the results of these changes.
   a A crowd of 8000 people increases by 20%.
   b The price of a $43 000 car decreases by 6%.
   c The mass of a 3.20 kg baby increases by 80%.

7 Read what Mia is saying.
   Explain why she is correct.

A price can increase by 150% but it cannot decrease by 150%.

8 Before tax, the price of fuel is $3.40 per litre.
   Tax of 30% is added.
   Work out the cost of 28 litres of fuel, including tax.

9 A trader bought 12 shirts for $150 altogether. He sold 11 them for $20 each and one for $10.
   Work out his overall percentage profit or loss.

10 The price of a computer is $695. A shop offers 15% discount.
   Work out the discount price.

11 This year Justin earned $52 700.
   He must pay 28% tax on everything he earns over $12 800.
   a Work out how much tax he has to pay.
   b Work out the percentage of his income that he pays in tax.

Here are nine wallpaper patterns.

Key words

Make sure you learn and understand these key words:

tessellation
column vector
locus
loci

In the first pattern a shape has been **translated** to different positions.

In the second pattern a shape has been **rotated** through 180° degrees to a different position.

In the fourth pattern you can extend it by **reflection** in the thick vertical lines.

Can you see examples of translation, rotation and reflection in the other patterns?

Here is another repeating wallpaper pattern.

Look carefully. There is a pattern with three flowers on the left. What symmetry does this have?

The three-flower pattern on the left is rotated to form the middle three-flower unit. Where is the centre of rotation? What is the angle of rotation?

The three-flower pattern on the left can be reflected or translated to give the three-flower pattern on the right. Where is the mirror line for the reflection? How will the pattern continue?

In this unit you will carry out more transformations of 2D shapes, and learn how to describe combined transformations of 2D shapes. You will also learn about tessellating shapes and about loci.

12.1 Tessellating shapes

A **tessellation** is a pattern made of identical shapes. You can make your own tessellation by fitting copies of a shape together, without gaps or overlaps. You say that the shape tessellates, or is a tessellating shape.

Here are some examples of shapes that tessellate with themselves.

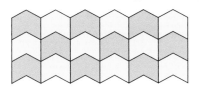 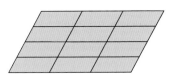 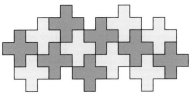

Here are some examples of shapes that do not tessellate with themselves. There are gaps between the shapes.

 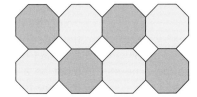 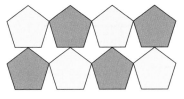

When you make a tessellation you can move the shape by translating, rotating or reflecting it.
For example, here are some of the ways you can tessellate a rectangle.

 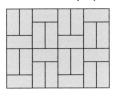 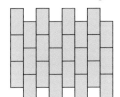 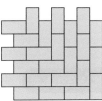

Many tessellations are made by repeating a shape and using half-turn rotations of the same shape.

For example, this triangle and a half-turn rotation of the same triangle fit together

exactly to make a tessellation like this.

In any tessellation, the sum of the angles at the point where the vertices of the shapes meet is 360°.
Look closely at three of the tessellations above.

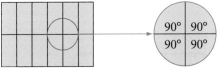

$90° + 90° + 90° + 90° = 360°$

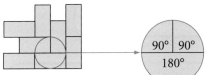

$90° + 90° + 180° = 360°$

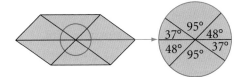

$37° + 95° + 48° + 37° + 95° + 48° = 360°$

Worked example 12.1

a Show that this triangle will tessellate by drawing a tessellation on squared paper.
b Explain why a regular pentagon will not tessellate.

a Rotate the triangle ◣ through half a turn to give this triangle ◥
These two triangles fit together to give a rectangle ◪ that can be easily repeated in the tessellation.

b
Exterior angle = 360° ÷ 5 = 72°
Interior angle = 180° − 72° = 108°
Angles around a point = 360°
360 ÷ 108 = 3.33...
Three pentagons: 3 × 108° = 324° < 360°
Four pentagons: 4 × 108° = 432° > 360°
Only three pentagons will fit around a point, leaving a gap of 360° − 324° = 36°, so pentagons will not tessellate.

Start by working out the interior angle of the pentagon. Then work out how many pentagons will fit around a point, by dividing 360° by the size of the interior angle. The answer is not an exact number, which means there must be a gap. Work out the size of the gap that is left and include that in the explanation. Make sure you draw diagrams and show all your working.

◆ **Exercise 12.1**

1 Show how each of these quadrilaterals and triangles will tessellate by drawing tessellations on squared paper.

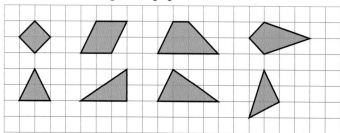

2 Explain how you know that a regular hexagon will tessellate.
Show all your working and include diagrams in your explanation.

3 Anders is talking to Maha about tessellations.
Read what he says.
  a Explain why Anders is correct.
    Show all your working and include diagrams in your explanation.
  Now read what Maha says to Anders.
  b Explain why Maha is correct.
    Show all your working and include diagrams in your explanation.

Regular octagons do not tessellate.

I have some square tiles and some octagonal tiles. The sides of all the tiles are the same length. It **is** possible to make a pattern with octagonal and square tiles and leave no gaps.

12.2 Solving transformation problems

You already know that a shape can be transformed by a reflection, rotation or translation.

When a shape undergoes any of these three transformations it only changes its position. Its shape and size stay the same. Under these three transformations, an object and its image are <u>always</u> congruent.

When you reflect a shape on a coordinate grid you need to know the <u>equation</u> of the mirror line.

All vertical lines are parallel to the y-axis and have the equation x = 'a number'.

All horizontal lines are parallel to the x-axis and have the equation y = 'a number'.

Some examples are shown on the grid on the right.

When you rotate a shape on a coordinate grid you need to know the <u>coordinates</u> of the centre of rotation, and the <u>size and direction</u> of the turn.

When you translate a shape on a coordinate grid, you can describe its movement with a **column vector**.

This is an example of a column vector: $\begin{pmatrix} 4 \\ 5 \end{pmatrix}$

The top number states how many units to move the shape right (positive number) or left (negative number).

The bottom number states how many units to move the shape up (positive number) or down (negative number).

For example: $\begin{pmatrix} 4 \\ 5 \end{pmatrix}$ means 'move the shape 4 units right and 5 units up'

$\begin{pmatrix} -2 \\ -3 \end{pmatrix}$ means 'move the shape 2 units left and 3 units down'.

> If the scale on the grid is one square to one unit, the numbers tell you how many squares to move the object up or across.

You can use any of these three transformations to solve all sorts of problem.

Worked example 12.2a

The diagram shows a triangle on a coordinate grid.
Draw the image of the triangle after each of these translations.

a $\begin{pmatrix} 3 \\ 2 \end{pmatrix}$ **b** $\begin{pmatrix} 2 \\ -1 \end{pmatrix}$ **c** $\begin{pmatrix} -3 \\ 1 \end{pmatrix}$ **d** $\begin{pmatrix} -1 \\ -3 \end{pmatrix}$

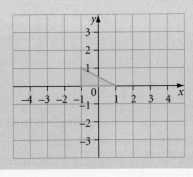

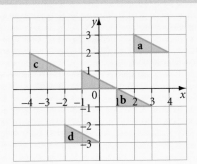

a Move the original triangle (object) 3 squares right and 2 squares up.
b Move the original triangle 2 squares right and 1 square down.
c Move the original triangle 3 squares left and 1 square up.
d Move the original triangle 1 square left and 3 squares down.

Worked example 12.2b

The diagram shows shape A on a coordinate grid.
One corner of shape A is marked with a red cross.
Harsha rotated shape A 90° clockwise about the point (4, 1) and labelled
the image shape B.
She reflected shape A in the line $x = 4$ and labelled the image shape C.

The red crosses on shapes B and C
have exactly the same coordinates.

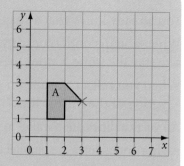

a Show that what Harsha said is correct.
b Write down the coordinates of the red cross on shapes B and C.

a

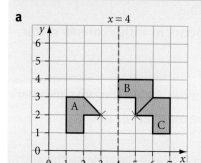

First, rotate shape A through 90° clockwise about the point (4, 1).
The easiest way to do this is to use tracing paper. Carefully trace shape
A, then put the point of the pencil on the point (4, 1). Turn the tracing
paper 90° clockwise, then draw the image of shape A.
Label this image shape B.
Draw the line $x = 4$ onto the grid and reflect shape A in the line.
Draw the image and label it shape C.
It is clear that the red cross on shapes B and C have exactly the same
coordinates.

b The coordinates of the red cross on shapes B and C are (5, 2).

⬥ Exercise 12.2

1 The diagram shows shape A on a coordinate grid.
Copy the grid, then draw the image of shape A after each translation.

a $\begin{pmatrix} 3 \\ 2 \end{pmatrix}$ **b** $\begin{pmatrix} 4 \\ -2 \end{pmatrix}$ **c** $\begin{pmatrix} -2 \\ 2 \end{pmatrix}$ **d** $\begin{pmatrix} -1 \\ -2 \end{pmatrix}$

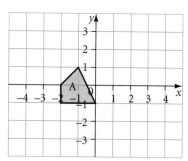

2 The diagram shows triangle B on a coordinate grid.
Make two copies of the grid.
a On the first copy, draw the image of triangle B after reflection
in the line:
  i $x = 4$ **ii** $y = 3$ **iii** $x = 4.5$ **iv** $y = 4$
b On the second copy, draw the image of triangle B after a rotation:
  i 90° clockwise about the point (4, 1)
  ii 90° anticlockwise about the point (1, 1)
  iii 180° about the point (2, 4)
  iv 180° about the point (4, 3)

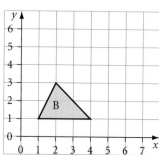

3 This is part of Oditi's homework.

> <u>Question</u>   Draw a reflection of the orange triangle on the coordinate grid in the line with equation $x = 4$. Explain your method.
>
> <u>Answer</u>   Reflected triangle drawn on grid in green. I reflected each corner of the triangle in the line, then joined the three corners together.

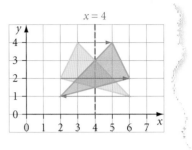

Make a copy of this grid.
Use Oditi's method to draw these reflections.
a Reflect the triangle in the line $x = 4$.
b Reflect the parallelogram in the line $y = 5$.
c Reflect the kite in the line $x = 8$.

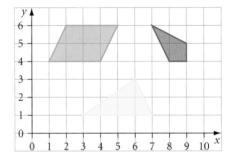

4 The diagram shows shape X on a coordinate grid.
One corner of shape X is marked with a red cross.
Razi rotated shape X 180° about the point $(-1, 0)$ and labelled it shape Y.
He translated shape X by the column vector $\begin{pmatrix} 4 \\ -4 \end{pmatrix}$ and labelled the image shape Z.

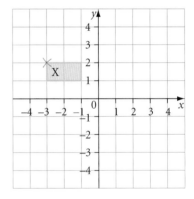

> The red crosses on shapes Y and Z have exactly the same coordinates.

a Show that what Razi said is correct.
b Write down the coordinates of the red crosses on shapes Y and Z.

5 The diagram shows shape ABCD on a coordinate grid.
  a Write down the coordinates of the points A, B, C and D.
The diagram also shows the line with equation $y = x$.
  b Copy the diagram. Reflect shape ABCD in the line $y = x$. Label the
  c Write down the coordinates of the points A', B', C' and D'.
  d Compare your answers to parts **a** and **c**. What do you notice about the coordinates of ABCD and its image A'B'C'D'?

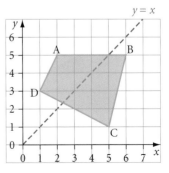

12.3 Transforming shapes

You can use a <u>combination</u> of reflections, translations and rotations to transform a shape.

You can also describe the transformation that maps an object onto its image.

To describe a reflection you must give: • the equation of the mirror line.

To describe a translation you must give: • the column vector.

To describe a rotation you must give: • the centre of rotation
  • the number of degrees of the rotation (or fraction of a whole turn)
  • the direction of the rotation (clockwise or anticlockwise).

> Note that when a rotation is 180° (half a turn) you do not need to give the direction of the rotation as the image of the object will be the same whether you rotate it clockwise or anticlockwise.

Worked example 12.3

The diagram shows triangles A, B, C and D.
a Draw the image of triangle A after a reflection in the y-axis followed by a rotation 90° clockwise, centre (−1, 1). Label the image E.
b Describe the transformation that transforms:
  i triangle A to triangle B
  ii triangle B to triangle C
  iii triangle C to triangle D.

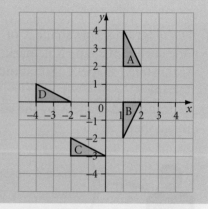

a

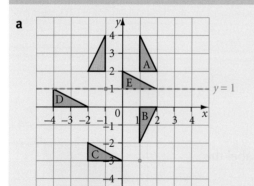

First, reflect triangle A in the y-axis to give the blue triangle shown on the diagram. Then rotate the blue triangle 90° clockwise about (−1, 1), shown by a red dot, to give the red triangle.

Remember to label the final triangle E.

b i Triangle A to triangle B is a reflection in the line $y = 1$, shown in orange.
ii Triangle B to triangle C is a rotation 90° anticlockwise, centre (1, −3), shown by a pink dot.
iii Triangle C to triangle D is a translation two squares left and three squares up, so the column vector is $\begin{pmatrix} -2 \\ 3 \end{pmatrix}$.

◆ **Exercise 12.3**

1 The diagram shows shape A on a coordinate grid.
Make two copies of the diagram.
On different copies of the diagram, draw the image of
A after each of these combinations of transformations.

   a Reflection in the y-axis followed by the translation $\begin{pmatrix} 1 \\ -2 \end{pmatrix}$

   b Rotation of 90° anticlockwise, centre $(-1, 2)$ followed
      by a reflection in the line $x = 1$

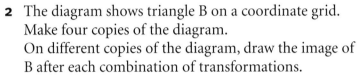

2 The diagram shows triangle B on a coordinate grid.
Make four copies of the diagram.
On different copies of the diagram, draw the image of
B after each combination of transformations.

   a Translation $\begin{pmatrix} 5 \\ 1 \end{pmatrix}$, followed by a reflection in the x-axis

   b Rotation of 180°, centre $(-3, -2)$ followed by a
      reflection in the y-axis

   c Translation $\begin{pmatrix} -1 \\ 5 \end{pmatrix}$, followed by a rotation of
      90° clockwise, centre $(-2, 1)$

   d Reflection in the line $y = -1$, followed by a rotation 90°
      anticlockwise, centre $(2, 2)$.

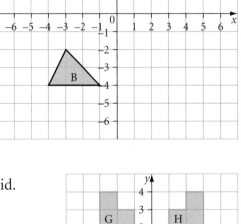

3 The diagram shows shapes G, H, I, J and K on a coordinate grid.
Describe the reflection that transforms:
   a shape G to shape H
   b shape G to shape K
   c shape H to shape J
   d shape J to shape I.

4 The diagram shows shapes L, M, N, P and Q on a coordinate grid.
Describe the translation that transforms:
   a shape N to shape L   **b** shape N to shape P
   c shape N to shape Q   **d** shape N to shape M
   e shape L to shape P   **f** shape P to shape M.

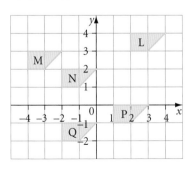

5 The diagram shows triangles R, S, T, U, V and W on a coordinate grid.
Describe the rotation that transforms:

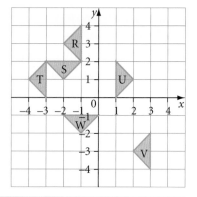

a triangle R to triangle S
b triangle S to triangle T
c triangle T to triangle U
d triangle U to triangle V
e triangle V to triangle W.

6 The diagram shows three shapes X, Y and Z
on a coordinate grid.
Make three copies of the grid.
On the first grid draw shape X, on the second grid draw
shape Y and on the third grid draw shape Z.

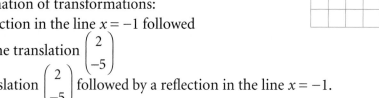

a On the first grid draw the image of X after the
combination of transformations:
   i reflection in the line $y = 1$ followed by a rotation 90°
anticlockwise, centre $(2, -3)$
   ii rotation 90° anticlockwise, centre $(2, -3)$, followed
by a reflection in the line $y = 1$.

b On the second grid draw the image of Y after the
combination of transformations:
   i reflection in the line $x = -1$ followed
by the translation $\begin{pmatrix} 2 \\ -5 \end{pmatrix}$

   ii translation $\begin{pmatrix} 2 \\ -5 \end{pmatrix}$ followed by a reflection in the line $x = -1$.

c On the third grid draw the image of Z after the combination of transformations:
   i a rotation of 180°, centre $(0, 0)$, followed by a reflection in the line $y = 2$
   ii a reflection in the line $y = 2$ followed by a rotation of 180°, centre $(0, 0)$.

d **i** What do you notice about your answers to **i** and **ii** in parts **a**, **b** and **c**?
   ii Does it matter in which order you carry out combined transformations? Explain your answer.
   iii Write down two different transformations that you can carry out on shape Z so that the final
image is the same, whatever order you do the transformations.

7 The diagram shows shapes A, B, C, D and E on a
coordinate grid.

a Describe the single transformation that transforms:
   i shape A to shape B
   ii shape B to shape C
   iii shape C to shape D.

b Describe a combined transformation that transforms:
   i shape A to shape D
   ii shape B to shape E.

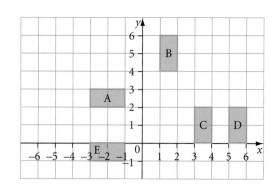

12.4 Enlarging shapes

When you enlarge a shape, all the lengths of the sides of the shape increase in the same proportion. This is called the <u>scale factor</u>. All the angles in the shape stay the same size.

When you describe an enlargement you must give:
- the scale factor of the enlargement
- the position of the centre of enlargement.

Worked example 12.4

a The diagram shows a trapezium.

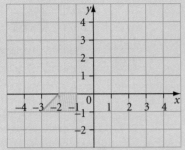

Draw an enlargement of the trapezium, with scale factor 3 and centre of enlargement (−3, −2).

b The diagram shows two triangles A and B.

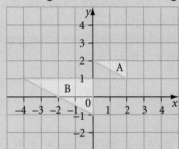

Triangle B is an enlargement of triangle A. Describe the enlargement.

---

a

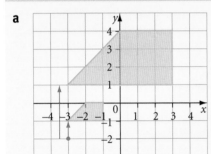

First, mark the centre of enlargement at (−3, −2), shown as a red dot on the diagram. The closest vertex of the trapezium is one square up from the centre of enlargement.
On the enlarged trapezium this vertex will be three squares up from the centre of enlargement (shown by the red arrows).
Mark this vertex on the diagram then complete the trapezium by drawing each side with length three times that of the original.

b

First, work out the scale factor of the enlargement.
Compare matching sides of the triangles, for example, the two sides shown by the red arrows. In triangle A, the length is 2 squares and in triangle B the length is 4 squares.
$4 \div 2 = 2$, so the scale factor is 2.
Now find the centre of enlargement by drawing lines (rays) through the matching vertices of the triangles, shown by the blue lines. The blue lines all meet at (4, 3).
So, the enlargement has scale factor 2, centre (4, 3).

◆ **Exercise 12.4**

1 The diagram shows a triangle on a coordinate grid.
Make a copy of the diagram on squared paper.
On the copy, draw an enlargement of the triangle with
scale factor 3, centre (−2, 0).

2 The diagram shows a shape on a coordinate grid.
Make three copies of the diagram on squared paper.
  a On the first copy, draw an enlargement of the shape with
  scale factor 2, centre (2, 2).
  b On the second copy, draw an enlargement of the shape with
  scale factor 3, centre (3, 3).
  c On the third copy, draw an enlargement of the shape with
  scale factor 2, centre (3, 4).

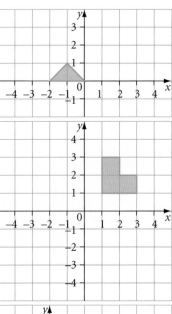

3 The diagram shows three triangles, A, B and C, on
a coordinate grid.
  a Triangle B is an enlargement of triangle A.
  Describe the enlargement.
  b Triangle C is an enlargement of triangle A.
  Describe the enlargement.

 4 The vertices of rectangle X are at (1, −2), (1, −3), (3, −3)
and (3, −2).
The vertices of rectangle Y are at (−5, 4), (−5, 1), (1, 1)
and (1, 4).
Rectangle Y is an enlargement of rectangle X. Describe
the enlargement.

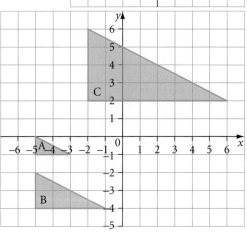

 5 Sasha drew a triangle with vertices at (1, 1), (2, 1) and (1, 3).
She enlarged the shape by a scale factor of 3, centre (0, 0). Read what Sasha said.

> If I multiply the coordinates of each vertex by 3 it will give me the
> coordinates of the enlarged triangle, which are at (3, 3), (6, 3) and (3, 9).

  a Show, by drawing, that in this case Sasha is correct.
  Read what Ahmad said.

> This means that, for any enlargement, with any scale factor and centre
> of enlargement, I can multiply the coordinates of each vertex by the
> scale factor to work out the coordinates of the enlarged shape.

  b Use a counter-example to show that
  Ahmad is wrong.

> Remember that a counter-example is just one
> example that shows a statement is not true.

12.5 Drawing a locus

A **locus** is a set of points that follow a given rule. The plural of locus is **loci**.

You need a ruler and compasses to draw loci accurately.

Worked example 12.5

a   A is a fixed point. Draw the locus of points that are all 2 cm from A.
b   Draw the locus of points that are exactly 3 cm from:
   i   a given line   ii   a given line segment BC.

---

a

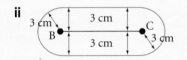

Use compasses to draw a circle of radius 2 cm with centre A.
All the points on the circle are 2 cm from A, so this is the required locus of points.
All the points <u>inside</u> the circle are <u>less than</u> 2 cm from A. All the points <u>outside</u> the circle are <u>more than</u> 2 cm from A.

b i

3 cm   3 cm
3 cm   3 cm

Using a ruler, on either side of the given line, measure and mark two points that are 3 cm from the line. Then join the points on each side of the given line to draw two parallel lines. These lines, shown in red, are the required locus of points exactly 3 cm from the line.
A straight line has infinite length, so the locus of points also has infinite length.

ii

3 cm   3 cm   C
B   3 cm   3 cm

The line segment BC has endpoints at B and C. Follow the steps in part **i** to draw the parallel lines either side of the line segment. From points B and C draw semicircles of radius 3 cm to complete the locus of points, shown in red, that are 3 cm from the given line segment.

◆ Exercise 12.5

1   The diagram shows a point P. Copy the diagram on plain paper.   P •
    Draw the locus of points that are exactly 5 cm from point P.

2   Draw a straight, horizontal line.
    Draw the locus of points that are exactly 2 cm from the line.   _____

3   Draw a line segment AB, 6 cm long.
    Draw the locus of points that are exactly 3 cm from AB.
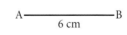

4   A donkey is tied by a rope to a post in a field. The rope is 8 m long.
    Draw the locus of points that the donkey can reach when the rope is tight.
    Use a scale of 1 cm to 2 m.

5   A coin has radius 1.5 cm.
    The coin is rolled around the inside of a rectangular box, so
    that it is always touching a side of the box.
    The box measures 10 cm by 12 cm.
    Draw the locus of C, the centre of the coin.
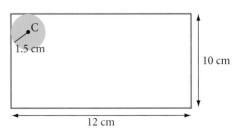

6 Draw the capital letters T, L and C on centimetre-squared paper.
For each letter, draw the locus of points that are 1 cm from the letter.

7 The diagram shows a rectangular field WXYZ.
There is a fence around the perimeter of the field.
Gary the goat is tied by a rope to corner X of the field.
When the rope is tight, Gary can just reach corner Y.
Copy the diagram on plain paper.
   a Draw the locus of points that Gary can reach when
   the rope is tight.
   b Shade the region inside which Gary can move.

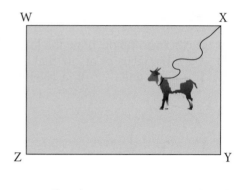

8 The diagram shows two schools, P and Q, 70 km apart.
Students can go to a school if they live less than 40 km from that school.
Copy the diagram on plain paper. Use a scale of 1 cm to 5 km.
   a Draw the locus of points that are exactly 40 km from P.
   b Draw the locus of points that are exactly 40 km from Q.
   c Tanesha can go to either school. Shade the region in which Tanesha must live.

Summary

You should now know that:

★ A tessellation is a repeating pattern made by fitting together copies of a given shape, without any gaps or overlaps. You can move the original shape by translating, rotating or reflecting it.

★ Many tessellations can be made by using the shape itself and a half-turn rotation of the shape.

★ In any tessellation, the sum of the angles where vertices of shapes meet is 360°.

★ A column vector describes a translation of a shape on a coordinate grid. The top number describes a move to the right or left. The bottom number describes a move up or down.

★ To describe a reflection, you state the equation of the mirror line.

★ To describe a translation you can use a column vector.

★ To describe a rotation, you state the centre of rotation, the number of degrees of the rotation and the direction of the rotation.

★ When you describe an enlargement you must state the scale factor of the enlargement and the position of the centre of enlargement.

★ A locus is a set of points that follow a given rule.

You should be able to:

★ Tessellate triangles and quadrilaterals and relate to angle sums and half-turn rotations; know which regular polygons tessellate and explain why others will not.

★ Use a coordinate grid to solve problems involving translations, rotations, reflections and enlargements.

★ Transform 2D shapes by combinations of rotations, reflections and translations; describe the transformation that maps an object to its image.

★ Enlarge 2D shapes, given a centre and scale factor; identify the scale factor of an enlargement.

★ Recognise that translations, rotations and reflections preserve length and angle, and map objects onto congruent images, and that enlargements preserve angle but not length.

★ Know what is needed to give a precise description of a reflection, rotation, translation or enlargement.

★ Find, by reasoning, the locus of a point that moves at a given distance from a fixed point, or at a given distance from a fixed straight line.

End-of-unit review

1 Explain why a regular pentagon will not tessellate.
  Show all your working and include diagrams in your explanation.

2 The diagram shows triangle A on a coordinate grid.
  Make a copy of the grid.

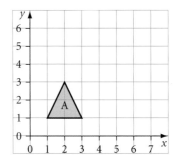

  a Draw the image of triangle A after a reflection in the
    line $x = 4$. Label the image B.
  b Draw the image of triangle A after a translation described
    by column vector $\begin{pmatrix} -1 \\ 3 \end{pmatrix}$. Label the image C.
  c Draw the image of triangle A after a reflection in the
    line $y = 4$ followed by a rotation 180° about the point $(3, 5)$.
    Label the image D.

3 The diagram shows triangles A, B, C, D, E and F o a coordinate grid.
  Describe the single transformation that transforms:
  a triangle A to triangle B
  b triangle C to triangle D
  c triangle E to triangle F
  d triangle A to triangle E
  e triangle C to triangle E.

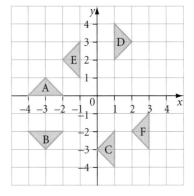

4 The diagram shows a shape on a coordinate grid.
  Make two copies of the diagram, on squared paper.
  a On the first copy, draw an enlargement of the shape with
    scale factor 2, centre $(0, 0)$.
  b On the second copy, draw an enlargement of the shape
    with scale factor 3, centre $(3, -2)$.

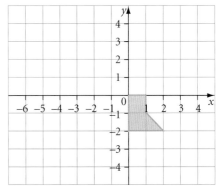

5 The vertices of triangle G are at $(3, 2)$, $(5, 2)$, and $(5, 3)$.
  The vertices of triangle H are at $(7, 2)$, $(13, 2)$, and $(13, 5)$.
  Triangle H is an enlargement of triangle G.
  Describe the enlargement.

6 On a piece of plain paper, mark a point Q.
  Draw the locus of points that are exactly 4 cm from point Q.

7 Draw a line segment XY, 8 cm long.
  Draw the locus of points that are exactly 2 cm from XY.

X ———————————— Y
          8 cm

13 Equations and inequalities

The **Rhind Papyrus** is a famous document that is kept in the British Museum in London. It was written in Egypt in 1650 BCE. It is a list of 84 practical problems and their solutions. It shows how the people of Ancient Egypt carried out mathematical calculations.

Some of the problems are easy to solve using algebra. This technique was not known in Egypt. They wrote their problems and solutions in words, not symbols.

Here, for example, is Problem 24.

> A quantity and its one-seventh added together make nineteen.
>
> What is the quantity?

The Egyptian solution was like this. See if you can understand it.

Start with 8 because 7 and $\frac{1}{7}$ of 7 makes 8.

Find how many eights make up 19.

Quantities of 8: $1 \rightarrow 8 \quad 2 \rightarrow 16$
$\frac{1}{2} \rightarrow 4 \quad \frac{1}{4} \rightarrow 2 \quad \frac{1}{8} \rightarrow 1$

19 is made up of 16 and 2 and 1. This is 2 and $\frac{1}{4}$ and $\frac{1}{8}$ 'lots' of 8. The same number of sevens gives the required quantity.

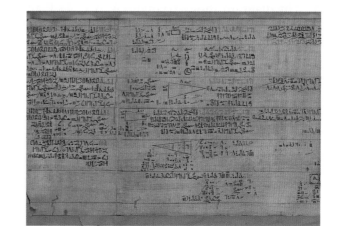

So now we must calculate 2 and $\frac{1}{4}$ and $\frac{1}{8}$ 'lots' of 7:

  1 lot is 2 and $\frac{1}{4}$ and $\frac{1}{8}$

  2 lots are 4 and $\frac{1}{2}$ and $\frac{1}{4}$

  4 lots are 8 and 1 and $\frac{1}{2}$

  Add these together to get 7 lots of 2 and $\frac{1}{4}$ and $\frac{1}{8}$

Total: 7 lots are 16 and $\frac{1}{2}$ and $\frac{1}{8}$.

This is the answer, which you would write as $16\frac{5}{8}$.

Here is a **modern solution**, using algebra.

Call the quantity x and write an equation:

$$x + \frac{x}{7} = 19$$

Multiply both sides by 7: $\quad 7x + x = 133$

$$\rightarrow 8x = 133$$

$$\rightarrow x = \frac{133}{8} = 16\frac{5}{8}$$

Algebra makes it much easier to solve mathematical problems!

You will learn more about using algebra in this unit.

13.1 Solving linear equations

In earlier work on solving equations, you may have noticed there can be more than one way to solve an equation. You can use any method you prefer, as long as it works. You should write out each step in your solution neatly and check your answer at the end.

> **Worked example 13.1**
>
> Solve the equation $2(x - 5) = 2 + 8x$.
>
> **First method**
> $$2(x - 5) = 2 + 8x$$
> $$\rightarrow 2x - 10 = 2 + 8x \qquad \text{Multiply out the brackets.}$$
> $$\rightarrow -10 = 2 + 6x \qquad \text{Subtract } 2x \text{ from each side.}$$
> $$\rightarrow -12 = 6x \qquad \text{Subtract 2 from each side.}$$
> $$\rightarrow \quad -2 = x \qquad \text{Divide each side by 6.}$$
>
> **Second method**
> $$2(x - 5) = 2 + 8x$$
> $$\rightarrow x - 5 = 1 + 4x \qquad \text{Divide each side by 2.}$$
> $$\rightarrow x - 6 = 4x \qquad \text{Subtract 1 from each side.}$$
> $$\rightarrow -6 = 3x \qquad \text{Subtract } x \text{ from each side.}$$
> $$\rightarrow -2 = x \qquad \text{Divide each side by 3.}$$
>
> **Check the answer:**
> $x = -2 \rightarrow 2(x - 5) = 2 \times (-2 - 5) = 2 \times -7 = -14$ Both sides of the equation have the same value, -14.
> and
> $x = -2 \rightarrow 2 + 8x = 2 + (8 \times -2) = 2 + -16 = -14$ There are other ways you could solve this equation. For example, in the first method you could subtract $8x$ instead of $2x$ and get $-6x - 10 = 2$. You should get the same answer.

◆ Exercise 13.1

1 Solve these equations.
   a $4x + 8 = 14$ **b** $4x + 14 = 8$ **c** $4x + 14 = -8$ **d** $-4x + 8 = 14$

2 Solve these equations.
   a $a + 15 = 4$ **b** $a + 15 = 4a$ **c** $a + 15 = 4a - 3$ **d** $a - 15 = 4a + 3$

3 Solve these equations.
   a $12 - y = 4$ **b** $12 - y = -4$ **c** $12 - 2y = 4$ **d** $12 - 2y = -4$

4 Solve these equations. Check each of your answers by substitution.
   a $6 = 2d - 4$ **b** $6 = 2(d - 4)$ **c** $6d = 2d - 4$ **d** $6d = 2(d - 4)$

5 Here is an equation.
   $2(x + 12) = 4x - 6$
   a Solve the equation by first multiplying out the brackets.
   b Solve the equation by first dividing both sides by 2.

6 Solve these equations. Check your answers.
   a $5 + 3x = 3 + 5x$ **b** $5 + 3x = 3 - 5x$ **c** $5 - 3x = 3 - 5x$

7 Solve these equations.
   a $4(2p + 3) = 16$ **b** $4(2p - 3) = 16$ **c** $4(2p + 3) = 16p$ **d** $4(2p - 3) = 16p$

8 Solve these equations. Give the answers as fractions.
   a $3x + 12 = 20 - 4x$ **b** $9(2 + 3y) = 39$ **c** $z + 15 = 5(7 - z)$

9 Look at Shen's homework.
   There is a mistake on each line of his solution.
   Copy out his working and correct the mistakes.

$2(x + 8) = 3(6 - x)$
$\rightarrow 2x + 8 = 18 - 3x$
$\rightarrow -x + 8 = 18$
$\rightarrow x = 26$

10 Here is an equation.
   $10(x - 4) = 5x + 25$
   a Jake starts to solve it by multiplying out the brackets. He writes:
   Complete Jake's solution.

$10x - 40 = 5x + 25$

   b Zalika starts to solve it by dividing both sides of
   $10(x - 4) = 5x + 25$ by 5.
   Complete Zalika's solution.
   c Whose method is better?

11 Dakarai and Mia start to solve the equation $6 - 2x = 3x + 25$.

Dakarai writes:
$6 - 2x = 3x + 25$
$\rightarrow 6 = 5x + 25$
$\rightarrow$

Mia writes:
$6 - 2x = 3x + 25$
$\rightarrow -2x = 3x + 19$
$\rightarrow$

   a What does Dakarai do first?
   b Complete Dakarai's solution.
   c What does Mia do first?
   d Complete Mia's solution.

12 The equations and the answers below are mixed up.
   Copy the equations and the answers, like this.

$$2(x + 3) + x = 0 \qquad x = 8$$
$$x + 2(x - 3) = 0 \qquad x = 6$$
$$3x - 2(x + 3) = 0 \qquad x = 2$$
$$-(x + 2) + 2(x - 3) = 0 \qquad x = 1$$
$$x - (2 - x) = 0 \qquad x = -2$$

   Draw a line from each equation to the correct answer.

13 Solve these equations.
   a $12 - (m - 3) = 4$ **b** $12 - (3 - m) = 4$ **c** $12 - 2(m - 3) = -4$

14 Solve these equations.
   a $x + 2(x + 1) + 3(x + 2) = 4(x + 3)$
   b $x + 2(x - 1) - 3(x - 2) = 4(x - 3)$

13.2 Solving problems

You can use equations to solve simple number problems.

Worked example 13.2

Xavier thinks of a number. He doubles the number. He adds 3. He doubles again. The answer is 70. What number did he think of?

Call the number N.	You can use any letter.
$2N + 3$	Double it and add 3.
$2(2N + 3) = 70$	Double $2N + 3$ is 70. Now solve the equation.
$2N + 3 = 35$	Divide both sides by 2.
$2N = 32$	Subtract 3.
$N = 16$	The number is 16.

◆ **Exercise 13.2**

1 Lynn picks three numbers and calls them a, $a + 2$ and $a + 4$.
  a Find the difference between the largest and smallest numbers.
  b The sum of the three numbers is 100. Write down an equation to show this.
  c Solve your equation to find the value of a.
  d Write down the values of the three numbers.

2 The length of this rectangle is x cm.
  a The width of the rectangle is 2 cm less than the length.
    Write down an expression for the width of the rectangle, in centimetres.
  b The perimeter of the rectangle is 84 cm. Write down an equation to show this.
  c Solve the equation.
  d Find the area of the rectangle.

x cm

3 $3N$ and $3N + 3$ are two consecutive multiples of three.
  a The sum of the two numbers is 141. Write down an equation to show this.
  b Solve the equation to find the value of N
  c Work out the values of the two initial numbers.

4 Adeline is A years old.
  a Write down an expression for:
    i Adeline's age in 10 years' time
    ii Adeline's age 6 years ago.
  b Write down an equation for A.
  c Solve the equation to find Adeline's age now.

In 10 years' time, I shall be twice as old as I was 6 years ago.

5 The sides of a triangle, in centimetres, are x, $2x - 3$ and $2x + 5$. The perimeter of the triangle is 57 cm.
  a Write down an equation for x.
  b Work out the lengths of the three sides of the triangle.

6 This equilateral triangle and square have equal perimeters.
  a Write down an equation to show this.
  b Solve the equation.
  c Find the lengths of the sides of the shapes.

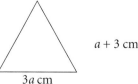

$a + 7$ cm

$a + 3$ cm

$3a$ cm

13.3 Simultaneous equations 1

The sum of two numbers is 83. The difference between the two numbers is 18. What are the numbers?

Call the numbers x and y. Then $\qquad x + y = 83$

$\qquad\qquad\qquad$ and $\qquad x - y = 18$

Now you have <u>two</u> equations and <u>two</u> unknowns. These are **simultaneous equations**.

> Simultaneous equations are both true at the same time, or simultaneously, for the two variables.

You need to find values of x and y that solve both equations simultaneously.

Rewrite the second equation: $\qquad\qquad\qquad\qquad\qquad x = 18 + y$

Substitute this into the first equation: $\qquad\qquad\qquad 18 + y + y = 83$

$$\rightarrow 2y = 83 - 18 = 65$$

$$\rightarrow y = 32.5$$

Then substitute this value to find x: $\qquad x = 18 + y = 18 + 32.5 = 50.5$

Check: $x + y = 50.5 + 32.5 = 83$ and $x - y = 50.5 - 32.5 = 18$.

Worked example 13.3

Solve these simultaneous equations. $\qquad 3x + 2y = 60$
$$y = 2x - 5$$

Substitute the second equation into the first.
$\quad 3x + 2(2x - 5) = 60 \qquad$ Put $2x - 5$ inside a pair of brackets.
$\quad 3x + 4x - 10 = 60 \qquad$ Multiply out the brackets.
$\qquad\qquad 7x = 70 \qquad$ Add $3x$ and $4x$; add 10 to both sides.
$\qquad\qquad\quad x = 10 \qquad$ Divide by 7.
Substitute this into the second equation.
$\quad y = 2 \times 10 - 5 = 15 \qquad$ Check these values in the first equation: $(3 \times 10) + (2 \times 15) = 60$

Exercise 13.3

1. Solve these simultaneous equations. $\qquad y = 2x - 1 \qquad y = x + 4$
   > Start with $2x - 1 = x + 4$.

2. Solve these simultaneous equations. $\qquad y = x - 9 \qquad y = 3x + 1$

3. Solve these simultaneous equations. $\qquad y = 9 - 2x \qquad y = x - 12$

4. Solve each pair of simultaneous equations.
   a $\quad x + y = 1 \qquad$ b $\quad x + y = 19 \qquad$ c $\quad x + y = -2$
   $\qquad\quad y = 2x - 8 \qquad\qquad\quad y = 5x + 1 \qquad\qquad\qquad y = x - 10$

5. Solve these simultaneous equations. $\qquad 3x = y \qquad\qquad x = y - 16$

6. Solve these simultaneous equations. $\qquad y = 2x \qquad\qquad x = 2y - 9$

7. Solve these simultaneous equations. $\qquad y = 3(x + 5) \qquad 2x + y = 0$

8. Solve these simultaneous equations. $\qquad 2x + 5y = 22 \qquad y = x - 4$

13.4 Simultaneous equations 2

Look again at these simultaneous equations from the last topic.

$$x + y = 83$$
$$x - y = 18$$

Another way to solve them is to <u>add</u> the equations together.

$$(x + y) + (x - y) = 83 + 18$$
$$\rightarrow 2x = 101$$
$$\rightarrow x = 50.5$$

The two y terms cancel.

Substitute this value in the first equation: $50.5 + y = 83 \rightarrow y = 83 - 50.5 = 32.5$

This method works because the coefficients of y (1 and -1) add up to 0.

The coefficient is the number multiplying the unknown.

Worked example 13.4

Solve the simultaneous equations: $5x + y = 27$
$2x + y = 6$

Subtract the second equation from the first.
$(5x + y) - (2x + y) = 27 - 6$ Subtraction cancels out the y terms.
$3x = 21$ Collect like terms.
$\rightarrow x = 7$
Substitute in the second equation.
$2 \times 7 + y = 6$ You could also substitute into the first equation.
$\rightarrow y = 6 - 14 = -8$

Exercise 13.4

1 Solve each of these pairs of simultaneous equations. Use any method you like.
   a $x + y = 15$ **b** $x + y = 30$ **c** $x + y = 2$
   $x - y = 3$ $x - y = 1$ $x - y = 14$

2 Here are two simultaneous equations. $2x + y = 19$
   $3x - y = 21$
   a Add the two sides of these equations and use the result to find the value of x.
   b Find the value of y.

3 Here are two simultaneous equations. $x + 6y = 9$
   $x + 2y = 1$
   a Subtract the two sides of the equations and use the result to find the value of y.
   b Find the value of x.

4 Here are two simultaneous equations. $3x + 2y = 38$
   $x - 2y = 2$
   a Find the value of $4x$.
   b Find the values of x and y.

Will you add or subtract to eliminate y?

5 Solve these simultaneous equations. Use any method you wish.
   a $2x + y = 22$ **b** $y = 2x - 12$ **c** $2x + y = 0$
   $x - y = 5$ $x + y = 3$ $x + 2y = 12$

13.5 Trial and improvement

Look at these three equations.

- **$2x + 3 = 28$**

The solution of this equation is $x = (28 - 3) \div 2 = 12.5$

- **$x^2 + 3x = 28$**

You cannot solve this by rearranging the terms. One way to solve it is to try different values of x.

A solution is $x = 4$ because $4^2 + (3 \times 4) = 16 + 12 = 28$

- **$x^2 + 3x = 36$**

Again, you cannot solve this by rearranging the terms. Try different values of x.

If $x = 4$, $x^2 + 3x = 28$	This is too small.
If $x = 5$, $x^2 + 3x = 5^2 + (3 \times 5) = 40$	This is too large.

Try a value between 4 and 5. Try $x = 4.5$.

If $x = 4.5$, $x^2 + 3x = 4.5^2 + (3 \times 4.5) = 33.75$	This is too small.

Try a value between 4.5 and 5. Try 4.6.

If $x = 4.6$, $x^2 + 3x = 4.6^2 + (3 \times 4.6) = 34.96$	This is too small.

Try 4.7

If $x = 4.7$, $x^2 + 3x = 4.7^2 + (3 \times 4.7) = 36.19$	This is too large.

This method is called **trial and improvement**.

You try to get closer and closer to the exact answer.

The table on the right gives answers closer and closer to 36.

4.65 was chosen because it is halfway between 4.6 and 4.7.

The exact answer is between 4.68 and 4.69.

The answer, to one decimal place, is 4.7.

x	value	
4	28	too small
5	40	too large
4.5	33.75	too small
4.6	34.96	too small
4.7	36.19	too large
4.65	35.5725	too small
4.68	35.9424	too small
4.69	36.0661	too large

Worked example 13.5

Use trial and improvement to find a positive solution to the equation $x(x - 2) = 60$.
Give the answer correct to one decimal place.

x	$x(x - 2)$	
6	$6 \times 4 = 24$	too small
8	$8 \times 6 = 48$	too small
9	63	too large
8.8	59.84	too small
8.9	61.41	too large
8.85	60.6225	too large

The table shows the values tried.

It is a good idea to put the results in a table.

The value of x is between 8 and 9. It is closer to 9.

The value of x is between 8.8 and 8.9.

8.8 is closer than 8.9.

The solution, to one decimal place, is $x = 8.8$.

 **Exercise 13.5**

1   Find the exact positive solution of each of these equations.
  a $x^2 + x = 30$ **b** $x^2 + 4x = 140$ **c** $x^3 - x = 60$ **d** $x(x + 6) = 91$

2   Work out a positive solution of each of these equations by trial and improvement.
  a $x^2 + x = 3.75$ **b** $x^2 - 2x = 19.25$ **c** $x^3 + x = 95.625$ **d** $x(x + 1)(x + 2) = 1320$

3   **a** Copy this table.
      Put in the value of $x^2 - 3x$ when $x = 6$.
  b Use trial and improvement to find a solution of the equation $x^2 - 3x = 16$.
      Record your trials in the table. Add more rows if you need them.
      Give the answer correct to one decimal place.

x	$x^2 - 3x$
5	10
6	

4   The table shows values of $w^2 - 6w$.
    Use the table to find a solution to each of these equations.
    Give each answer correct to one decimal place.
  a $w^2 - 6w = 7$ **b** $w^2 - 6w = 9$ **c** $w^2 = 6w + 10$

w	$w^2 - 6w$
7	7
7.1	7.81
7.2	8.64
7.3	9.49
7.4	10.36

5   Use trial and improvement to find a solution of the equation $2a^2 + a = 30$.
    Start with $a = 4$. Record your trials in a table.
    Give your answer correct to one decimal place.

6   Use trial and improvement to find a positive solution of the equation $5x + x^2 = 40$.
    Record your trials in a table.
    Give your answer correct to one decimal place.

7   **a** Read what Jake says. Show that he correct.

$x^2 + 10x = 150$ has a solution between 8 and 9.

  b Find the solution to Jake's equation, correct to one decimal place.

8   Use trial and improvement to find a solution of the equation $x^2(x + 1) = 6$.
    Record your trials in a table.
    Give your answer correct to one decimal place.

9   Use trial and improvement to find a solution of the equation $y^3 + y^2 = 100$.
    Give your answer correct to one decimal place.

10 The equation $10x - x^2 = 20$ has two solutions.
  a One solution is between 2 and 3. Use trial and improvement to find it.
      Give the answer correct to one decimal place.
  b The other solution is between 7 and 8. Find this, correct to one decimal place.

13.6 Inequalities

Here is an equation: $2x + 3 = 10$

To solve it, first subtract 3. $2x = 7$

Then divide by 2. $x = 3.5$

Now here is an **inequality**. $2x + 3 < 10$

You can solve an inequality in the same way as an equation.

First subtract 3. $2x < 7$

Then divide by 2. $x < 3.5$

The **solution set** is any value of x less than 3.5. You can show this on a number line.

> Remember: < means 'less than'.

The open circle (○) shows that 3.5 is <u>not</u> included.

You need to know the four inequality signs in the box.

< less than
> more than
≤ less than or equal to
≥ more than or equal to

Worked example 13.6

The perimeter of this triangle is at least 50 cm.
a Write an inequality to show this.
b Solve the inequality.
c Show the solution set on a number line.

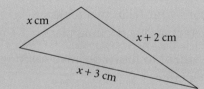

a $3x + 5 \geq 50$

b $3x \geq 45$

   $x \geq 15$

c

'At least 50' means '50 or more'.
Subtract 5 from both sides.
Divide both sides by 3.
The closed circle (●) shows that 15 <u>is</u> in the solution set.

◆ **Exercise 13.6**

1 Write down an inequality to describe each of these solution sets.

a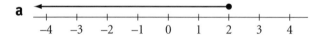

b

c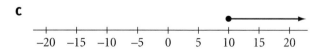

d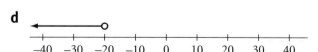

2 Show each of these solution sets on a number line.
   a $x > 3$ **b** $x \leq -3$ **c** $x < 0$ **d** $x \geq -20$

3 *N* is an integer. Work out:
a the smallest possible value of *N* if $N \geq 6.5$
b the largest possible value of *N* if $N < -3$
c the possible values of *N* if $N \geq -2$ and $N < 2$

4 Solve these inequalities.
a $5x > 7$ **b** $4x + 1 \leq 15$ **c** $3x + 1 < -6$ **d** $3(x + 1) \geq -6$

5 Show each solution set in question **4** on a number line.

 6 You are given that $z > 2$.
Write an inequality for each expression.
a $2z + 9$ **b** $3(z - 4)$ **c** $4 + 2z$ **d** $5(3z - 2)$

7 Solve these inequalities.
a $2(a + 4) < 15$ **b** $3b - 4 \geq b + 18$ **c** $c + 18 \leq 30 - c$ **d** $3(d + 5) > 2(d - 6)$

 8 The perimeter of this triangle is not more than 30 cm.
a Write an inequality to show this.
b Solve the inequality.
c What are the largest possible lengths of the sides?

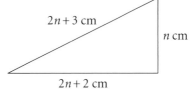

9 The diagram shows four angles round a point.
a Write an inequality for *x*.
b Solve the inequality.
c Explain why the angle labelled $x°$ cannot be a right angle.

 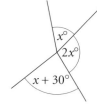

Summary

You should now know that:

★ Linear equations can be solved by algebraic manipulation, doing the same thing to each side of the equation.

★ Number problems can be solved by setting up equations and solving them.

★ Two equations with two unknowns are called simultaneous equations. They can be solved by eliminating one variable.

★ Some equations cannot easily be solved by algebraic manipulation. Solutions can be found by systematic trial and improvement.

★ Linear inequalities can be solved in a similar way to linear equations.

You should be able to:

★ Construct and solve linear equations with integer coefficients (with and without brackets, negative signs anywhere in the equation, positive or negative solution); solve a number problem by constructing and solving a linear equation.

★ Solve a simple pair of simultaneous linear equations by eliminating one variable.

★ Understand and use inequality signs ($<$, $>$, $\leq$, $\geq$); construct and solve linear inequalities in one variable; represent the solution set on a number line.

★ Use systematic trial and improvement methods to find approximate solutions of equations such as $x^2 + 2x = 20$.

 ★ Manipulate numbers, algebraic expressions and equations, and apply routine algorithms.

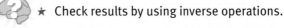 ★ Check results by using inverse operations.

End-of-unit review

1 Solve these equations.
   a $15 + 10x = 105$ **b** $10x - 105 = 15$ **c** $10(15 + x) = 105$ **d** $15 - 10x = 105$

2 Solve these equations.
   a $6m - 5 = 2m + 29$ **b** $6(m - 5) = 2(m + 29)$ **c** $6m - 5 = 29 - 2m$

3 The lengths in the diagram are in centimetres.
   The square and the rectangle have perimeters of the same length.
   a Write an equation to show this.
   b Solve the equation.
   c Find the length of the rectangle.

4 Read Zalika's number problem.

> I am thinking of a number, N.
> Twice $(N + 10)$ is the same as four times $(N - 10)$.

   a Write down an equation to show this.
   b Solve the equation to find the value of N.

5 Solve these simultaneous equations.
   a $x + y = 24$ **b** $2x + y = 100$ **c** $x + y = 26$
       $y = 2x$ $y = 2(x - 10)$ $3x + y = 56$

6 The sum of two numbers is 100.
   The difference between the two numbers is 95.
   Work out the two numbers.

7 The equation $3x + x^2 = 60$ has a solution between 5 and 10.
   Use trial and improvement to find the solution, correct to one decimal place. Show your trials.

8 Solve these inequalities.
   a $4x + 12 \geq 40$ **b** $3(x + 8) \leq 12$ **c** $5x - 14 > 3x + 15$

9 Show the solution sets from question **8** on a number line.

10 The lengths of the sides of this hexagon are in metres.
   a The perimeter is less than 50 metres. Write an inequality for this.
   b Solve the inequality.
   c If x is an integer, find its largest possible value.

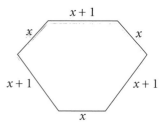

11 $x + 5.5 = 0$
   State whether these statements are true or false.
   a $2(x + 3) \leq -5$ **b** $3 - 2x > 12$ **c** $x^2 + x < 24.75$

Every musical note has a frequency. This is measured in hertz (Hz).

The frequency tells you how many times a string playing that note will vibrate every second.

This table shows the frequency of some of the notes in the musical scale, rounded to one decimal place.

Note	C	D	E	F	G	A	B	C^1
Frequency (Hz)	261.6	293.7	329.6	349.2	392.0	440.0	493.9	523.3

There are very simple ratios between the frequencies of some of these notes.

Frequency of C^1 : frequency of C = 2 : 1 because $523.3 \div 261.6 = 2.00$ or $\frac{2}{1}$ or 2 : 1

Frequency of G : frequency of C = 3 : 2 because $392.0 \div 261.6 = 1.50$ or $\frac{3}{2}$ or 3 : 2

Frequency of A : frequency of D = 3 : 2 because $440.0 \div 293.7 = 1.50$ or $\frac{3}{2}$ or 3 : 2

Frequency of A : frequency of E = 4 : 3 because $440.0 \div 329.6 = 1.33$ or $\frac{4}{3}$ or 4 : 3

The frequencies of G and C are in the same proportion as the frequencies of A and D; they both have the same ratio, 3 : 2.
Can you find some other ratios from the table that are equal to 3 : 2?

The frequencies of A and E are in the ratio 4 : 3.
Can you find some other pairs of notes in the same proportion, with a ratio of 4 : 3?

Can you find any notes where the frequencies are in the ratio 5 : 4?

When the ratio of the frequencies is 2 : 1, one note is an octave higher than the other.
C^1 is an octave higher than C.
Can you find the frequency of D^1, which is an octave higher than D? What about other notes?
Can you find the frequency of the note that is an octave **lower** than C?

In this unit you will compare ratios, and interpret and use ratios in a range of contexts. You will also solve problems involving direct proportion and learn how to recognise when two quantities are in direct proportion.

14.1 Comparing and using ratios

You see ratios used in a variety of situations, such as mixing ingredients in a recipe or sharing an amount among several people.

Ratios can also be used to make <u>comparisons</u>.

For example, suppose you wanted to compare two mixes of paint.

Pink paint is made from red and white paint in a certain ratio (red : white).

If two shades of pink paint have been mixed from red and white in the ratios $3:4$ and $2:3$, which shade is darker?

The best way to compare ratios is to write each ratio in the form $1:n$, where n is a number.

Then you can compare the ratios by comparing the values of n.

Worked example 14.1

Pablo mixes two shades of pink paint in the ratios of red : white paint, as shown opposite.
a Which shade of pink paint is darker?
b When Pablo mixes *Perfect pink* paint, he uses 4 litres of red paint. How much white paint does he use?
c Pablo makes 12 litres of *Rose pink* paint. How much white paint does he use?

Perfect pink	3:4
Rose pink	2:3

a *Perfect pink* *Rose pink*
   red : white   red : white

$\div 3 \overset{3:4}{\underset{1:1.\dot{3}}{\Big(\quad\Big)}} \div 3$ $\div 2 \overset{2:3}{\underset{1:1.5}{\Big(\quad\Big)}} \div 2$

First, write each ratio in the form $1:n$.
Divide 3 and 4 by 3 to get the ratio $1:1.333...$ or $1.\dot{3}$.
Divide 2 and 3 by 2 to get the ratio $1:1.5$.

$1.5 > 1.\dot{3}$, so there is more white in *Rose pink* than in *Perfect pink*.
This means that *Perfect pink* is darker.

Perfect pink is darker.

b red : white =
$\times 4 \overset{1:1.\dot{3}}{\underset{4:5.\dot{3}}{\Big(\quad\Big)}} \times 4$

First, write out the ratio of red : white in the form $1:n$.

Multiply both sides of the ratio by 4, as he uses 4 litres of red.

He uses $5\frac{1}{3}$ litres of white paint.

The answer is $5.\dot{3}$ which you can write as $5\frac{1}{3}$.

c Total number of parts = 2 + 3 = 5
$12 \div 5 = 2.4$ litres per part

First, work out the total number of parts.
Share the 12 litres into 5 equal parts to find the value of one part.

White = $3 \times 2.4 = 7.2$ litres

White has three out of the five parts, so multiply 2.4 litres by 3.

Exercise 14.1

1 Sanjay mixes two shades of blue paint in the following ratios of blue : white.
   a Write each ratio in the form $1:n$.
   b Which shade of blue paint is darker?

Sky blue 3:5   *Sea blue* 4:7

2 Angelica mixes a fruit drink using mango juice and orange juice in the ratio $2:5$.
Shani mixes a fruit drink using mango juice and orange juice in the ratio $5:11$.

  a Write each ratio in the form $1:n$.

  b Whose fruit drink has the higher proportion of orange juice?

3 In the Seals swimming club there are 13 girls and 18 boys.

  a Write the ratio of girls:boys in the form $1:n$.

  In the Sharks swimming club there are 17 girls and 23 boys.

  b Write the ratio of girls:boys in the form $1:n$.

  c Which swimming club has the higher proportion of boys?

4 When Marco makes a cake he uses sultanas and cherries in the ratio $5:2$.
Marco used 80 g of cherries when he made a cake last week.
What mass of sultanas did he use?

5 When Jerry makes concrete he uses cement, sand and gravel in the ratio $1:2:4$.
For one job he used 15 kg of sand.

  a How much cement and gravel did he use?

  b What is the total mass of the concrete he made?

6 The table shows the child-to-staff ratios in a kindergarten. It also shows the number of children in each age group.
At the kindergarten there are four rooms, one for each age group in the table.
What is the total number of staff that are needed to look after the children in this kindergarten?

Age of children	Child : staff ratios	Number of children
up to 18 months	3:1	10
18 months up to 3 years	4:1	18
3 years up to 5 years	8:1	15
5 years up to 7 years	14:1	24

7 This is part of Hassan's homework.
Use Hassan's method to check your answers to the questions below.

  a Purple gold is made from gold and aluminium in the ratio $4:1$.
A purple gold bracelet has a mass of 65 g.
What is the mass of the aluminium in the necklace?

  b Pink gold is made from silver, copper and gold in the ratio $1:4:15$.
A pink gold necklace has a mass of 80 g.
What is the mass of the copper in the necklace?

Question Red gold is made from gold and copper in the ratio 3:1.
A red gold necklace has a mass of 56 g.
What is the mass of the gold in the necklace?

Answer 3 + 1 = 4 parts
56 ÷ 4 = 14 g per part
Mass of gold = 3 × 14 = 42 g
Check: copper = 1 × 14 = 14 g,
so total = 42 + 14 = 56 g ✓

  c White gold is made from gold, palladium, nickel and zinc in the ratio $15:2:2:1$.
A white gold ring has a mass of 12 g.
What is the mass of the gold in the ring?

14.2 Solving problems

You already know that two quantities are in direct proportion when their ratios stay
the same as they increase or decrease. For example, when you buy a bottle of milk, the
more bottles you buy, the more it will cost you.

The two quantities, number of bottles and total cost, are in direct proportion.

When you own a car, the value of the car decreases each year that you own it.

So, as the number of years increases the value of the car decreases.

The two quantities, number of years and value of car, are not in direct proportion.

Worked example 14.2

a Are these quantities in direct proportion?
 i the cost of fuel and the number of litres bought
 ii the age of a house and the value of the house
b 12 sausages have a mass of 1.5 kg.
 What is the mass of 16 sausages?
c A 500 g box of cereal costs \$3.20. A 200 g box of the same cereal costs \$1.30.
 Which box is better value for money?
d When Greg went to Spain the exchange rate for dollars to euros was \$1 = €0.76.
 i Greg changed \$200 into euros. How many euros did he get?
 ii Greg changed €19 back into dollars. How many dollars did he get?

a	**i** Yes	The more litres of fuel you buy, the more it will cost. As both quantities increase, the ratio stays the same.
	ii No	As the years go by the value of a house may go up or down. The ratio does not stay the same.
b	1.5 ÷ 12 = 0.125 kg	First, use division to find the mass of one sausage.
	0.125 × 16 = 2 kg	Now use multiplication to find the mass of 16 sausages.
c	500 g box:	Compare the same quantity of cereal to work out which is the better value.
	\$3.20 ÷ 5 = \$0.64/100 g	Divide the cost by 5 to work out the price of 100 g of cereal.
	200 g box:	
	\$1.30 ÷ 2 = \$0.65/100 g	Divide the cost by 2 to work out the price of 100 g of cereal.
	500 g box is better value.	\$0.64 < \$0.65, so the bigger box is better value for money.
d	**i** 200 × 0.76 = €152	Multiply the number of dollars by the exchange rate to convert to euros.
	ii 19 ÷ 0.76 = \$25	Divide the number of euros by the exchange rate to convert to dollars.

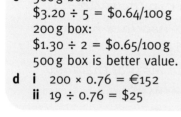
Exercise 14.2

1 Are these quantities in direct proportion? Explain your answers.
   a the total cost of cartons of orange juice and the number of cartons bought
   b the number of girls in a school and the number of boys in a school
   c the total cost of cinema tickets and the number of tickets bought
   d the distance travelled in a car and the number of litres of fuel used by the car during the journey
   e the number of goals scored by a football team and the number of supporters watching the match
   f the amount of work a person does in a day and the number of cups of coffee they drink

2 Lian delivers leaflets. She is paid $12 for delivering 400 leaflets.
How much is she paid for delivering: **a** 200 leaflets **b** 600 leaflets **c** 150 leaflets?

3 Six packets of biscuits cost $11.40.
a How much do 15 packets of biscuits cost? **b** How much do 7 packets of biscuits cost?

4 A shop sells apple juice in cartons of two sizes.
A 500 ml carton costs $1.30.
a Work out the cost of 250 ml of this apple juice.
A 750 ml carton costs $1.86.
b Work out the cost of 250 ml of this apple juice.
c Which carton is better value for money?

 500 ml $1.30

 750 ml $1.86

5 This is part of Oditi's homework.
She used inverse operations
to check each calculation.
Use Oditi's method to check your
answers to these questions. Show
all your working.

Question A pack of 60 food bags costs $5.40.
A pack of 50 food bags costs $4.25.
Which pack is better value for money?

Answer 5.40 ÷ 6 = $0.90 for 10 bags.
Check: 6 × 0.90 = $5.40
4.25 ÷ 5 = $0.85 for 10 bags.
Check: 5 × 0.85 = $4.25
The pack of 50 bags is better value for money.

a A box of 150 paper towels
costs $2.70.
A box of 250 paper towels
costs $4.75.
Which box gives you better
value for money?
b A 400 g pack of cheese costs
$3.20. A 350 g pack of cheese costs $2.87.
Which pack is better value for money?

6 Carlos travelled between the UK and Spain when the exchange rate
was £1 = €1.18.
a When he went to Spain he changed £325 into euros (€).
How many euros did he get?
b When he went back to the UK he changed €80 into British pounds (£).
How many pounds did he get? Give your answer to the nearest pound.

7 When Adriana travelled to America the exchange rate was €1 = $1.31,
Adriana saw a camera in a shop for $449.
The same camera cost €359 in Madrid.
Where should Adriana buy the camera? Show your working and check your answer.

Summary

You should now know that:

★ The best way to compare ratios is to write each
ratio in the form 1 : n, where n is a number. Then
you can compare the ratios by comparing the
values of n.

★ Two quantities are in direct proportion when their
ratios stay the same as they increase or decrease.

You should be able to:

★ Compare two ratios.

★ Interpret and use ratios in a range of contexts.

★ Recognise when two quantities are directly
proportional.

★ Solve problems involving proportionality.

End-of-unit review

1 Sanjay mixes two shades of green paint in the following ratios of green:white.
   a Write each ratio in the form $1:n$.
   b Which shade of green paint is darker?

Sea green 5:7   Fern green 8:11

2 In 'The Havens' gymnastic club there are 12 boys and 18 girls.
   a Write the ratio of boys:girls in the form $1:n$.
   In 'The Dales' gymnastic club there are 8 boys and 14 girls.
   b Write the ratio of boys:girls in the form $1:n$.
   c Which gymnastic club has the higher proportion of girls?

3 When Maria makes a flan she uses milk and cream in the ratio 3:2.
   Maria used 240 ml of milk for the flan she made yesterday.
   How much cream did she use?

4 Green gold is made from gold and silver in the ratio 3:1.
   A green gold bracelet has mass 56 g.
   a What is the mass of the gold in the necklace?
   b Show how to check your answer to part a.

5 Are these quantities in direct proportion? Explain your answers.
   a the total cost of packets of biscuits and the number of packets bought
   b the number of girls in an athletics club and the number of boys in an athletics club
   c the number of litres of fuel bought and the total cost of the fuel
   d the amount of TV a person watches in a day and the length of time they brush their teeth

6 Eight jars of jam cost $22.
   a How much do 16 jars of jam cost?
   b How much do 5 jars of jam cost?

7 A shop sells jars of coffee in two sizes.
   A 200 g jar costs $6.56.
   a Work out the cost of 100 g of this coffee.
   A 300 g jar costs $9.48.
   b Work out the cost of 100 g of this coffee.
   c Which jar is better value for money?

200 g
$6.56

300 g
$9.48

8 a Jean-Paul travelled from the UK to France when the exchange rate was £1 = €1.16.
      He changed £450 into euros (€).
      How many euros did he get?
      Show your working and check your answer.
   b When he travelled back to the UK from France the exchange rate
      was €1 = £0.84.
      He changed €65 into British pounds (£).
      How many pounds did he get? Give your answer to the nearest pound.
      Show your working and check your answer.

9 Lewis travelled to America when the exchange rate was £1 = $1.58.
   Lewis saw a laptop in a shop for $695.
   The same laptop cost £479 in London.
   Where should Lewis buy the laptop? Show your working and check your answer.

Use this brief summary to remind yourself of the work you have done on area, perimeter and volume.

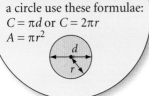

To work out the area (A) and circumference (C) of a circle use these formulae:
$C = \pi d$ or $C = 2\pi r$
$A = \pi r^2$

To work out the area (A) of a triangle use this formula:
$A = \frac{1}{2}bh$

To work out the area (A) of a parallelogram use this formula:
$A = bh$

To work out the area (A) of a trapezium use this formula:
$A = \frac{1}{2} \times (a + b) \times h$

The lengths in this diagram are in centimetres.
Find the area of each part.
The area of the square is $8 \times 8 = 64\,\text{cm}^2$.

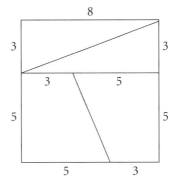

The parts are rearranged to make a rectangle.
The area of the rectangle is $5 \times 13 = 65\,\text{cm}^2$.
It should be $64\,\text{cm}^2$!
Where is the extra $1\,\text{cm}^2$?

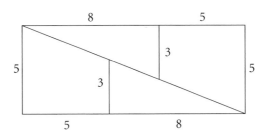

In this unit you will convert metric units of area and of volume. You will also solve problems involving the circumference and area of circles, as well as working with right-angled prisms and cylinders.

15.1 Converting units of area and volume

Before you can convert units of area and volume you need to know the conversion factors.

You have already used conversion factors for units of area. Here is a reminder of how to work them out.

This square has a side length of 1 cm.

The area of the square is 1 cm × 1 cm = 1 cm².

The area of the square is also 10 mm × 10 mm = 100 mm².

This shows that <u>1 cm² = 100 mm²</u>.

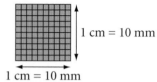

This square has a side length of 1 m.

The area of the square is 1 m × 1 m = 1 m².

The area of the square is also 100 cm × 100 cm = 10 000 cm².

This shows that <u>1 m² = 10 000 cm²</u>.

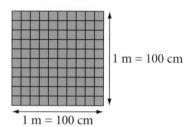

You can use a similar method to work out the conversion factors for volume.

This cube has a side length of 1 cm.

The volume of the cube is 1 cm × 1 cm × 1 cm = 1 cm³.

The volume of the cube is 10 mm × 10 mm × 10 mm = 1000 mm³.

This shows that <u>1 cm³ = 1000 mm³</u>.

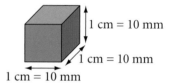

This cube has a side length of 1 m.

The volume of the cube is 1 m × 1 m × 1 m = 1 m³.

The volume of the cube is 100 cm × 100 cm × 100 cm = 1 000 000 cm³.

This shows that <u>1 m³ = 1 000 000 cm³</u>.

You already know that 1 litre = 1000 ml.

You also need to know that <u>1 cm³ = 1 ml</u>.

This means that 1 litre = 1000 cm³.

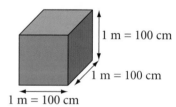

Worked example 15.1

Convert: **a** 6 m² to cm²   **b** 450 mm² to cm²   **c** 5.3 m³ to cm³   **d** 2300 cm³ to litres.

a 1 m² = 10 000 cm²	Write down the conversion factor for m² and cm².
6 × 10 000 = 60 000 cm²	Multiply by 10 000 to convert from m² to cm².
b 1 cm² = 100 mm²	Write down the conversion factor for cm² and mm².
450 ÷ 100 = 4.5 cm²	Divide by 100 to convert from mm² to cm².
c 1 m³ = 1 000 000 cm³	Write down the conversion factor for m³ and cm³.
5.3 × 1 000 000 = 5 300 000 cm³	Multiply by 1 000 000 to convert from m³ to cm³.
d 1 cm³ = 1 ml	Write down the conversion factor for cm³ and millilitres.
2300 cm³ = 2300 ml	Convert from cm³ to ml.
1 litre = 1000 ml	Write down the conversion factor for litres and millilitres.
2300 ÷ 1000 = 2.3 litres	Divide by 1000 to convert from millilitres to litres.

◆ Exercise 15.1

1 Convert:
  a $4\,m^2$ to cm^2 **b** $0.5\,m^2$ to cm^2 **c** $1.65\,m^2$ to cm^2
  d $8\,cm^2$ to mm^2 **e** $0.8\,cm^2$ to mm^2 **f** $12.4\,cm^2$ to mm^2
  g $50\,000\,cm^2$ to m^2 **h** $42\,000\,cm^2$ to m^2 **i** $8000\,cm^2$ to m^2
  j $900\,mm^2$ to cm^2 **k** $760\,mm^2$ to cm^2 **l** $20\,mm^2$ to cm^2.

2 Convert:
  a $7\,m^3$ to cm^3 **b** $0.75\,m^3$ to cm^3 **c** $1.2\,m^3$ to cm^3
  d $3\,cm^3$ to mm^3 **e** $0.4\,cm^3$ to mm^3 **f** $6.35\,cm^3$ to mm^3
  g $6\,000\,000\,cm^3$ to m^3 **h** $350\,000\,cm^3$ to m^3 **i** $12\,300\,000\,cm^3$ to m^3
  j $4000\,mm^3$ to cm^3 **k** $540\,mm^3$ to cm^3 **l** $62\,500\,mm^3$ to cm^3.

3 Convert:
  a $60\,cm^3$ to ml   **b** $125\,cm^3$ to ml   **c** $4700\,cm^3$ to ml
  d $8000\,cm^3$ to litres   **e** $2400\,cm^3$ to litres   **f** $850\,cm^3$ to litres
  g 3 litres to cm^3 **h** 4.2 litres to cm^3 **i** 0.75 litres to cm^3.

4 The shape of Tina's kitchen is a rectangle 925 cm long by 485 cm wide.
  a Work out the area of Tina's kitchen in square metres.
    Show how to use estimation to check your answer.
  Flooring costs $56 per square metre.
  It is only sold in whole numbers of square metres.
  b How much does Tina pay to buy flooring for her kitchen floor?
    Show how to use inverse operations to check your answer.

> **Remember** to use estimation to check your answer; round each number in the question to one significant figure.

5 Li is going to paint a door that measures 195 cm by 74 cm.
  He is going to give it two layers of paint on each side.
  One tin of paint covers $5\,m^2$.
  How many tins of paint does Li need to buy?
  Show how to check your answer.

Covers
5 m²

6 Chin-Mae has a fishtank that measures 75 cm by 45 cm by 35 cm.
  He also has a jug that holds 1.75 litres.
  He uses the jug to fill the fishtank with water.
  How many full jugs of water does it take to fill the fishtank?
  Show how to check your answer.

35 cm
45 cm
75 cm

7 Eloise makes 1.2 litres of salad dressing.
  She stores the salad dressing in jars of two different sizes, as shown.
  Each jar has a square base.
  She fills the jars to the heights shown.
  a Work out the volume of the large jar.
  Eloise works out that she can fill at least 10 large jars with salad dressing.
  b Without actually calculating the number of large jars
    that Eloise can fill, explain whether you think
    this is a reasonable answer or not.
  Eloise wants to store the dressing in a mixture of large
  and small jars.
  c What is the best way for Eloise to do this?

Large jar
Small jar
12 cm
16 cm
2.5 cm
3.5 cm

15.2 Using hectares

You may need to measure areas of land. You use **hectares** to do this.

A hectare is the area of a square field, of side 100 metres.

A football pitch is about half a hectare.

The abbreviation for hectare is ha.

You need to know this conversion.

> 1 hectare (ha) = 10 000 m²

> ### Worked example 15.2
>
> **a** Copy and complete these statements. **i** 2.4 ha = ☐ m²   **ii** 125 000 m² = ☐ ha
> **b** A rectangular piece of land measures 850 m by 1.4 km.
>   Work out the area of the land. Give your answer in hectares.
>
> **a** **i** 2.4 × 10 000 = 24 000   Multiply the number of hectares by 10 000 to convert to square metres.
>   2.4 ha = 24 000 m²
> **ii** 125 000 ÷ 10 000 = 12.5   Divide the number of square metres by 10 000 to convert to hectares.
>   125 000 m² = 12.5 ha
>
> **b** 1.4 km = 1400 m   First, find the area of the land in square metres. Then change the answer
>   to hectares. Start by converting 1.4 km to metres.
>   area = 850 × 1400   Then work out the area of the land.
>   = 1 190 000 m²   This answer is in square metres.
>   1 190 000 ÷ 10 000 = 119 ha   Divide by 10 000 to convert square metres into hectares.

> ### ◆ Exercise 15.2

1 Copy and complete these conversions.
    a 3 ha = ☐ m²   **b** 4.6 ha = ☐ m²   **c** 0.8 ha = ☐ m²
    d 12.4 ha = ☐ m²   **e** 0.75 ha = ☐ m²   **f** 0.025 ha = ☐ m²

2 Copy and complete these conversions.
    a 50 000 m² = ☐ ha   **b** 89 000 m² = ☐ ha   **c** 240 000 m² = ☐ ha
    d 1500 m² = ☐ ha   **e** 900 m² = ☐ ha   **f** 1 265 000 m² = ☐ ha

3 A rectangular piece of land measures 780 m by 550 m.
    Work out the area of the land in: **a** square metres   **b** hectares.

4 A farmer has an L-shaped field.
    The dimensions of the field are shown in the diagram.
    a Work out the area of the field, in hectares.
    The farmer sells the field for $3950 per hectare.
    b How much money does the farmer receive?
    c Show how to use estimation to check your answer.

5 A company wants to build a theme park.
    The diagram shows a plan of the land it wants to buy.
    The company wants to pay no more than $16 million
    for the land.
    The price of the land is $5120 per hectare.
    Can the company afford to buy the land?
    Show all your working and use estimation to check your answer.

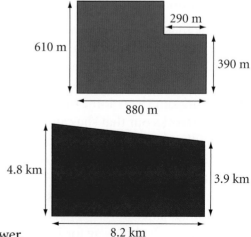

15.3 Solving circle problems

When you used the formulae for the circumference and area of a circle, you took the value of π as 3.14. Every scientific calculator has a 'π' button. The value given by the 'π' button on a calculator is more accurate than 3.14. Try it out. What do you notice? Using the 'π' button will give a more accurate answer.

When you solve circle problems, use the 'π' button on your calculator and make sure you use the correct formulae for circumference and area.

Circumference:	$C = \pi d$ or $C = 2\pi r$
Area:	$A = \pi r^2$

Worked example 15.3

Use the 'π' button on the calculator. Give all answers correct to one decimal place (1 d.p.).
a Work out the area and circumference of a circle with diameter 6.8 cm.
b Work out the area and perimeter of a semicircle with radius 7 m.
c A circle has circumference 12 mm. What is the diameter of the circle?
d A circle has area 24 cm². What is the radius of the circle?

a $r = 6.8 \div 2 = 3.4$ cm   Divide the diameter by 2 to work out the radius.
$A = \pi r^2 = \pi \times 3.4^2$ Write down the formula for the area and substitute the value for r.
  $= 36.3$ cm² (1 d.p.)   Write the answer correct to one decimal place.
$C = \pi d = \pi \times 6.8$ Write down the formula for the circumference and substitute the value for d.
  $= 21.4$ cm (1 d.p.)   Write the answer correct to one decimal place.

b 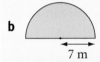   It is often helpful to draw a diagram to help you answer the question. In this case, draw a semicircle and mark on the radius 7 m.

Area $= \dfrac{\pi r^2}{2}$ The area of a semicircle is half the area of a circle. Write down the formula,

  $= \dfrac{\pi \times 7^2}{2}$ then substitute in the value for r.

  $= 77.0$ m² (1 d.p.)   Write the answer correct to one decimal place.

Perimeter $= \dfrac{2\pi r}{2} + 2r$ The perimeter of a semicircle is half the circumference of the circle plus the

  $= \dfrac{2 \times \pi \times 7}{2} + 2 \times 7$ diameter of the circle. Write down the formula and substitute the value for r. Write the answer correct to one decimal place.

  $= 36.0$ m (1 d.p.)

c $C = \pi d$, so $12 = \pi \times d$ Write down the formula for the circumference and substitute the value for C.
$d = \dfrac{12}{\pi}$ Rearrange the equation to make d the subject, then work out the answer.
  $= 3.8$ mm (1 d.p.)   Write the answer correct to one decimal place.

d $A = \pi r^2$, so $24 = \pi \times r^2$ Write down the formula for the area and substitute the value for A.
$r^2 = \dfrac{24}{\pi}$ Rearrange the equation to make r^2 the subject, then work out the value of r^2.

$r^2 = 7.639\,437\,268$ Write down the full value of r^2. You must only round the final value for r.
$r = \sqrt{7.639\,437\,268}$ Rearrange the equation to make r the subject, then work out the answer.
$r = 2.8$ cm (1 d.p.)   Write the final answer correct to one decimal place.

◆ **Exercise 15.3**

Throughout this exercise use the 'π' button on your calculator.

1 Work out the area and the circumference of each circle.
Give your answers correct to one decimal place (1 d.p.).
a radius = 8 cm **b** radius = 15 cm **c** radius = 3.5 m
d diameter = 12 cm **e** diameter = 9 m **f** diameter = 25 mm

2 Work out the area and the perimeter of each semicircle.
Give your answers correct to two decimal places (2 d.p.).
a radius = 6 cm **b** radius = 10 cm **c** radius = 4.5 m
d diameter = 18 cm **e** diameter = 24 mm **f** diameter = 3.6 m

3 Work out the diameter of each circle.
Give your answers correct to the nearest whole number.
a circumference = 56.5 cm **b** circumference = 78.5 mm **c** circumference = 40.84 m
d circumference = 6.28 m **e** circumference = 283 mm **f** circumference = 201 cm

4 Work out the radius of each circle.
Give your answers correct to one decimal place.
a area = 238 cm^2 **b** area = 117 cm^2 **c** area = 19.6 m^2
d area = 6.16 m^2 **e** area = 254 mm^2 **f** area = 486.8 cm^2

 5 A circular ring has a circumference of 5.65 cm.
Work out the radius of the ring.
Give your answer correct to the nearest millimetre.

 6 The area of a circular pond is 21.5 m^2.
Work out the diameter of the circle.
Give your answer correct to the nearest centimetre.

 7 The circumference of a circular disc is 39 cm.
Work out the area of the disc.
Give your answer correct to the nearest square centimetre.

 8 Work out the areas of each compound shape.
Give your answers correct to two decimal places.

a

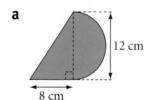

12 cm

8 cm

b

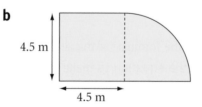

4.5 m

4.5 m

c

28 mm   28 mm

d

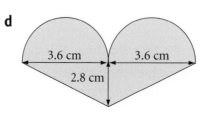

3.6 cm   3.6 cm

2.8 cm

15.4 Calculating with prisms and cylinders

A **prism** is a 3D shape that has the same **cross-section** along its length.

Here are some examples of prisms. The cross-section of each one is shaded.

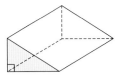

Cross-section is a right-angled triangle.

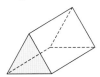

Cross-section is an equilateral triangle.

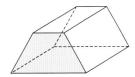

Cross-section is a trapezium.

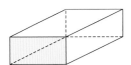

Cross-section is rectangle.

You can work out the <u>volume</u> of a prism using the formula:

volume = area of cross-section × length

You can work out the <u>surface area</u> of a prism by finding the total area of all the faces of the prism.

Worked example 15.4a

a Work out the volume of each prism.

b A prism has a volume of 91 cm³.
The area of the cross-section is 13 cm².
What is the length of the prism?

c Work out the surface area of this prism.

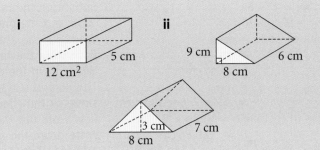

a i V = area of cross-section × length
    = 12 × 5
    = 60 cm³

The diagram shows the area of the cross-section of the cuboid. Substitute the area and length into the formula for the volume. Work out the answer and remember the units, cm³.

ii Area of triangle = $\frac{1}{2}$ × base × height

First, work out the area of the cross-section of the prism.

    = $\frac{1}{2}$ × 8 × 9

Substitute base and height measurements in the area formula.

    = 36 cm²

Work out the answer and remember the units, cm².

V = area of cross-section × length
    = 36 × 6
    = 216 cm³

Now work out the volume of the prism, by substituting the area and length into the volume formula. Work out the answer and remember the units, cm³.

b V = area of cross-section × length

Write down the formula for the volume of a prism.

91 = 13 × l

Substitute the volume and the area in the formula.

$l = \frac{91}{13}$

Rearrange the equation to make l the subject.

l = 7 cm

Work out the answer and remember the units, cm.

c Area of triangle = $\frac{1}{2}$ × base × height

First, work out the area of the triangular face.

    = $\frac{1}{2}$ × 8 × 3

Substitute base and height measurements in the area formula.

    = 12 cm²

Work out the answer.

Area of base = 8 × 7 = 56 cm²
Area of sloping side = 5 × 7 = 35 cm²
Surface area = 2 × 12 + 56 + 2 × 35
    = 150 cm²

The base is a rectangle, so work out the area (length × width). The side is a rectangle, so work out the area (length × width). Now work out the total area. There are two triangular faces, one base and two sloping sides. Remember the units, cm².

A cylinder is also a prism. The cross-section is a circle.

The formula for the area of a circle is: $\boxed{A = \pi r^2}$

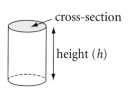

The formula for the volume of a prism is: $\boxed{\text{volume} = \text{area of cross-section} \times \text{length}}$

So the formula for the volume of a cylinder is: $\boxed{\text{volume} = \pi r^2 \times \text{height}}$

or simply $\boxed{V = \pi r^2 h}$

Worked example 15.4b

a Work out: **i** the volume
ii the surface area of this cylinder.

b A cylinder has volume $552.2\,\text{cm}^3$. The radius of the circular end is $5.2\,\text{cm}$.
What is the height of the cylinder? Give your answer in centimetres.

a i $V = \pi r^2 h$	Write down the formula for the volume of a cylinder.
$= \pi \times 3^2 \times 8$	Substitute the radius and height measurements in the formula.
$= 226.2\,\text{cm}^3$	Work out the answer and remember the units, cm^3.
ii Area of circle $= \pi r^2$	Work out the area of one of the circular ends.
$= \pi \times 3^2$	Substitute the radius measurement in the formula.
$= 28.27\,\text{cm}^2$	Write down the answer, correct to at least two decimal places.
$C = 2\pi r$	The curved surface of a cylinder is a rectangle with length the
$= 2 \times \pi \times 3 = 18.85\,\text{cm}$	same as the circumference of the circle. Work this out first.
Area of rectangle $= 18.85 \times 8$	Now work out the area of the curved surface (length × height).
$= 150.80\,\text{cm}^2$	Write down the answer, correct to at least two decimal places.
Total area $= 2 \times 28.27 + 150.80$	Add together the area of the two ends and the curved surface.
$= 207.3\,\text{cm}^2$	Write down the final answer, correct to one decimal place.
b $\quad V = \pi r^2 h$	Write down the formula for the volume of a cylinder.
$552.2 = \pi \times 5.2^2 \times h$	Substitute the volume and radius in the formula.
$h = \dfrac{552.2}{\pi \times 5.2^2}$	Rearrange the formula to make h the subject.
$= 6.5\,\text{cm}$	Work out the answer and remember the units, cm.

◆ Exercise 15.4

1 Work out the volume of each prism.

a

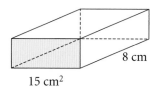

b

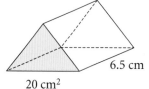

c

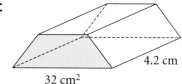

2 Copy and complete this table.

	Area of cross-section	Length of prism	Volume of prism
a	$12\,\text{cm}^2$	$10\,\text{cm}$	$\square\,\text{cm}^3$
b	$24\,\text{cm}^2$	$\square\,\text{cm}$	$204\,\text{cm}^3$
c	$\square\,\text{m}^2$	$6.2\,\text{m}$	$114.7\,\text{m}^3$

3 Work out the volume and surface area of each prism.

a
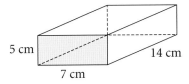
5 cm
14 cm
7 cm

b
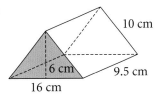
10 cm
6 cm
9.5 cm
16 cm

c
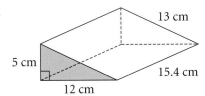
13 cm
5 cm
15.4 cm
12 cm

4 Work out the volume and surface area of each cylinder.
Give your answers correct to one decimal place (1 d.p.).

a
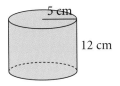
5 cm
12 cm

b
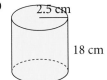
2.5 cm
18 cm

c
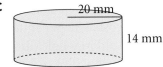
20 mm
14 mm

5 Copy and complete this table. Give your answers correct to two decimal places (2 d.p).

	Radius of circle	Area of circle	Height of cylinder	Volume of cylinder
a	2.5 m	☐ m²	4.2 m	☐ m³
b	6 cm	☐ cm²	☐ cm	507 cm³
c	☐ m	20 m²	2.5 m	☐ m³
d	☐ mm	☐ mm²	16 mm	1044 mm³

6 Each of these prisms has a volume of 256 cm³.
Work out the length marked x in each diagram. Give your answers correct to one decimal
place (1 d.p.).

a
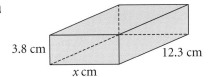
3.8 cm
12.3 cm
x cm

b
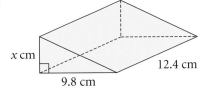
x cm
12.4 cm
9.8 cm

c
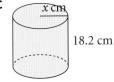
x cm
18.2 cm

Summary

You should now know that:

★ 1 cm² = 100 mm²   1 m² = 10 000 cm²
 1 cm³ = 1000 mm³   1 m³ = 1 000 000 cm³
 1 cm³ = 1 ml

★ 1 hectare = 10 000 m²

★ A prism is a 3D shape that has the same cross-section along its length.

★ Volume of a prism = area of cross-section × length

★ Surface area of a prism = sum of the areas of all the faces

★ Volume of a cylinder = $\pi r^2 h$

You should be able to:

★ Convert between metric units of area and volume; know and use the relationship 1 cm³ = 1 ml.

★ Know that land area is measured in hectares (ha); convert between hectares and square metres.

★ Solve problems involving the circumference and area of circles, including by using the 'π' button on a calculator.

★ Calculate lengths, surface areas and volumes in right-angled prisms and cylinders.

End-of-unit review

1 Convert:
  a 5 m² to cm²
  b 40 000 cm² to m²
  c 9 cm² to mm²
  d 820 mm² to cm²
  e 9 m³ to cm³
  f 24 500 000 cm³ to m³
  g 7 cm³ to mm³
  h 270 mm³ to cm³
  i 80 cm³ into ml
  j 450 ml to cm³
  k 9000 cm³ to litres
  l 3.6 litres to cm³.

2 The shape of Greg's study is a rectangle 575 cm long by 325 cm wide.
  a Work out the area of Greg's study in square metres.
    Show how to use estimation to check your answer.
  Flooring costs $52 per square metre.
  It is only sold in whole numbers of square metres.
  b How much will it cost Greg to buy flooring for his study?
    Show how to use inverse operations to check your answer.

3 Copy and complete these statements.
  a 3 ha = □ m²
  b 4.6 ha = □ m²
  c 0.8 ha = □ m²
  d 20 000 m² = □ ha
  e 94 000 m² = □ ha
  f 5600 m² = □ ha

4 The radius of a circle is 7 cm.
  Work out: **a** the area   **b** the circumference of the circle.
  Give your answers correct to one decimal place. Use the 'π' button on your calculator.

5 The circumference of a circle is 21.4 cm. Work out the diameter of the circle.
  Give your answer correct to the nearest whole number. Use the 'π' button on your calculator.

6 The area of a circle is 36.3 cm². Work out the radius of the circle.
  Give your answer correct to one decimal place. Use the 'π' button on your calculator.

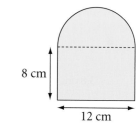

7 A compound shape is made from a rectangle and a semicircle.
  Work out:
  a the area   **b** the perimeter of the compound shape.
  Give your answers correct to one decimal place.
  Use the 'π' button on your calculator.

8 cm

12 cm

8 Work out the volume of each prism.

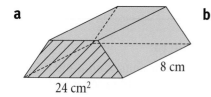

a

8 cm

24 cm²

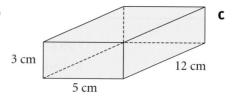

b

3 cm

5 cm

12 cm

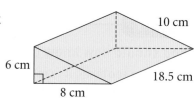

c

10 cm

6 cm

8 cm

18.5 cm

9 Work out the surface area of the prisms in parts **b** and **c** of question **8**.

10 Work out the volume and surface area of this cylinder.
  Give your answers to the nearest whole number.

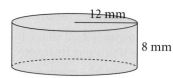

12 mm

8 mm

11 A cylinder has volume 1000 cm³ and height 11.8 cm.
  What is the radius of the cylinder? Give your answer correct to one decimal place.

On Sunday 3 June 2012 there was a Jubilee Pageant in London. 1000 boats travelled down the River Thames through the city of London.

The pageant was held to celebrate the fact that Queen Elizabeth II had been on the throne for 60 years.

The pageant started at 14:30 and lasted about 3 hours.

The chart below shows a weather forecast for London on that day.

City of Londen Youth Hostel
Sun 3 Jun

UK local time	Regional warnings	Weather	Temperature (°C)	Wind speed & direction (mph)	Wind gusts (mph)	Visibility	Humidity (%)	Precipitation Probability (%)	Feels like (°C)	UV index	Air Quality index [BETA]
0100	No warnings		10	11	24	Moderate	91	80	8	0	
0400	No warnings		10	12	26	Moderate	95	80	8	0	
0700	No warnings		10	11	24	Moderate	95	80	7	1	
1000	No warnings		10	10	No gusts	Moderate	93	80	8	1	2
1300	No warnings		10	8	No gusts	Moderate	94	80	8	1	
1600	No warnings		10	7	No gusts	Moderate	92	80	8	1	
1900	No warnings		10	6	No gusts	Moderate	91	60	8	1	
2200	No warnings		9	5	No gusts	Moderate	93	60	8	0	

Issued at 0900 on Fri 1 Jun 2012

The forecast was made on Friday morning, two days before the pageant. It predicted the weather every two hours through the day.

One column show the probability of precipitation – that means rain or snow.

The probability is given as a percentage.

The forecast reported an 80% chance of heavy rain during the pageant. It advised that the thousands of spectators should take umbrellas. There should be no gusts of wind during the pageant.

Weather forecasts are produced by complex computer programs. They are available for thousands of places throughout the world. They are updated regularly. You can easily find them on the internet. Try to find one for a place near where you live.

On the day of the pageant it was dry until about 16:00. After that it rained steadily. There were no gusts of wind.

In this unit, you will learn more about predicting probabilities.

16.1 Calculating probabilities

When a football team play a match, they can win, draw or lose.

These are **mutually exclusive** outcomes. This means that if one outcome happens, the others cannot.

These three are all the possible outcomes. One of them must happen.

The probabilities of all the mutually exclusive outcomes add up to 1.

Worked example 16.1

The probability that City will win its next football match is 0.65.
The probability City will draw is 0.2. Work out the probability that City will:
a not win   **b** win or draw   **c** lose.

a $1 - 0.65 = 0.35$ If the probability of an outcome is p, the probability it will <u>not</u> occur is $1 - p$.
b $0.65 + 0.2 = 0.85$ The two outcomes are mutually exclusive so add the probabilities.
c $1 - (0.65 + 0.2) = 0.15$ The probabilities for win, draw and lose add up to 1.

◆ Exercise 16.1

1 The temperature each day can be average, above average or below average.
Work out the probability that the temperature will be:
a below average   **b** not above average   **c** not below average.

> The probability that tomorrow's temperature will be average is 60%. The probability that the temperature will be above average is 35%.

2 When Sasha throws two dice, the probability of her scoring two sixes is $\frac{1}{36}$. The probability of her scoring one six is $\frac{5}{18}$.
Find the probability of Sasha scoring: **a** at least one six   **b** no sixes.

3 Mia spins a coin until she gets a head. The probability she needs just one spin is $\frac{1}{2}$. The probability she needs two spins is $\frac{1}{4}$. The probability she needs three spins is $\frac{1}{8}$. Work out the probability that she needs:
a more than one spin   **b** more than two spins   **c** more than three spins.

4 This table shows the probability that a train will be late.
a Work out the missing probability.
b Find the probability that the train is: **i** not early   **ii** not late.

Outcome	Early	On time	Less than 5 minutes late	At least 5 minutes late
Probability	0.10	0.74	0.12	

5 A teacher is setting a test for the class next week. These are the probabilities for the day of the test.

Day	Monday	Tuesday	Wednesday	Thursday	Friday
Probability	10%	20%	45%	15%	

Work out the probability that the test will be on:
a Monday or Tuesday   **b** Wednesday or Thursday   **c** Friday.

16.2 Sample space diagrams

When you throw a fair dice there are six equally likely outcomes: 1, 2, 3, 4, 5 or 6.

When you spin a fair coin there are two equally likely outcomes: heads (H) and tails (T).

When you throw the dice and the coin together, there are 12 possible outcomes.

You can show all possible outcomes in a **sample space diagram**.

Each mark (+) shows one outcome. They are all equally likely.

To find the probability of a particular outcome, look for all the possible ways of achieving it.

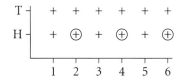

This diagram shows the outcomes for 'a head and an even number'.

The probability of scoring a head and an even number is $\frac{3}{12} = \frac{1}{4}$.

Worked example 16.2

One fair spinner has three sections marked with the numbers 1, 2 and 3.

Another fair spinner has five sections marked with the numbers 1, 2, 3, 4 and 5.

a Draw a sample space diagram to show all the possible outcomes.

b Work out the probability of scoring: **i** two 2s   **ii** two odd numbers   **iii** a total of 5.

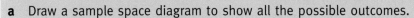

a

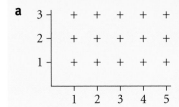

b i $\frac{1}{15}$

ii $\frac{6}{15} = \frac{2}{5}$

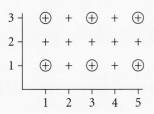

iii $\frac{3}{15} = \frac{1}{5}$

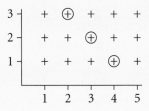

◆ **Exercise 16.2**

1 Xavier throws a coin and a six-sided dice at the same time.
   a Draw a sample space diagram to show all the possible outcomes.
   b On your diagram, circle points that show a tail and an odd number.
   c Work out the probability of his scoring:
      i an odd number   **ii** a tail and an odd number   **iii** <u>not</u> a tail and <u>not</u> an odd number.

2 This is a sample space diagram for two dice thrown at the same time. Work out the probability of both dice showing:
   a 5 or more   **b** 4 or more   **c** 3 or more.

3 Draw a probability space diagram for two dice being thrown together. Use your diagram to find the probability of scoring:
   a two odd numbers   **b** two even numbers
   c one odd number and one even number.

4 This is the sample space diagram for the scores on two spinners.
   a Write down the numbers on each spinner.
   b Both spinners are fair. Find the probability of scoring:
      i two odd numbers   **ii** at least one 3   **iii** 2 or less on both spinners.

5 a Draw a sample space diagram for these two spinners.
   b Find the probability of scoring:
      i two even numbers   **ii** two odd numbers
      iii a total of 5   **iv** a total of more than 5.

6 There are four girls and three boys in a group. Their names are shown in the sample space diagram. One girl and one boy are chosen at random. Find the probability that:
   a Maha is <u>not</u> chosen   **b** Shen is <u>not</u> chosen.
   c <u>neither</u> Maha <u>nor</u> Shen is chosen.

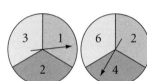

7 A computer chooses two random digits. Each digit can be 0, 1, 2, 3, 4, 5, 6, 7, 8 or 9.
   a Show the possible choices on a sample space diagram.
   b Find the probability that:
      i both digits are 7   **ii** at least one digit is 7   **iii** neither digit is 7   **iv** both digits are odd.

8 Anders throws a 10-faced dice with numbers from 1 to 10. Then he spins a coin.
   a Draw a sample space diagram to show all the possible outcomes.
   b Find the probability of scoring: **i** a head and a multiple of 3   **ii** a tail and a prime number.

9 Tanesha chooses one letter at random from the word DEAR. Dakarai chooses one letter at random from the word ROAD.
   a Draw a sample space diagram to show all the possible outcomes.
   b Find the probability that:
      i both choose R   **ii** at least one chooses R
      iii both choose the same letter   **iv** they each choose different letters.

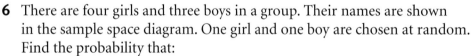

16.3 Using relative frequency

Have you ever used drawing pins to fix notices to boards?

If you drop a drawing pin it can land point up or point down.

Point up   Point down

However, you <u>cannot</u> assume these outcomes are both equally likely.

You can <u>estimate</u> the probability that a drawing pin will land point up by dropping it a number of times and finding the **relative frequency**. The more times you drop it, the better the estimate will be.

If you cannot use equally likely outcomes to work out a probability, you can use relative frequency.

Worked example 16.3

Xavier does a survey of the number of passengers in cars passing his school in the morning.

Number of passengers	1	2	3	4	5 or more
Frequency	42	28	7	12	4

Estimate the probability that the number of passengers is: **a** 2   **b** more than 2.

a The number of cars is 93. $42 + 28 + 7 + 12 + 4 = 93$
The relative frequency is $\frac{28}{93}$.
The probability is 0.30 (2 d.p.). $28 \div 93 = 0.3010...$ It is sensible to round this to two decimal places.
b The relative frequency is $\frac{23}{93}$. $7 + 12 + 4 = 23$
The probability is 0.25 (2 d.p.) $23 \div 93 = 0.2473...$ Give the estimated probability as a decimal.

◆ Exercise 16.3

1 Look again at the table in Worked example 16.3.
   Estimate the probability of there being: **a** 1 passenger   **b** 1 or 2 passengers.

2 Each of the faces on a cardboard cube is a different colour. Hassan throws the cube 150 times and records the colour on the top. The results are shown in the table.
   Estimate the probability of getting:
   a black   **b** red, white or blue   **c** neither black nor white.

Score	Red	Blue	Yellow	Green	White	Black
Frequency	29	17	33	15	25	31

3 This table shows the heights of some plants grown from seed.
   A plant is picked at random. Estimate the probability that the height will be:
   a less than 5 cm   **b** 10 cm or more.

Height (cm)	0–	5–	10–	15–20
Frequency	6	25	11	3

4 In 2009 in the UK 781 000 women gave birth.
   12 595 had twins. 172 had triplets. Five had four or more babies.
   Estimate the probability of having: **a** twins   **b** one baby.

Twins means 2 babies.

Triplets means 3 babies.

5 Two types of rechargeable battery are tested to see how long they will last.

Time (hours)	Up to 5	At least 5 but less than 10	At least 10 but less than 15	At least 15 but less than 20
Battery A	6	12	16	12
Battery B	18	20	15	12

a For each type of battery, estimate the probability that it lasts:
  i 15 hours or more   **ii** less than 10 hours.
b Which battery lasts longer? Give a reason for your answer.

6 A shop sells three makes of computer. This table shows how many were faulty within one year.

Make	Solong	HQ	Tooloo
Number sold	420	105	681
Faulty within one year	28	19	32

  a Estimate the probability that each make will be faulty.
  b The shop started to stock a new brand, called Dill computers. It sold 63, but 7 were faulty within a year. How does this make compare to the others?

7 Lynn planted three packets of seeds. The table shows how many germinated.

Packet of seeds	Type A	Type B	Type C
Number of seeds	24	38	19
Number that germinated	17	21	16

A seed germinates when it starts to grow.

Which type is the most likely to germinate? Give a reason for your answer.

8 In archery you score up to 10 points for each arrow. In a competion you shoot 60 arrows. The table shows the results for one competitor.

Score	10	9	8	Fewer than 8
First 20 arrows	8	5	5	2
Last 40 arrows	27	4	5	4

  a Find the probability of scoring 9 or 10, using:
    i the first 20 arrows   **ii** all 60 arrows.
  b Did the competitor become more accurate as the competition went on? Give a reason for your answer.

Summary

You should now know that:
- ★ If outcomes are mutually exclusive then only one of them can happen.
- ★ If a list of mutually exclusive outcomes covers all possible cases, then the probabilities add up to one.
- ★ You cannot always find probabilities by using equally likely outcomes.
- ★ You can use relative frequency to estimate probability.

You should be able to:
- ★ Know that the sum of probabilities of all mutually exclusive outcomes is 1 and use this when solving probability problems.
- ★ Record and find all outcomes for two successive events in a sample space diagram.
- ★ Understand relative frequency as an estimate of probability and use this to compare outcomes of experiments in a range of contexts.
- ★ Check results by considering whether the answer is reasonable in the context of the problem.

End-of-unit review

1 Six coins are spun together. There can be up to six heads.
The table shows the probabilities of different numbers
of heads.
Find the probability of scoring fewer than:
a 6 heads **b** 5 heads **c** 4 heads.

Number of heads	6	5	4
Probability	0.02	0.09	0.23

2 Mia throws five dice.
The table shows the probabilities for the number of sixes.
Find the probability of scoring:
a at least 1 six **b** at least 2 sixes **c** more than 2 sixes.

Number of sixes	0	1	2
Probability	0.40	0.40	0.16

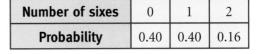

3 Two identical spinners have five sections numbered 1, 2, 3, 4 and 5.
  a Draw a sample space diagram.
  b Find the probability that the difference between the numbers is:
    i 0 **ii** 1 **iii** 2.
  c Find the probability that the product of the numbers is:
    i more than 9 **ii** less than 9 **iii** equal to 9.

4 Zalika spins a coin and throws a dice with eight faces numbered from 1 to 8.
  a Draw a sample space diagram.
  b Find the probability of scoring:
    i a head and an even number
    ii a tail and a prime number
    iii a head but not an 8.

5 Ahmad has two attempts to score a basket in
basketball. He tries this 25 times. The table
shows the results.
  a Find the probability that Ahmad will score:
    i two baskets **ii** at least one basket.
  Hassan gets these results from 40 tries.
  b Find the probability that Hassan scores at at least
    one basket.
  c Who is better? Give a reason for your answer.

Baskets scored	2	1	0
Frequency	10	8	7

Baskets scored	2	1	0
Frequency	20	15	5

Here are some drawings and pictures.

Each one has a different scale.

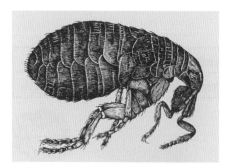

Key words

Make sure you learn and understand this key word:

bearing

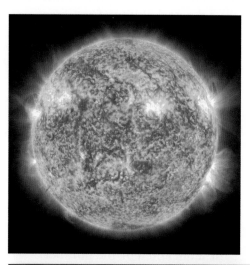

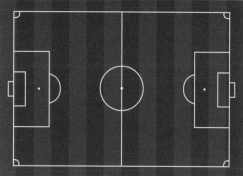

Estimate what length 1 cm represents on each one.

Here are some clues to help you.

- The length of a flea is between 2 and 3 mm.
- The diameter of the Sun is about 1 400 000 km.
- The length of Africa from north to south is about 8000 km.
- A football pitch is about 100 m long.

In this unit you will practise making and using scale drawings. You will also look at how scales are used in maps. The skill of working out real-life distances between places shown on a map is very useful. It enables you to estimate the distance to travel and how long it will take you. You will also learn about bearings. These are important in map reading. They give the angle of travel, from one place to another.

17.1 Using bearings

A **bearing** describes the direction of one object from another.

It is an angle measured from <u>north</u> in a <u>clockwise</u> direction.

A bearing can have any value from 0° to 360°. It is always written with three figures.

In this diagram the bearing from A to B is 120°. 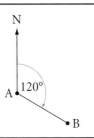	In this diagram the bearing from A to B is 065°. 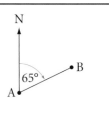

Worked example 17.1

The diagram shows three towns, A, B and C.
a   Write down the bearing of B from A.
b   Write down the bearing from A to C.
c   Write down the bearing of B from C.

A•

•B

C •

a   Draw a north arrow from A, and a line joining A to B. Measure the angle from the north arrow clockwise to the line joining A to B.

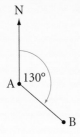

The bearing is 130°.

b   Draw a north arrow from A, and a line joining A to C. Measure the angle from the north arrow clockwise to the line joining A to C.

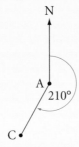

The bearing is 210°.

c   Draw a north arrow from C, and a line joining C to B. Measure the angle from the north arrow clockwise to the line joining C to B.

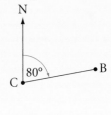

The bearing is 080°.

◆ Exercise 17.1

1   For each diagram, write down the bearing of B from A.

a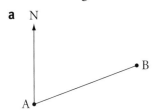

b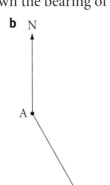

c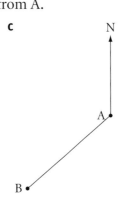

d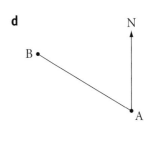

2 The diagram shows the positions of a shop and a school.
   a Write down the bearing of the shop from the school.
   b Write down the bearing of the school from the shop.

3 Ahmad goes for a walk.
The diagram shows the initial position of Ahmad (A), a farm (F), a pond (P), a tree (T) and a waterfall (W).
Write down the bearing that Ahmad follows to walk from:
   a A to F   **b** F to P
   c P to T   **d** T to W
   e W to A.

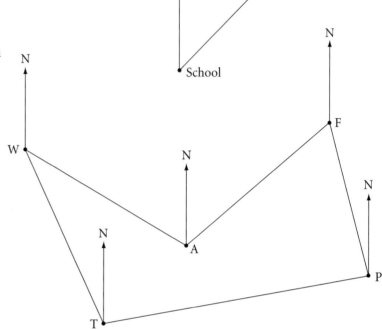

4 **a** For each diagram, write down the bearing of Y from X and X from Y.

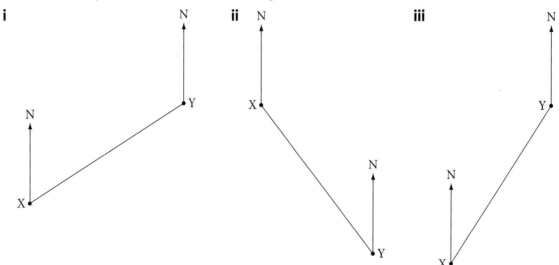

   b Draw two different diagrams of your own, plotting two points X and Y.
      In each diagram, the bearing of Y from X must be less than 180°.
      For each of your diagrams write down the bearing of Y from X and of X from Y.
   c What do you notice about each pair of answers you have given in parts **a** and **b**?
   d Copy and complete this rule for two points X and Y, when the bearing of Y from X is less than 180°.
      When the bearing of Y from X is $m°$, the bearing of X from Y is ____°.

5 This is part of Dakarai's homework.

Question   i *Write down the bearing of B from A.*
           ii *Work out the bearing of A from B.*

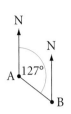

Answer   i *Bearing of B from A is 127°.*
        ii *Bearing of B from A is 180° + 127° = 307°.*

Dakarai knows that any two north arrows are always parallel so he uses alternate angles to work out the bearing of A from B.
For each of these diagrams:
i   write down the bearing of B from A
ii   work out the bearing of A from B.

a   **b** 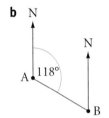   **c**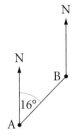

6 This is part of Harsha's homework.

Question   i *Write down the bearing of P from Q.*
           ii *Work out the bearing of Q from P.*

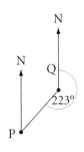
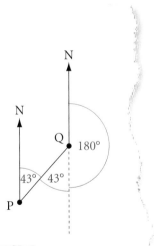

Answer   i *Bearing of P from Q is 223°.*
        ii *Bearing of Q from P is 223° - 180° = 043°.*

Harsha uses alternate angles to work out the bearing of Q from P.
For each of these diagrams:
i   write down the bearing of P from Q
ii   work out the bearing of Q from P.

a 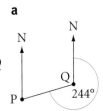   **b** 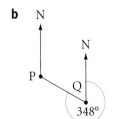   **c**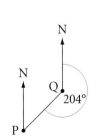

17.2 Making scale drawings

You can use bearings in scale drawings to help you solve problems. When you make a scale drawing, always measure all the lengths and angles accurately.

Scales are also used on maps. Maps often have scales such as 1 : 50 000 or 1 : 800 000. When you convert between a distance on a map and the actual distance you need to convert between units such as centimetres and kilometres.

> The scale on a map is often much bigger than the scale on a scale drawing, because maps represent areas that are very big, such as countries.

Worked example 17.2

a A ship leaves harbour and sails 120 km on a bearing of 085°. It then sails 90 km on a bearing of 135°.
   i Make a scale drawing of the ship's journey. Use a scale of '1 cm represents 10 km'.
   ii How far and on what bearing must the ship now sail to return to the harbour?

b A map has a scale of 1 : 50 000.
   i On the map a footpath is 12 cm long. What is the length, in kilometres, of the footpath in real life?
   ii In real life a road is 24 km long. What is the length, in centimetres, of the road on the map?

a i

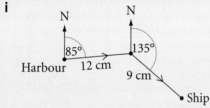

First, draw a north arrow and measure a bearing of 085°.
120 ÷ 10 = 12, so draw a line 12 cm long to represent the first part of the journey. Now draw another north arrow at the end of the first line, and measure a bearing of 135°. 90 ÷ 10 = 9, so draw a line 9 cm long to represent the second part of the journey.

ii

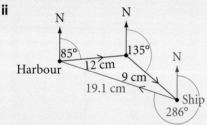

Draw a straight line joining the ship to the harbour and measure the length of the line, in centimetres.
Multiply by the scale to work out the distance the ship has to sail.
Draw a north arrow from the position of the ship and measure the angle, to give the bearing on which the ship needs to sail to return to the harbour.

Distance: 19.1 × 10 = 191 km
Bearing: 286°

b i 12 × 50 000 = 600 000 cm
600 000 cm ÷ 100 = 6000 m
6000 m ÷ 1000 = 6 km

Multiply by the scale to get the real-life distance in centimetres.
Divide by 100 to convert from centimetres to metres.
Divide by 1000 to convert from metres to kilometres.

ii 24 km × 1000 = 24 000 m
24 000 m × 100 = 2 400 000 cm
2 400 000 ÷ 50 000 = 48 cm

Multiply the real-life distance by 1000 to convert from kilometres to metres, then by 100 to convert from metres to centimetres. Divide by the scale to get the distance on the map, in centimetres.

◆ **Exercise 17.2**

1 A ship leaves harbour and sails 80 km on a bearing of 120°. It then sails 100 km on a bearing of 030°.
   a Make a scale drawing of the ship's journey. Use a scale where 1 cm represents 10 km.
   b How far must the ship now sail to return to the harbour?
   c What bearing must the ship now sail on, to return to the harbour?

2 Mark leaves his tent and walks 12 km on a bearing of 045°.
He then walks 16 km on a bearing of 275°.

   a Make a scale drawing of Mark's walk.
Use a scale where 1 cm represents 2 km.

   b How far must Mark now walk to return to his tent?

   c On what bearing must Mark now walk to return to his tent?

3 Jun lives 8 km south of Yue.
Jun leaves home and walks 6 km to a lake.
She walks on a bearing of 070°.
Yue leaves home and walks to meet Jun at the lake.
How far, and on what bearing, must she walk?

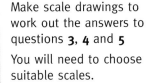

Make scale drawings to work out the answers to questions **3**, **4** and **5**
You will need to choose suitable scales.

4 A yacht is 70 km west of a speedboat.
The yacht sails on a bearing of 082°.
The speedboat travels on a bearing of 252°.
Could the yacht and the speedboat collide? Explain your answer.

5 A lighthouse is 85 km north of a port.
The captain of a ship knows he is on a bearing of 145° from the lighthouse.
He also knows he is on a bearing of 052° from the port.

   a How far is the ship from the lighthouse?

   b How far is the ship from the port?

6 A map has a scale of 1 : 50 000.

   a On the map, a footpath is 9 cm long. What is the length, in kilometres, of the footpath in real life?

   b In real life a road is 18 km long. What is the length, in centimetres, of the road on the map?

7 Alicia is participating in a charity sailing race on the Mar Menor.
The map shows the route she takes.
The map has a scale of 1 : 250 000.

   a What is the total distance that Alicia sails?

   Alicia earns €56 for charity, for every kilometre she sails.

   b What is the total amount that Alicia raises for charity?

Summary

You should now know that:

★ A bearing gives the direction of one object from another. It is an angle measured from north in a clockwise direction.

★ A bearing can have any value from 000° to 360°. It must always be written with three figures.

You should be able to:

★ Use bearings to solve problems involving distance and direction.

★ Make and use scale drawings and interpret maps.

End-of-unit review

1 For each diagram, write down the bearing of B from A.

a 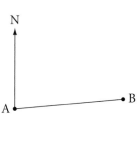   **b** 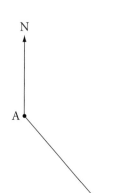   **c** 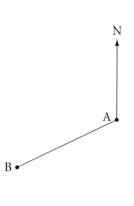   **d**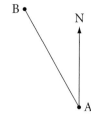

2 For each diagram:
   i write down the bearing of Q from P
   ii work out the bearing of P from Q.

a 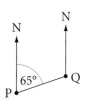   **b** 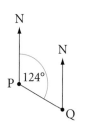   **c** 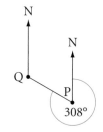   **d**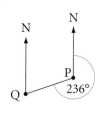

3 A ship leaves harbour and sails 90 km on a bearing of 140°. It then sails 120 km on a bearing of 050°.
   a Make a scale drawing of the ship's journey. Use a scale where 1 cm represents 10 km.
   b How far must the ship now sail to return to the harbour?
   c On what bearing must the ship now sail to return to the harbour?

 4 Sion lives 12 km north of Amir.
   Sion leaves home and cycles 18 km to Newtown.
   He cycles on a bearing of 145°.
   Amir leaves home and cycles to meet Sion at Newtown.
   How far, and on what bearing does he cycle?

5 A map has a scale of 1 : 25 000.
   a On the map a footpath is 22 cm long. What is the length, in km, of the footpath in real life?
   b In real life a road is 14 km long. What is the length, in cm, of the road on the map?

 6 Rhodri takes part in a charity cycle ride.
   The table shows the distances, on the map, between
   consecutive checkpoints on the cycle route.
   The map has a scale of 1 : 500 000.
   Rhodri raises $24 for charity for every kilometre he cycles.
   What is the total amount that Rhodri raises for charity?

Checkpoints	Distance on map (cm)
Start to A	3.4
A to B	5.6
B to C	4.7
C to Finish	2.3

18 Graphs

What can you say about the equation $y = 0.5x + 5$?

You should recognise it as the equation of a straight line.

To draw the line you need to find some points. Start with a table of values.

x	−20	−15	−10	−5	0	5	10	15	20
$0.5x + 5$	−5	−2.5	0	2.5	5	7.5	10	12.5	15

Key words

Make sure you learn and understand these key words:

gradient
coefficient
direct proportion

Now you can plot these points on a graph and draw a straight line through them.

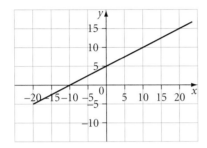

But what would you use a linear graph for?

Here are some practical examples.

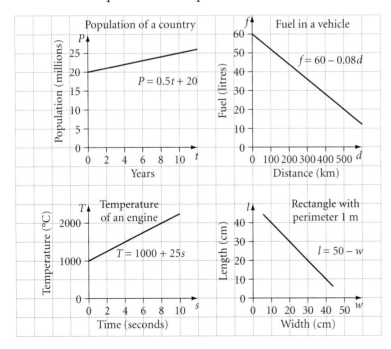

From these, you can see that the variables do not have to be x and y. You can use any letters.

In this unit you will learn more about interpreting, drawing and using all sorts of graphs.

18.1 Gradient of a graph

Look at these two straight-line graphs.

Both lines are sloping, but one is steeper than the other.

The steepness of a graph is described by its **gradient**.

To find the gradient of the line, you can draw a right-angled triangle.

Use part of the line itself as the hypotenuse, and position the triangle so that its other two sides are on the coordinate grid lines.

Find the difference between the x-coordinates and the y-coordinates of the endpoints of the line segment you have used.

The gradient is: $\dfrac{\text{change in } y}{\text{change in } x}$.

The gradient of line 1 is $\dfrac{2}{3}$.

The gradient of line 2 is $\dfrac{-4}{2} = -2$.

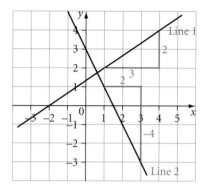

> The gradient of line 2 is negative because it goes <u>down</u> from left to right.

Worked example 18.1

A straight-line graph goes through the points (0, 5) and (6, 2). Find the gradient of the graph.

Plot the points and draw the line.

Draw a triangle.

The gradient is $-\dfrac{3}{6} = -\dfrac{1}{2}$.

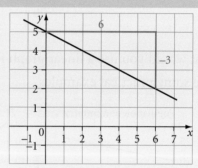

◆ **Exercise 18.1**

1 Calculate the gradients of line **a** and line **b**.

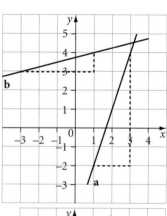

2 Work out the gradients of lines **a**, **b** and **c**.

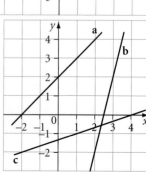

3 Work out the gradients of lines **a**, **b** and **c**.

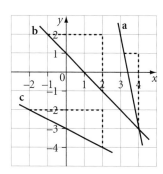

> The gradients are negative.

4 Work out the gradients of lines **p**, **q** and **r**.

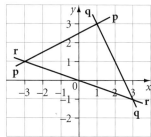

5 a Show that the gradient of line **d** is 2.5.
  b Find the gradients of lines **e** and **f**.

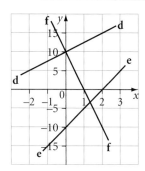

> Look at the numbers on the axes.

6 Work out the gradients of lines **a**, **b** and **c**.

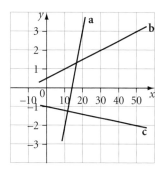

7 A straight line goes through the points $(-4, 2)$, $(2, 5)$ and $(4, 6)$.
  a Draw the line on a grid.
  b Find the gradient of the line.

8 Find the gradient of the straight line through each set of points.
  a $(3, -4)$, $(6, 2)$ and $(4, -2)$ **b** $(3, 6)$, $(-6, -3)$ and $(-3, 0)$
  c $(-1, -6)$, $(-4, 6)$ and $(-3, 2)$ **d** $(5, 3)$, $(2, 3)$ and $(-4, 3)$

> Plot the points on a graph.

9 Find the gradient of the straight line through each set of points.
  a $(0, 0)$, $(2, 12)$ and $(-5, -30)$ **b** $(10, 0)$, $(5, 20)$ and $(0, 40)$
  c $(10, 0)$, $(9, -12)$ and $(12, 24)$ **d** $(-10, 10)$, $(0, 11)$ and $(5, 11.5)$

18.2 The graph of $y = mx + c$

The graph shows three straight lines.

The gradient of each line is $\frac{1}{2}$.

The equations of the lines are: $y = \frac{1}{2}x$ $y = \frac{1}{2}x + 3$ $y = \frac{1}{2}x - 2$

The equations are in the form $y = mx + c$, where m and c are numbers.

The **coefficient** of x is m. It is the gradient of the line.

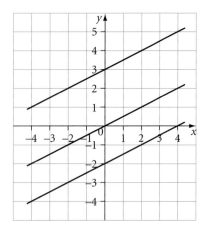

Worked example 18.2

a   Find the gradient of the line with the equation $y = 5x - 15$.
b   Find the gradient of the line with the equation $y = -3x - 15$.

The gradient is 5   The coefficient of x is 5.
The gradient is –3   The coefficient of x is –3.

◆ **Exercise 18.2**

1   **a**   Draw the straight line with the equation $y = 1.5x$.
    b   On the same grid, draw the line with equation $y = 1.5x + 2.5$.
    c   On the same grid, draw the line with equation $y = 1.5x - 3$.
    d   Find the gradient of each line.

2   Find the gradients of the lines with these equations.
    a $y = 2x + 5$ **b** $y = -2x + 5$ **c** $y = 3x + 5$ **d** $y = -3x - 5$

3   Below are the equations of four straight lines.
    A: $y = 4x + 10$ B: $y = 10x - 4$ C: $y = 4x - 4$ D: $y = -10x + 4$
    Write down the letters of:
    a   two parallel lines   **b**   a line that passes through $(0, 10)$
    c   two lines that pass through $(0, -4)$ **d**   a line with a negative gradient.

4   The equation of a straight line is $y = 6x - 4$.
    a   Find the equation of a line, parallel to this, that passes through the origin $(0, 0)$.
    b   Find the equation of a line, parallel to this, that passes through the point $(0, 8)$.

5   Find the gradients of the lines with these equations.
    a $y = 5x + 2$ **b** $y = 5 + 2x$ **c** $y = -5x + 2$ **d** $y = 5 - 2x$

6   Below are the equations of five lines.
    A: $y = 2x + 3$ B: $y = 3 - 2x$ C: $y = 2x - 3$ D: $y = -3 - 2x$ E: $y = -2x + 2$
    Which lines are parallel?

18.3 Drawing graphs

This is the equation of a straight-line graph. $y = -2x + 3$

The gradient of the straight line is -2.

You can write the equation in different ways.

Change the order.	$y = 3 - 2x$
Add $2x$ to both sides.	$y + 2x = 3$
Change the order.	$2x + y = 3$
Subtract 3 from both sides.	$2x + y - 3 = 0$

These are all different ways to write the equation of the line.

Worked example 18.3

The equation of a line is $2y - 3x + 4 = 0$.
a Show that this is the equation of a straight line.   **b** Find its gradient.   **c** Draw a graph of the line.

a $2y + 4 = 3x$ Add $3x$ to both sides.
    $2y = 3x - 4$ Subtract 4 from both sides.
     $y = 1.5x - 2$ Divide both sides by 2.
    This is the equation of a straight line.   It is in the form $y = mx + c$.

b The gradient is 1.5. m is the gradient.

c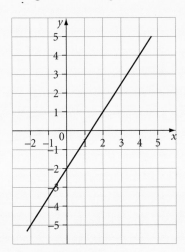

Make a table of values.
Three points are enough.

x	0	4	-2
$1.5x - 2$	-2	4	-5

Exercise 18.3

1 Write these equations in the form $y = mx + c$.
   a $x + y = 10$ **b** $2x + y = 10$ **c** $x + 2y = 10$ **d** $2x + 4y = 10$

2 A graph has the equation $2x - y = 5$.
   a Show that this is the equation of a straight line.
   b Find the gradient of the line.
   c Draw a graph of the line.

3 A graph has the equation $x + 2y + 4 = 0$.
  a Show that this is the equation of a straight line.
  b Find the gradient of the line.
  c Draw a graph of the line.

4 a Show that the equation of this line is $2x + 3y = 24$.
  b Find the gradient of the line.

5 a Write each of these equations in the form $y = mx + c$.
  i $x - y + 6 = 0$ **ii** $2x - 3y + 6 = 0$
  b Draw the graph of each line.
  c Find the gradient of each line.

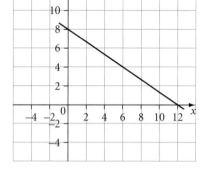

6 Match each equation to the correct line.
  a $x + 2y = 8$
  b $x - 2y = 8$
  c $y + 2x = 8$
  d $2y - x = 8$

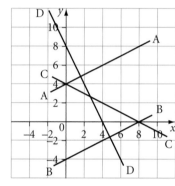

7 a Write $x + 4y = 40$ in the form $y = mx + c$.
  b Which line has the equation $x + 4y = 40$?
  c Find the equations of the other two lines.

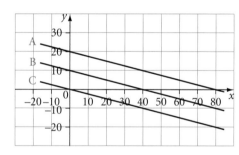

8 a Rewrite these equations in the form $y = mx + c$.
  i $20x = 2y + 15$ **ii** $x = 20y + 60$
  b Find the gradient of each line in part **a**.
  c Draw the graph of each line.

Choose a sensible scale for each axis.

9 The equation of line A is $x = 20y$.
  a Find the gradient of line A.
  b Find the coordinates of point P.
  c Find the equation of line B.

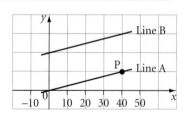

10 a Draw a graph of each of these lines. Use the same set of axes.
    Your graphs must show where each line crosses the axes.
    i $5x + 2y = 100$ **ii** $2x + 5y = 100$
  b Find the gradient of each line.
  c Where do the lines cross?

Choose the same scale on each axis.

18.4 Simultaneous equations

Here is a pair of equations. $y = 0.5x + 4$ $y = 2.5x - 3$

In Unit 13 you learnt how to use algebra to solve these simultaneously.

You can write: $0.5x + 4 = 2.5x - 3$

Subtract $0.5x$ from both sides: $4 = 2x - 3$

Add 3 to both sides: $7 = 2x$

Divide both sides by 2: $x = 3.5$

Find y by substitution: $y = 0.5x + 4 = 0.5 \times 3.5 + 4 = 5.75$

You can also use a graph to solve equations like these.

Worked example 18.4

a Draw a graph of the lines with equations $y = 0.5x + 4$ and $y = 2.5x - 3$.
b Use your graph to solve the equations $y = 0.5x + 4$ and $y = 2.5x - 3$ simultaneously.

a

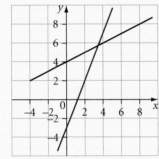

Start with a table of values
Choose at least three values for x.

x	0	2	4
$0.5x + 4$	4	5	6
$2.5x - 3$	−3	2	7

b The lines cross at approximately (3.5, 5.8).
The approximate solution is $x = 3.5$ and $y = 5.8$.
The solution may not be exact because it is
based on a graph.

Exercise 18.4

1 The graph shows the lines with equations $y = 2x - 2$,
$y = x - 4$ and $y + x = 4$.
Use the graph to solve these pairs of equations simultaneously.
a $y = 2x - 2$ and $y = x - 4$
b $y = 2x - 2$ and $y + x = 4$
c $y = x - 4$ and $y + x = 4$

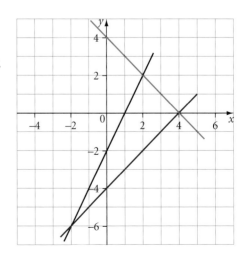

2 Use this graph to solve these pairs of equations simultaneously.

a $y = 2x + 1$ and $y = \frac{1}{2}x - 2$

b $y = 2x + 1$ and $y = -\frac{1}{2}x + 6$

c $y = \frac{1}{2}x - 2$ and $y = -\frac{1}{2}x + 6$

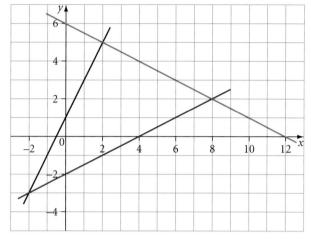

3 a Draw the lines with these equations. Draw all of them on the same grid.

i $y = x - 3$ **ii** $y = 7 - x$ **iii** $y = \frac{1}{2}x + 1$

b Use the graphs to solve these pairs of equations simultaneously.

i $y = x - 3$ and $y = 7 - x$ **ii** $y = x - 3$ and $y = \frac{1}{2}x + 1$ **iii** $y = 7 - x$ and $y = \frac{1}{2}x + 1$

4 Use this graph to find approximate solutions of the following pairs of simultaneous equations.

a $y = 0.5x - 5$ and $y = -1.5x + 30$

b $y = 0.5x - 5$ and $y = -0.67x + 20$

c $y = -0.67x + 20$ and $y = -1.5x + 30$

The solutions are approximate because you are reading them from a graph.

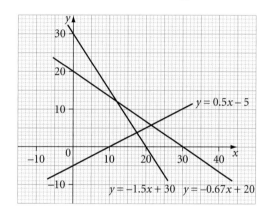

5 Look at these two simultaneous equations. Draw graphs to find approximate solutions. $y = 3x - 2$ $y = \frac{1}{3}x + 4$

6 Look at these two simultaneous equations. Draw graphs to find approximate solutions. $y = \frac{1}{2}x - 3$ $y = -\frac{5}{2}x + 6$

7 a Write the equation $3x + 2y = 12$ in the form $y = mx + c$.

b Write the equation $x + 3y + 3 = 0$ in the form $y = mx + c$.

c Use this graph to solve the equations $3x + 2y = 12$ and $x + 3y + 3 = 0$ simultaneously.

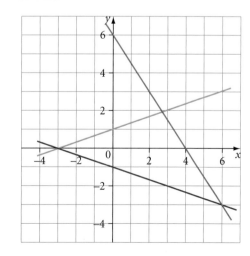

18.5 Direct proportion

When two variables are in **direct proportion**, the graph of the relation is a straight line through the origin.

It is easy to find the equation of the line. Then the equation can be used to find missing values algebraically.

Worked example 18.5

The cost of petrol is $2.85 per litre.
a   Write a formula for the cost in dollars (C) of L litres.
b   Show that the graph of this formula passes through the origin.
c   Use the formula to find the number of litres you can buy for $500.

a $C = 2.85\,L$

Multiply the number of litres by 2.85 to find the cost, in dollars.

b   If $L = 0$ then $C = 0$

The origin is (0, 0).

c $500 = 2.85\,L \rightarrow L = \dfrac{500}{2.85} = 175.44$

Substitute $C = 500$ into the formula and rearrange to find L.

You can buy 175.44 litres.

Exercise 18.5

1   Metal wire costs $6.20 per metre.
   a   Draw a graph to show the cost of up to 10 metres.
   b   Work out the gradient of the graph.
   c   Write down a formula for the cost in dollars (C) of M metres.
   d   Use the formula to find: i the cost of 12.5 metres   ii how many metres you can buy for $200.

2   A photocopier can copy 16 pages per minute.
   a   Write down a formula for the number of pages (p) that can be photocopied in m minutes.
   b   Draw a graph to show the number of pages that can be photocopied in up to 5 minutes.
   c   Work out the gradient of the graph.
   d   Use the formula to find:
      i how many pages can be copied in $7\frac{1}{2}$ minutes   ii the time to photocopy 312 pages.

3   A packet of 500 sheets of paper has mass 2.5 kg.
   a   Find the mass, in grams, of one sheet of paper.
   b   Write down a formula for the mass (m), in grams, of n sheets of paper.
   c   Draw a graph to show the mass, in grams, of up to 500 sheets of paper.
   d   Mia weighs some sheets of paper. The mass is 0.385 kg. How many sheets are there?

4   Greg buys 83 litres of fuel. It costs him $346.11.
   a   Work out the cost of one litre of fuel.
   b   Draw a graph to show the cost of up to 100 litres of fuel.
   c   Write down the gradient of the graph.
   d   How many litres can Greg buy for $500?

18.6 Practical graphs

When you solve a real-life problem, you may need to use a function where the graph is a straight line. In this topic, you will investigate some real-life problems.

Worked example 18.6

The cost of a car is $20 000. The value falls by $1500 each year.
a Write a formula to show the value (V), in thousands of dollars, as a function of time (t), in years.
b Draw a graph of the function.
c When will the value fall to $11 000?

a $V = 20 - 1.5\,t$

When $t = 0$, $V = 20$.
V decreases by 1.5 every time t increases by 1.

b

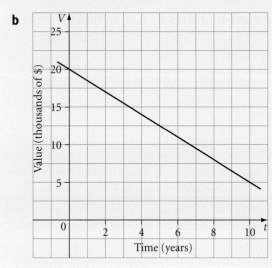

Plot a few values to draw the graph.
Use V and t instead of y and x.
Negative values are not needed.
The gradient is –1.5.

c After 6 years

The value of t when $V = 11$

In the worked example, the gradient is –1.5. This means that the value falls by $1500 dollars each year.

Exercise 18.6

1 A tree is 6 metres high. It grows 0.5 metres each year.
   a Write down a formula to show the height (y), in metres, as a function of time (x), in years.
   b Draw a graph of the formula.
   c Use the graph to find:
      i the height of the tree after 5 years   **ii** the number of years until the tree is 10 metres high.

2 A candle is 30 centimetres long. It burns down 2 centimetres every hour.
   a Write down a formula to show the height (h), in centimetres, as a function of time (t), in hours.
   b Draw a graph to show the height of the candle.
   c Use the graph to find:
      i the height of the candle after 4 hours   **ii** the time until the candle is half its original height.

3 The cost of a taxi is $5 for each kilometre.
   a Write down a formula for the cost (c), in dollars, in terms of the distance (d), in kilometres.
   b Draw a graph to show the cost.
   c Use the graph to find: **i** the cost of a journey of 6.5 kilometres   **ii** the distance travelled for $55.

4 There are six cars in a car park. Every minute another two cars enter the car park. No cars leave.
  a Write down a formula to show the number of cars (y) in the car park after t minutes.
  b Draw a graph to show the number of cars in the car park.
  c Use the graph to find:
    i the number of cars after 5 minutes   **ii** the time before there are 24 cars in the car park.
  d The car park only has spaces for 24 cars. Show this on the graph.

5 Anders has $20 credit on a mobile phone. Each text costs $0.50.
  a Write down a formula for the credit (c), in dollars, after sending t texts.
  b Draw a graph to show the credit.
  c Anders sends 11 texts. How much credit is left?

6 The population of an animal in a wildlife reserve is 8000. The population decreases by 500 each year.
  a Write a formula to show the population (P) as a function of the number of years (Y).
  b Draw a graph to show how the population changes over time.
  c Use your graph to find the population after four years.
  d How long will it be until the population is halved?

7 This graph shows the predicted population of a country.
  a What is the population now?
  b Find the estimated population in 30 years' time.
  c Work out the gradient of the graph.
  d Find a formula for P as a function of t.

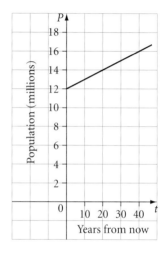

8 Sasha puts $2000 in a bank. The bank pays her $50 every year.
  a Work out a formula for the amount she has in dollars (A) after t years.
  b Draw a graph to show how her money increases.
  c How much does she have after five years?
  d How long is it until she has $2600?

Summary

You should now know that:

★ An equation of the form $y = mx + c$ gives a straight-line graph.

★ The value of m is the gradient of the line. It can be positive or negative.

★ You can use graphs to solve simultaneous equations.

★ Real-life problems can give rise to straight-line graphs.

★ You can draw a straight-line graph accurately by using a table of values.

You should be able to:

★ Construct tables of values and plot graphs of linear functions, where y is given implicitly in terms of x, rearranging the equation into the form $y = mx + c$.

★ Know the significance of m in $y = mx + c$ and find the gradient of a straight-line graph.

★ Find the approximate solution of a pair of simultaneous equations by finding the point of intersection of their graphs.

★ Construct functions arising from real-life problems; draw and interpret their graphs.

★ Manipulate algebraic expressions and equations.

★ Draw accurate mathematical graphs.

★ Recognise connections with similar situations and outcomes.

End-of-unit review

1 Work out the gradient of each line on the graph.

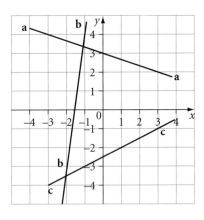

2 Find the gradient of a straight line between:
   a $(0, 0)$ and $(10, 2)$ **b** $(0, 6)$ and $(6, -6)$ **c** $(5, 2)$ and $(-3, -2)$.

3 Find the gradients of the lines with these equations.
   a $y = 4x - 5$ **b** $y = 4 - 5x$ **c** $2 + 3x = y$ **d** $x + y = 20$

4 Write each formula in the form $y = mx + c$.
   a $2x + y = 4$ **b** $x + 4y = 2$ **c** $2y + 4 = x$ **d** $3(x - y) = 2$

5 These are the equations of three straight lines. Find the gradient of each one.
   a $2x + y = 9$ **b** $x = 2y + 4$ **c** $\frac{1}{4} y = \frac{1}{2} x - 12$

6 These are the equations of five straight lines.
   A: $y + 2x = 5$ B: $y + 5 = 2x$ C: $2y = 7 - 4x$ D: $2x + 2y = 5$ E: $2x - y = 1$
   Which lines are parallel?

7 Use the graph to find solutions to each pair of simultaneous
   equations.
   a $x + 2y = 5$ and $3x + y = 13$
   b $y + 20 = 3x$ and $x + 2y = 5$
   c $3x + y = 13$ and $y + 20 = 3x$

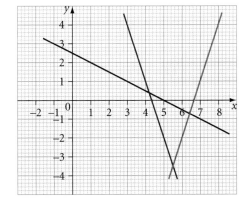

8 **a** Draw graphs of the straight lines with these equations.
         Draw both lines on the same grid.
         i $y = 3x + 7$ **ii** $2y + x = 2$
   b Use your graph to find approximate solutions to these
         simultaneous equations.
         $y = 3x + 7$ and $2y + x = 2$

9 The cost of hiring a car is $40 plus a charge of $30 per day.
   a How much will it cost to hire a car for two days?
   b Find a formula to show the cost (c), in dollars, of hiring a car for d days.
   c Draw a graph to show the cost of hiring a car.
   d A driver pays $220 to hire a car. Use the graph to find the number of days she had the car.

10 The exchange rate between Hong Kong dollars (HK$) and Pakistani rupees (PR) is HK$1 = 12.2 PR.
   a Draw a graph to show the exchange rate. Put HK$ on the horizontal axis. Go up to 100 HK$.
   b Use the graph to convert 500 PR to HK$.
   c Use a calculation to get a more accurate answer to part **b**.

19 Interpreting and discussing results

Here are the results for the football teams Manchester United, Chelsea and Liverpool in the English Premiership in 2011–12.

The table shows how many games were won, drawn or lost.

	Won	Drawn	Lost
Man U	28	5	5
Chelsea	18	10	10
Liverpool	14	10	14

Key words

Make sure you learn and understand these key words:

frequency polygon
midpoint
scatter graph
correlation

Students were asked to use computer software to draw charts of these results.

Here are some of the charts they drew.

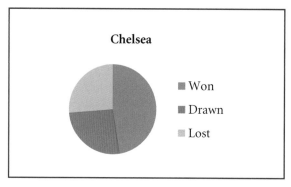

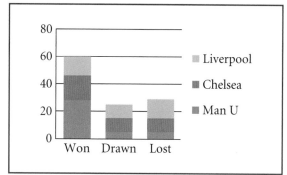

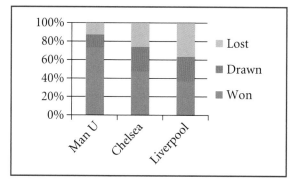

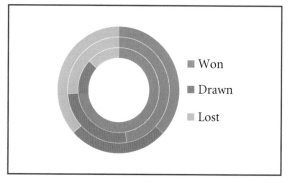

Which is the best chart?

Which chart is not very useful?

How could you improve the charts?

What chart would you draw?

In this unit you will draw and interpret more diagrams and graphs. You will also learn how to draw and interpret scatter graphs and back-to-back stem-and-leaf diagrams.

19.1 Interpreting and drawing frequency diagrams

In stage 8 you drew frequency diagrams for discrete and continuous data.

> The frequency diagrams you drew in stage 8 were bar charts.

You can also draw a **frequency polygon** for continuous data.

This is a useful way to show patterns, or trends, in the data.

To draw a frequency polygon, you plot the frequency against the **midpoint** of the class interval.

Worked example 19.1

Jeff grew 40 seedlings.
He grew 20 in a greenhouse and 20 outdoors. The heights of the 20 seedlings grown in the greenhouse are shown in the table.
a Draw a frequency polygon for the data in the table.
The frequency polygon shows the heights of the 20 seedlings grown outdoors.

Height, h (cm)	Frequency
$0 \le h < 10$	2
$10 \le h < 20$	4
$20 \le h < 30$	8
$30 \le h < 40$	6

Heights of seedlings grown outdoors

b Compare the two frequency polygons (this one and the one you have drawn).
What can you say about the heights of the two sets of seedlings?

a

Height, h (cm)	Frequency	Midpoint
$0 \le h < 10$	2	5
$10 \le h < 20$	4	15
$20 \le h < 30$	8	25
$30 \le h < 40$	6	35

Before you can draw the frequency polygon you need to work out the midpoints. Add an extra column to the table for these values. The midpoint of the class $0 \le h < 10$ is 5. The midpoint of the class $10 \le h < 20$ is 15, and so on.

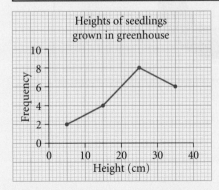

Now draw the frequency polygon. Extend the horizontal scale to 40 cm. Extend to vertical scale to at least 8. Plot the midpoints against the frequency, then join the points in order with straight lines. Remember to give the chart a title and label the axes.

b The seedlings that were grown in the greenhouse grew higher than the seedlings that were grown outdoors. 14 of the seedlings grown in the greenhouse were over 20 cm tall, whereas only 6 of the seedlings grown outdoors were over 20 cm tall.

Compare the two polygons and make a general comment, describing the similarities or differences. Include a numerical comparison to show that you clearly understand what the charts show.

Exercise 19.1

1 The table shows the masses of the students in class 9T.
  a Copy and complete the table.
  b Draw a frequency polygon for this data.
  c How many students are there in class 9T?
  d What fraction of the students have a mass less than 60 kg?

Mass, m (kg)	Frequency	Midpoint
$40 \le m < 50$	4	
$50 \le m < 60$	12	
$60 \le m < 70$	8	

2 Ahmad carried out a survey on the length of time patients had to wait to see a doctor at two different doctors' surgeries. The tables show the results of his survey.

Oaklands Surgery			Birchfields Surgery		
Time, t (minutes)	Frequency	Midpoint	Time, t (minutes)	Frequency	Midpoint
$0 \le t < 10$	25		$0 \le t < 10$	8	
$10 \le t < 20$	10		$10 \le t < 20$	14	
$20 \le t < 30$	12		$20 \le t < 30$	17	
$30 \le t < 40$	3		$30 \le t < 40$	11	

  a How many people were surveyed at each surgery?
  b Copy and complete the tables.
  c On the same grid, draw a frequency polygon for each set of data.
     Make sure you show clearly which frequency polygon represents which surgery.
  d Compare the two frequency polygons. What can you say about the waiting times at the two surgeries?

3 Liza carried out a survey on the number of hours that some students spent doing homework each week. The frequency diagrams show the results of her survey.

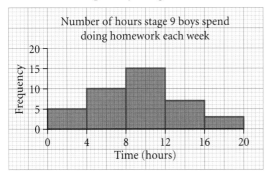

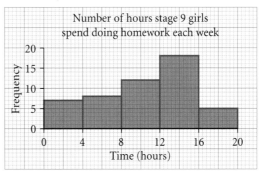

  a On the same grid, draw a frequency polygon for each set of data.
  b Compare the two frequency polygons.
     What can you say about the amount of time that boys and girls spend doing homework?
  c How many boys and how many girls were surveyed?
  d Do you think it is fair to make a comparison using these sets of data? Explain your answer.

19.2 Interpreting and drawing line graphs

Line graphs show how data changes over a period of time. A line graph shows a trend.

You can draw more than one line on a line graph, to help you to compare two sets of data.

You can also use a line graph to predict what will happen in the future.

Worked example 19.2

The table shows the population of the USA, every 10 years, from 1950 to 2010.
Each figure has been rounded to the nearest 10 million.

Year	1950	1960	1970	1980	1990	2000	2010
Population (millions)	150	180	200	230	250	280	310

a Draw a line graph for this data.
b Describe the trend in the population.
c Use your graph to estimate the population of the USA in 1985.
d Use your graph to predict the population of the USA in 2020.

a

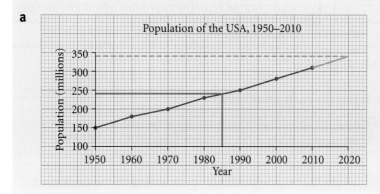

Plot time on the horizontal axis. Start at 1950 and extend the axis as far as 2020 so that you can answer part d of the question.

Plot population on the vertical axis. Start at 100 (million) and extend the axis to approximately 350 (million) so that you can answer part d of the question.

Plot all the points and join them, in order, with straight lines.

Remember to label the axis and give the graph a title.

b The population of the USA is increasing. Every 10 years the population increases by 20 or 30 million.

Describe what the line graph is showing. Give some figures in your answer to show you clearly understand the graph.

c 240 million

Draw a line on the graph (shown in red) up from 1985 and across to the population axis, and read the value.

d 340 million

Extend the line on the graph (shown in green). Make sure it follows the trend. Read the value from the population axis (shown by the green dotted line).

Exercise 19.2

1 The table shows the average monthly rainfall in Lima, Peru.

Month	Jan	Feb	Mar	Apr	May	Jun	Jul	Aug	Sep	Oct	Nov	Dec
Rainfall (mm)	1.2	0.9	0.7	0.4	0.6	1.8	4.4	3.1	3.3	1.7	0.5	0.7

  a Draw a line graph for this data.
  b Describe the trend in the data.
  c Between which two months was the greatest increase in rainfall?

2 The table shows the number of tourists, worldwide, from 2002 to 2010.
Each figure is rounded to the nearest 10 million.

Year	2002	2004	2006	2008	2010
Number of tourists (millions)	700	760	840	920	940

   a Draw a line graph for this data. Extend the horizontal axis to 2012.
   b Describe the trend in the data.
   c Use your graph to estimate the number of tourists, worldwide, in 2007.
   d Use your graph to predict the number of tourists, worldwide, in 2012.

3 The table shows the maximum and minimum daily temperatures recorded in Athens,
Greece, during one week in April.

Day	Monday	Tuesday	Wednesday	Thursday	Friday	Saturday	Sunday
Maximum temperature (°C)	17	18	20	22	21	20	18
Minimum temperature (°C)	13	13	14	16	14	15	14

   a Using the same set of axes, draw line graphs to show this data.
   b Describe the trend in both sets of data.
   c On which day was the difference between the maximum and minimum temperature greatest?

4 The line graph shows the number of visits made to Wales
by people from the rest of the UK from 1990 to 2010.

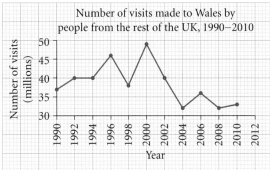

   a Use the graph to estimate the number of visits
made by people in the UK to Wales in 1995.
   b Between which two years was the biggest increase
in the number of visits made by people in
the UK to Wales?
   c Between which two years was the biggest decrease
in the number of visits made by people in
the UK to Wales?
   d Is it possible to use this graph to predict the number
of visits made by people in the UK to Wales in 2012?
Explain your answer.

5 The line graph shows the average mass of a girl from
newborn to 18 years old.

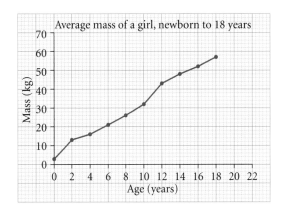

   a Describe the trend in the data.
   b During which two-year period does a girl gain
the most mass?
   c Use the graph to estimate the mass of a girl aged 15.
   d Is it possible to predict the mass of a girl aged 22?
Explain your answer.

19.3 Interpreting and drawing scatter graphs

A **scatter graph** is a useful way to compare two sets of data.
You can use a scatter graph to find out whether there is a **correlation**,
or relationship, between the two sets of data.

Two sets of data may have:

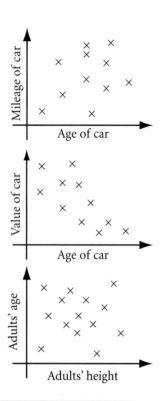

- positive correlation – as one value increases, so does the other. For
  example, as a car gets older, the greater the distance it will have travelled.
  The scatter graph on the right shows what this graph may look like.

- negative correlation – as one value increases, the other decreases.
  For example, as a car gets older, the less it will be worth. The
  scatter graph on the right shows what this graph may look like.

- no correlation – there is no relationship between one set of
  values and the other. For example, adults' heights do not relate
  to their ages. The scatter graph on the right shows what
  this graph may look like.

Worked example 19.3

The table shows the maths and science test results of 12 students. Each test was marked out of 10.

Maths result	8	5	2	10	5	8	9	3	6	6	7	3
Science result	7	4	3	9	6	8	8	4	5	4	8	2

a Draw a scatter graph to show this data.
b What type of correlation does the scatter graph show? Explain your answer.

a

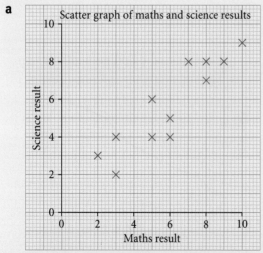

Mark each axis with a scale from 0 to 10.
Take the horizontal axis as the 'Maths result'
and the vertical axis as the 'Science result'.
Plot each point and mark it with a cross.
Start with the point (8, 7), then (10, 8), etc.
Make sure you plot all the points; there
should be 12 crosses on the scatter graph,
one for each student.

Remember to give the graph a title.

b The graph shows positive correlation, because
the higher the maths score, the higher the
science score.

The graph shows that the better a student
does in maths, the better they do in science,
so it shows positive correlation.

⬥ **Exercise 19.3**

1 Hassan carried out a survey on 15 students in his class. He asked them how many hours a week they spend on homework, and how many hours a week they watch the TV.
The table shows the results of his survey.

Hours doing homework	14	11	19	6	10	3	9	4	12	8	6	15	18	7	12
Hours watching TV	7	12	4	15	11	18	15	17	8	14	16	7	5	16	10

a Draw a scatter graph to show this data. Mark each axis with a scale from 0 to 20. Show 'Hours doing homework' on the horizontal axis and 'Hours watching TV' on the vertical axis.
b What type of correlation does the scatter graph show? Explain your answer.

2 The table shows the history and music exam results of 15 students.
The results for both subjects are given as percentages.

History result	12	15	22	25	32	36	45	52	58	68	75	77	80	82	85
Music result	25	64	18	42	65	23	48	24	60	45	68	55	42	32	76

a Draw a scatter graph to show this data. Mark a scale from 0 to 100 on each axis.
Show 'History result' on the horizontal axis as and 'Music result' on the vertical axis.
b What type of correlation does the scatter graph show? Explain your answer.

3 The table shows the maximum daytime temperature in a town over a period of 14 days.
It also shows the number of cold drinks sold at a vending machine each day over the same 14-day period.

Maximum daytime temperature (°C)	28	26	30	31	34	32	27	25	26	28	29	30	33	27
Number of cold drinks sold	25	22	26	28	29	27	24	23	24	27	26	29	31	23

a Draw a scatter graph to show this data.
Show 'Maximum daytime temperature' on the horizontal axis, with a scale from 25 to 35.
Show 'Number of cold drinks sold' on the vertical axis, with a scale from 20 to 32.
b What type of correlation does the scatter graph show? Explain your answer.

4 The scatter graph shows the distance travelled and the time taken by a taxi driver for the 12 journeys he made on one day.
a What type of correlation does the scatter graph show? Explain your answer.
b One of the journeys doesn't seem to fit the correlation. Which journey is this?
Explain why you think this journey may have been different from the others.

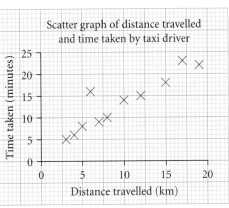

19.4 Interpreting and drawing stem-and-leaf diagrams

You already know how to use ordered stem-and-leaf diagrams to display a set of data.

You can use a back-to-back stem-and-leaf diagram to display two sets of data.

In a back-to-back stem-and-leaf diagram, you write one set of data with its 'leaves' to the right of the stem. Then you write the second set of data with its 'leaves' to the left of the stem. Both sets of numbers count from the stem, so the second set is written 'backwards'.

Remember, when you draw an ordered stem-and-leaf diagram, you should:
- write the numbers in order of size, smallest nearest the stem
- write a key to explain what the numbers mean
- keep all the numbers in line, vertically and horizontally.

Worked example 19.4

The results of a maths test taken by classes 9A and 9B are shown below.

Class 9A test results									
10	33	6	26	14	25	4	23	5	39
7	15	8	26	34	8	15	26	34	14

Class 9B test results									
12	21	8	17	32	19	9	21	7	33
8	13	20	18	32	21	33	18	25	14

a Draw a back-to-back stem-and-leaf diagram to show this data.
b For both sets of test results work out:
   i the mode   **ii** the median   **iii** the range   **iv** the mean.
c Compare and comment on the test results of both classes.

a

Class 9A test results							Class 9B test results					
8	8	7	6	5	4	**0**	7	8	8	9		
	5	5	4	4	0	**1**	2	3	4	7	8	8	9
		6	6	6	5	3	**2**	0	1	1	1	5
			9	4	4	3	**3**	2	2	3	3

Key: For class 9A, 4 | 0 means 04 marks
For class 9B, 0 | 7 means 07 marks

The test results vary between 4 and 39, so 0, 1, 2 and 3 need to form the stem. The leaves for class 9A need to come out from the stem, in order of size, to the left. The leaves for class 9B come out from the stem, to the right. Write a key for each set of data to explain how the diagram works.

b i Class 9A mode = 26
Class 9B mode = 21
ii 20 students: median = 21 ÷ 2 = 10.5th value
Class 9A: 10th = 15, 11th = 15, so median = 15
Class 9B: 10th = 18, 11th = 19, so median = 18.5
iii Class 9A range = 39 − 4 = 35
Class 9B range = 33 − 7 = 26
iv Class 9A mean = 372 ÷ 20 = 18.6
Class 9B mean = 381 ÷ 20 = 19.05

Look for the test result that appears the most often, and write down the mode for each set of data. There are 20 students in each class, so the median is the mean of the 10th and 11th students' results.

Range is the difference between the highest result and the lowest result.

To work out the mean, add all the scores together then divide by the number of scores (20).

c On average, Class 9B had better results than class 9A as their median and mean were higher. The median shows that in Class 9B 50% of the students had a result greater than 18.5 compared to 15 for Class 9A. Class 9A had a higher modal (most common) score than Class 9B. Class 9A had more variation in their scores as they had the higher range.

Write a few sentences comparing the test results of the two classes. Use the mode, median, range and means that you have just worked out and explain what they mean.

Decide which class you think had the better results and give reasons for your answer.

Exercise 19.4

1 Antonino sells ice-creams. He records the numbers of ice-creams
he sells at different locations.
The figures below show how many ice-creams he sold each day
over a two-week period at two different locations.

Beach car park						
56	46	60	47	57	46	62
60	57	45	61	46	59	62

City car park						
68	54	45	45	56	30	69
39	42	45	59	68	47	34

a Draw a back-to-back stem-and-leaf diagram to show this data.
b For both sets of data, work out:
  i the mode   **ii** the median   **iii** the range.
c Compare and comment on the ice-cream sales at the different locations.
d Antonino thinks that his sales are better at the City car park.
  Do you agree? Explain your answer.

2 The stem-and-leaf diagram shows the times taken by the students in a stage 9 class to run 100 m.

Boys' times						Girls' times			
7	5	5	1	15	9			
8	3	2	2	0	16	7	8	8	8
6	4	4	4	3	17	3	5	5	6	7
				0	18	1	4	4	5
					19	6	9

Key: For the boys' times, 1 | 15 means 15.1 seconds
    For the girls' times, 15 | 9 means 15.9 seconds

a For both sets of times work out:
  i the mode   **ii** the median   **iii** the range   **iv** the mean.
b Compare and comment on the times taken
  by the boys and the girls to run 100 m.
c Read what Alicia says.
  Do you agree? Explain your answer.

The girls are faster than the boys, as their mode is higher.

3 A business trials two different websites. Each website records the
number of 'hits' it has over a period of 21 days. The figures below show
the number of hits per day on each website.

A 'hit' is when a person looks at the website.

Website A						
141	152	134	161	130	153	142
130	158	159	145	133	145	147
145	148	153	155	146	160	152

Website B						
134	129	145	156	145	128	138
166	136	146	154	146	157	145
148	158	169	157	168	155	167

a Draw a back-to-back stem-and-leaf diagram to show this data.
b Compare and comment on the number of hits on each website.
c The manager of the business thinks that they should use website A because the number of hits
  was more consistent than website B.
  Do you agree? Explain your answer.

19.5 Comparing distributions and drawing conclusions

You can compare two or more sets of data by looking at the <u>distribution</u> of the data.

To do this, you draw graphs to show the distributions, then look for differences between the graph.

You can also work out statistics such as the mean, median, mode and range, and use these values to compare the distributions.

Worked example 19.5

a A gardener plants two different types of daffodil bulb. When they are fully grown he measures the heights of the daffodils. The frequency polygons show the heights of the two different types of daffodils.
Look at the shape of the distributions. Write three sentences to compare the heights of the two different types of daffodil.

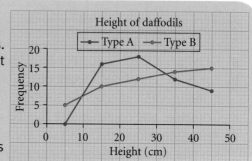

b Sally wants to buy a holiday apartment in Malaga or Madrid. The table shows the average monthly maximum temperatures in Malaga and Madrid.

Average monthly maximum temperatures (°C)												
	Jan	Feb	Mar	Apr	May	Jun	Jul	Aug	Sep	Oct	Nov	Dec
Malaga	17	17	19	20	23	27	29	30	28	24	20	17
Madrid	11	12	16	17	22	28	32	32	28	20	14	11

Sally decides to buy an apartment in Malaga because she says that, on average, the temperatures are higher and more consistent than in Madrid. Has Sally made the right decision? Explain your answer.

a The heights of the type B daffodils are more varied. Six more of the type B daffodils than the type A daffodils reached the greatest height of 40–50 cm. All of the type A daffodils grew taller than 10 cm, whereas four of the type B daffodils were below 10 cm in height.

When you compare frequency polygons, look at the width, or spread, of the data to see which set of values is more varied. Also compare specific height intervals, and give numerical comparisons to show that you fully understand the graphs.

b

	Mean	Median	Mode	Range
Malaga	22.6 °C	21.5 °C	17 °C	13 °C
Madrid	20.3 °C	18.5 °C	none	21 °C

The mean and median temperatures for Malaga are both higher than those for Madrid so, on average, Malaga is warmer. It is not possible to compare the modes as Madrid does not have one. The range for Malaga is lower than that for Madrid, which means that the temperatures are more consistent. So Sally is correct and has made the right decision.

Sally is talking about averages, which means you need to work out the mean, median and mode. She also mentions consistency, which means you need to work out the range. Once you have worked out the averages and ranges, present your results in a table. You can then use the data in the table to make comparisons. Make sure you explain clearly the decisions you have taken.

◆ Exercise 19.5

1 The frequency polygons show the heights of 60 stage 7 and 60 stage 8 students.
Look at the shape of the distributions.
Write three sentences to compare the heights of the stage 7 and stage 8 students.

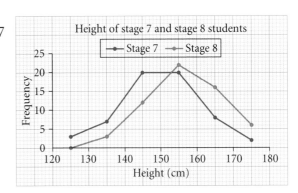

2 The frequency diagrams show the number of goals scored by a hockey team in 15 home matches and 15 away matches.

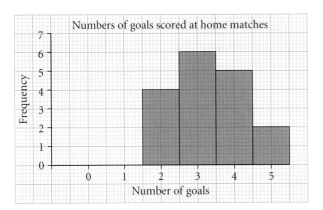

Look at the shapes of the distributions. Write three sentences to compare the numbers of goals scored at home matches and at away matches.

3 Claude is a dairy farmer. He has drawn these two scatter graphs to show his monthly milk production, the monthly average daytime temperature and the monthly average rainfall.

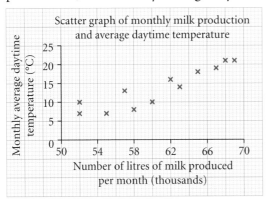 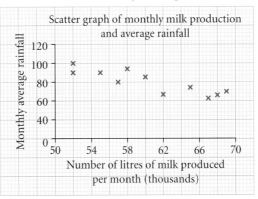

a Compare these two scatter graphs. Make two comments.

b Claude says that his cows produce more milk in the months when the temperature is higher and rainfall is lower. Is Claude correct? Explain your answer.

These are Claude's monthly milk production figures for 2010 and 2011.

Monthly milk production (thousands of litres) for 2010 and 2011												
	Jan	**Feb**	**Mar**	**Apr**	**May**	**Jun**	**Jul**	**Aug**	**Sep**	**Oct**	**Nov**	**Dec**
2010	55	53	59	59	69	71	73	72	70	59	59	57
2011	52	55	52	57	62	67	68	69	65	63	60	58

Claude says that, on average, his cows produced more milk per month in 2010 than 2011, but his milk production was more consistent in 2011.

c Is Claude correct? Explain your answer.

4 The frequency diagrams show the population of a village by age group in 1960 and 2010.

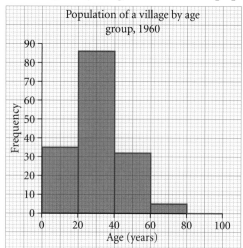

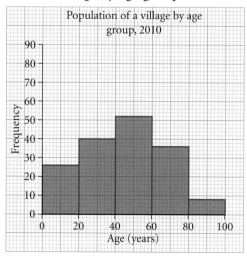

a Look at the shape of the distributions. Write three sentences to compare the age groups in the population in 1960 and 2010.

b Read what Anders says. Is Anders correct? Show working to support your answer.

> Approximately 25% of the population were over the age of 40 in 1960, compared with approximately 60% in 2010.

c Give reasons why you think the distributions of the ages of the population have changed from 1960 to 2010.

Summary

You should now know that:

★ A frequency polygon shows patterns, or trends, in continuous data. To draw a frequency polygon for continuous data, plot the frequency against the midpoint of the class interval.

★ You can draw more than one line on a line graph in order to compare two sets of data. You can also use a line graph to predict what will happen in the future.

★ A scatter graph is a way of comparing two sets of data. A scatter graph shows whether there is a correlation, or a relationship, between the two sets of data. Data may have positive correlation, negative correlation or no correlation.

★ You can display two sets of data on a back-to-back stem-and-leaf diagram. In a back-to-back stem-and-leaf diagram, one set of data has its leaves to the right of the stem, the other set of data has its leaves to the left of the stem.

You should be able to:

★ Select, draw and interpret diagrams and graphs, including:
  • frequency diagrams such as bar charts
  • line graphs
  • scatter graphs
  • back-to-back stem-and-leaf diagrams.

★ Interpret tables, graphs and diagrams and make inferences to support or cast doubt on initial conjectures; have a basic understanding of correlation.

★ Compare two or more distributions; make inferences, using the shape of the distributions and appropriate statistics.

★ Relate results and conclusions to the original questions.

End-of-unit review

1 Marina carried out a survey on the length of time it took employees to travel to work at two different supermarkets. The tables show the results of her survey.

Andersons Supermarket		
Time, t (minutes)	Frequency	Midpoint
$0 \leq t < 15$	5	7.5
$15 \leq t < 30$	8	
$30 \leq t < 45$	38	
$45 \leq t < 60$	9	

Chattersals Supermarket		
Time, t (minutes)	Frequency	Midpoint
$0 \leq t < 15$	32	7.5
$15 \leq t < 30$	13	
$30 \leq t < 45$	10	
$45 \leq t < 60$	5	

  a How many people were surveyed at each supermarket?
  b Copy and complete the tables.
  c On the same grid, draw a frequency polygon for each set of data.
  d Compare the travelling times to the two supermarkets. Use the frequency polygons to help you.

> Make sure you show clearly which frequency polygon represents which supermarket.

2 The table shows the numbers of visitors to a theme park from 2002 to 2010.
   Each figure is rounded to the nearest 0.1 million.

Year	2002	2004	2006	2008	2010
Number of visitors (millions)	1.3	1.5	1.8	2.0	2.3

  a Draw a line graph for this data. Include 2012 on the horizontal axis.
  b Describe the trend in the data.
  c Use your graph to estimate the number of visitors to the theme park in 2005.
  d Use your graph to predict the number of visitors to the theme park in 2012.

3 Some stage 9 students were asked to estimate a time of 60 seconds.
   They each had to close their eyes and raise their hand when they thought 60 seconds had passed.
   The stem-and-leaf diagram shows the actual times estimated by the students.

```
        Boys' times              Girls' times
                            4 | 9
              6   5   3   | 5 | 6   6   7   9
      9   7   7   4   3   | 6 | 0   1   3   4   7
      8   6   5   3   2   | 7 | 2   3   4   5
                  5   4   | 8 | 1
```

   Key: For the boys' times, 3 | 5 means 53 seconds
   For the girls' times, 4 | 9 means 49 seconds

  a For both sets of times work out:
     i the mode   ii the median   iii the range   iv the mean.
  b Compare and comment on the boys' and the girls' estimates for 60 seconds.
  c Read what Hassan says.
     Do you agree? Explain your answer.

> The boys are better at estimating 60 seconds as their median is higher.

End-of-year review

1 Work these out.
  a $6 + {-5}$
  b $-4 - {-6}$
  c $3 \times {-4}$
  d $-18 \div 6$

2 Copy and complete each statement.
  a $6^3 \times 6^7 = 6^\square$
  b $8^5 \div 8^2 = 8^\square$
  c $9^{-1} = \frac{1}{\square}$
  d $15^0 = \square$

3 a The first term of a sequence is 4 and the term-to-term rule is 'add 6'.
   Write down the first four terms of this sequence.
  b A sequence has the position-to-term rule: term = 3 × position number − 2.
   Write down the first four terms of this sequence.

4 Jim thinks of a number.
  He adds 5 to the number then multiplies the result by 7.
  a Write this as a function using a mapping.
  The answer Jim gets is 91.
  b Use inverse functions to work out the number Jim thought of.
   Show all your working.

5 Work these out mentally.
  a 9×0.2
  b 12×0.04
  c $6 \div 0.2$
  d $24 \div 0.06$
  e 0.4×0.8
  f $0.4 \div 0.02$

6 Work these out.
  a 26×10^3
  b 0.07×10^{-1}
  c $24 \div 10^4$
  d $0.8 \div 10^{-2}$

7 Round each number to the given degree of accuracy.
  a 15.264 (1 d.p.)
  b 0.0681 (1 s.f.)
  c $45\,776$ (2 s.f.)

8 Write the correct sign, =, < or >, that goes in the box between the expressions.
  a $20 - 3 \times 5 \ \square\ 1 + \frac{45}{15}$
  b $40 - 5^2 \ \square\ 3(38 - 33)$

9 A green gold bracelet weighs 56 g.
  The bracelet is made from 75% gold, 20% silver and 5% copper.
  a What is the mass of the gold in the bracelet?
  b What is the mass of the copper in the bracelet?

10 A motorist drives at an average speed of 90 km/h.
  How far does he travel in $2\frac{1}{2}$ hours?

11 A 500 g bag of pasta costs $0.82.
  A 2 kg bag of the same pasta costs $3.30.
  Which bag is the better value for money?
  Show your working.

500 g   2 kg

12 Calculate:
  a the exterior angle of a regular pentagon
  b the interior angle of a regular pentagon.

13 Work out the size of each unknown angle in these diagrams.
Explain how you worked out your answers.

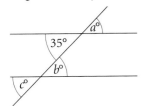 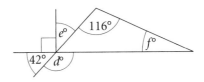

14 Copy these 3D shapes and draw on them their planes of symmetry.

a  **b**   **c**

15 Ceri is looking into the age of the children at a youth club. She uses this data-collection sheet.
She asks the children to say which age group they are in.
  a Give two reasons why her data collection sheet is not suitable.
  b Design a better data-collection sheet.

Age (years)	Tally	Frequency
12–14		
14–16		
16–18		
Total		

16 Sarah sews together two pieces of material to make a curtain.

The first piece of material is $1\frac{3}{5}$ m wide, the second is $2\frac{2}{3}$ m wide.

  a What is the total width of the curtain?
  b Show how to check your answer is correct.

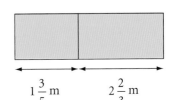
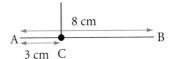

17 Work out the answers to these.
Write each answer in its simplest form and as a mixed number when appropriate.

  a $\frac{1}{8} \times 36$ **b** $\frac{2}{5} \times \frac{15}{16}$ **c** $9 \div \frac{3}{8}$ **d** $\frac{4}{5} \div \frac{12}{25}$

18 Draw a line AB 8 cm long.
Mark the point C on the line, 3 cm from A.
Construct the perpendicular at C, as shown in the diagram.

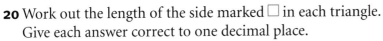

19 a Draw a circle of radius 5 cm.
  b Using a straight edge and compasses, construct an inscribed regular hexagon.
Make sure you leave all your construction lines on your diagram.

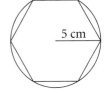

20 Work out the length of the side marked □ in each triangle.
Give each answer correct to one decimal place.

  a 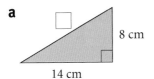 **b**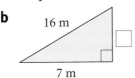

21 Simplify each expression.   **a** $x^6 \times x^4$ **b** $25t^9 \div 5t^3$

22 Write an expression for:
  a the perimeter   **b** the area of this rectangle.
  Write each expression in its simplest form.

$2x + 3$

4

23 Use the formula $T = ma + w$ to work out the value of:
  a T when $m = 8$, $a = 5$ and $w = 12$ **b** a when $T = 46$, $w = 18$ and $m = 4$.

24 a Factorise each expression.   **i** $5x - 15$ **ii** $12xy - 8y$

  b Simplify each expression.   **i** $\frac{x}{2} + \frac{x}{5}$ **ii** $\frac{2x}{3} + \frac{y}{4}$

  c Expand and simplify each expression.   **i** $(x + 6)(x - 2)$ **ii** $(x + 4)^2$

25 An athletics coach must pick either Taj or Aadi to represent the athletics club in a long-jump competition.
  These are the distances, in cm, that the boys have jumped in their last 10 training sessions.

Taj	295	265	273	297	305	265	290	265	315	286
Aadi	295	294	275	282	275	296	280	276	284	308

  a Calculate the mean, median, mode and range of both sets of data.
  b Who do you think the coach should choose to represent the athletics club? Explain your decision.

26 The diagram shows shapes A, B, C, D, E, F and G on a grid.
  Describe the single translation, reflection, rotation or enlargement that transforms:
  a shape A to shape B   **b** shape B to shape C
  c shape C to shape D   **d** shape B to shape E
  e shape F to shape G.

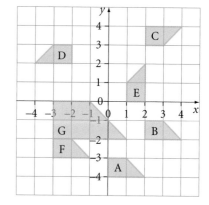

27 Brad buys a house for $130 000.
  Five years later he sells it for $140 400.
  a What is his percentage profit?
  b Show how to check your answer.

28 A goat is tied by a rope to a post in a field. The rope is 12 m long.
  Draw the locus of points that the goat can reach when the rope is tight.
  Use a scale of 1 cm to 3 m.

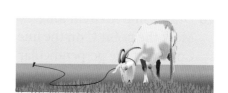

29 a Solve this equation. $5x - 3 = 3x + 11$
  b Solve these simultaneous equations. $2x + y = 11$
                                              $5x + 3y = 29$
  c Solve this inequality. $6x - 4 \leq 29$
  d The equation $x^2 - 3x = 13$ has a solution between $x = 5$ and $x = 6$.
    Use trial and improvement to find the solution to the equation, correct to one decimal place.

30 When Sven makes bread rolls he uses rye flour and wheat flour in the ratio $2:3$.
  Sven makes bread rolls using 250 g of rye flour.
  What mass of wheat flour does he use?

31 A shop sells pots of cream in two different sizes.
A 300 ml pot costs $1.53. A 500 ml pot costs $2.60.
Which size pot is better value for money?
Show all your working.

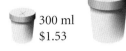

300 ml
$1.53

500 ml
$2.60

32 Copy and complete each statement.
  a $6\,m^2 = \square\,cm^2$ **b** $550\,mm^2 = \square\,cm^2$ **c** $0.8\,m^3 = \square\,cm^3$
  d $5.2\,cm^3 = \square\,mm^3$ **e** $450\,cm^3 = \square\,ml$ **f** $3.6\,ha = \square\,m^2$

33 A circle has a radius of 6.5 cm. Work out:
  a the area of the circle
  b the circumference of the circle.
  Give both your answers correct to one decimal place. Use the 'π' button on your calculator.

34 Work out: **i** the volume   **ii** the surface area
  of the triangular prism and the cylinder.
  Give your answers to part **b** correct to one decimal place.

  a
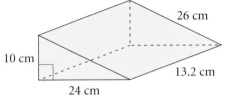

  26 cm
  10 cm
  13.2 cm
  24 cm

  b
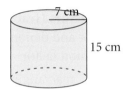

  7 cm
  15 cm

35 Mia has two spinners, as shown.
  She spins the spinners and then multiplies the numbers
  they land on to get a score.
  a Copy and complete the sample space diagram to
    show all the possible scores.
  b What is the probility that Mia scores 6?
  c What is the probility that Mia does <u>not</u> score 6?

×	2	3	4
2	4		
3			

36 An aeroplane leaves an airport and flies 400 km on a bearing of 140°.
  It then flies 320 km on a bearing of 050°.
  a Make a scale drawing of the aeroplane's journey. Use a scale where 1 cm represents 40 km.
  b How far is the aeroplane away from the airport?
  c On what bearing must the aeroplane fly to return to the airport?

37 a Copy and complete this table of values for the
    function $y = 3x - 1$.
  b On graph paper, draw the line $y = 3x - 1$ for
    values of x from -3 to $+3$.
  c What is the gradient of the line $y = 3x - 1$?

x	−3	−2	−1	0	1	2	3
y							

38 The table shows the times taken by some adults to complete
  a crossword.
  a How many adults completed the crossword?
  b What fraction of the adults completed the crossword
    in less than 8 minutes?
  c Draw a frequency polygon for this data.

Time, t (minutes)	Frequency
$0 \le t < 4$	9
$4 \le t < 8$	16
$8 \le t < 12$	8
$12 \le t < 16$	7

Glossary and index